Praise for Dirty Linen

'*Dirty Linen* is a powerfully affecting read, an encapsulation of the terror, the trauma, the hatred, the injustice, the terrible sadness and loss. But there is also the bravery and courage, and the very human struggles in these stories of individuals living their everyday lives. It's a kind and personal book, bringing it right down to the individual and hearing their voice and their truth ... The writing itself is wonderful, full of compassion and intelligence and revelation ... facing up to the reality of pain and yet bearing hope as well.'

Anna Burns

'*Dirty Linen* is shocking, riveting and compassionate.'

Roddy Doyle

'*Dirty Linen* is a milestone in writings about the Troubles. It doesn't rely on numbers, blame or anger to tell the remarkable, tragic stories of those who died violently in one single parish. Beautifully written, it captures the inhumanity of suffering and the powerful grace of those who – luckily and often randomly – survived. The long-lasting effects of the Troubles brought home to us at last.'

Joe Duffy

'Epic in impact and domestic in its details: the devastating thing about *Dirty Linen* is how Doyle gets into the grain and texture of people's lives to honour their damage and bring it close. Brilliantly written, fully human, hard to read and harder to put down – everyone should read this book.'

Anne Enright

'*Dirty Linen* is nothing short of superb. How hard it must have been at times to write, but how important a book.'

Wendy Erskine

'This is the finest memoir of the conflict I've ever read. But it is more than the story of the Troubles as they shattered lives in a small place. It is a story of all wars and how they haunt generations. Beautifully written and scrupulously fair-minded, this is an outstanding book.'

Fergal Keane

'… historical, political, artisitic, *Dirty Linen* is a phenomenal work.'

Martina Evans

'Sometimes the best way to perceive the broader truths of a conflict is to narrow your aperture, and Martin Doyle has done that, brilliantly, in *Dirty Linen*. By measuring the awful toll of violence on the lives of ordinary people in his own home parish, Doyle offers us a personal history of the Troubles that is as exacting as it is humane. An elegant, haunting book.'

Patrick Radden Keefe

'I thought nothing about the Troubles could shock me but this book has me floored. Doyle evokes the sinister machinations of state collusion, the grim predictability of tit for tat killings and the everyday anxiety of the inhabitants of his small community with humanity and compassion. Essential reading for anyone who wants to understand the way we lived then.'

Louise Kennedy

'You read Martin Doyle's memoir at moments almost with your hands up to protect your face from the lethal missiles of memory and specificity, the almost unbearably poignant and powerful details, small human details, huge human hurts, which keep coming, and coming, because that is what it is to tell a story of the Troubles from, and about, a place called home. These details come like a hail of bullets. But they're not gratuitous. And remarkably, this is not a depressing book. There is something redemptive, something life-affirming, about the space that *Dirty Linen* makes for these stories and about what it teaches us about the layers and the interwoven narratives of a place.'

Belinda McKeon

'A masterpiece, the very best book on the Troubles ... a seminal work, beautifully and sensitively written.'

Conor O'Clery

'All of us with Ulster family, and everyone who cares about Ireland, needs to read this fascinating, powerful, utterly moving book.'

Joseph O'Connor

'Superb, a really important and moving work that brings the reality of the Troubles to life and restores the human tragedy to its proper place in public memory ... a vital, potent and moving piece of work.'

Fintan O'Toole

'It will be hailed as an outstanding memoir of the Troubles.'

The Observer

'This is an important, humane book, stunning in its sweep and power.'

The Irish Times

'A powerful elegy, suffused with pity, humanity and authenticity.'

Sunday Independent

'Deeply compassionate ... a fine, and necessary, act of remembrance.'

The Sunday Times

'A book that mixes tragedy, victory, humanity, and clear-eyed assessment of the actions and savagery of some of those active in the name of one cause or another in a way that cannot be forgotten.'

Irish Examiner

'If Northern Ireland is ever to wake up from its nightmarish history ... then Martin Doyle's is the sort of moderate, intelligent and compassionate voice that must be heard.'

Sunday Business Post

In memory of Nikki and Marie

MARTIN DOYLE is Books Editor of *The Irish Times*, which he joined in 2007. He started his career in London in 1990 with *The Irish World*, joined *The Irish Post* in 1992 and became Editor before moving in 2001 to *The Times*. He edited *A History of The Irish Post*,which was published in 2000 to mark the newspaper's thirtieth anniversary. A native of Banbridge, County Down, he is a graduate of the University of St Andrews, where he studied French and German. He contributed an essay to *The 32: An Anthology of Irish Working-Class Voices* (Unbound, 2021) and to *The Routledge Handbook of the Northern Ireland Confl ict and Peace* (2023).

Dirty Linen

The Troubles in My Home Place

Martin Doyle

MERRION PRESS

First published in hardback in 2023 by
Merrion Press
10 George's Street
Newbridge
Co. Kildare
Ireland
www.merrionpress.ie

This revised paperback edition first published in 2024

978 1 78537 524 8 (Paperback)
978 1 78537 504 0 (Ebook)

A CIP catalogue record for this book is
available from the British Library.

Typeset in Minion Pro 11.5/17 pt

Cover design by Fiachra McCarthy.

Merrion Press is a member of Publishing Ireland.

Putrid currents floated trout to the loch,
Their bellies white as linen tablecloths

'Lint Water', *Seamus Heaney*

A nation is a very complex thing … it never has consisted solely of one blood or of one simple race. It is like a river, which rises far off in the hills and has many sources, many converging streams before it becomes one great stream.

Roger Casement

We have a common history, but not a common memory.

Éamon Phoenix

Contents

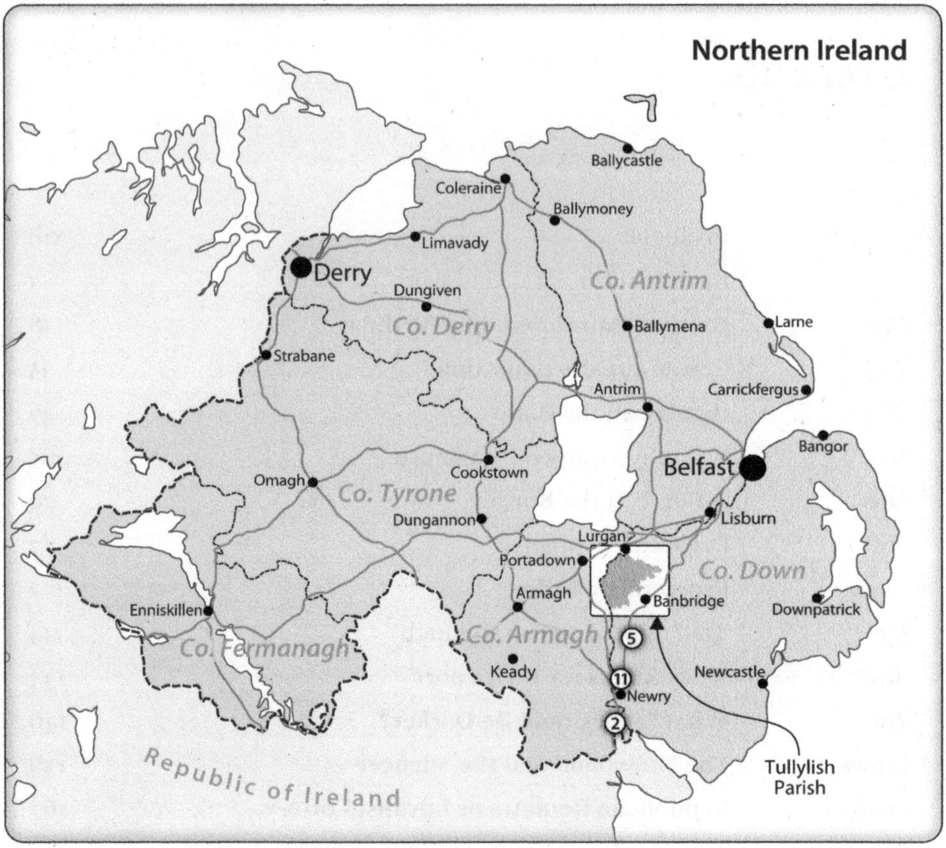

1 Sgt Maj. Arthur McMillan (37), Sgt Ian Mutch (31); and Lance Cpl Colin Leslie (26), *18 June 1972*

2 Joe Fegan (28), *22 August 1972*

3 Pat Campbell (34), *29 October 1973*

4 John Michael Feeney (45), Joseph Toman (48) and Brendan O'Hara (38), *27 April 1975*

5 Fran O'Toole (29), Tony Geraghty (23) and Brian McCoy (33), *31 July 1975*

6 Joe Toland (79), *1 August 1975*, Jimmy Marks (44), *7 January 1976*, and Rosie McConville (43), *13 March 1987*

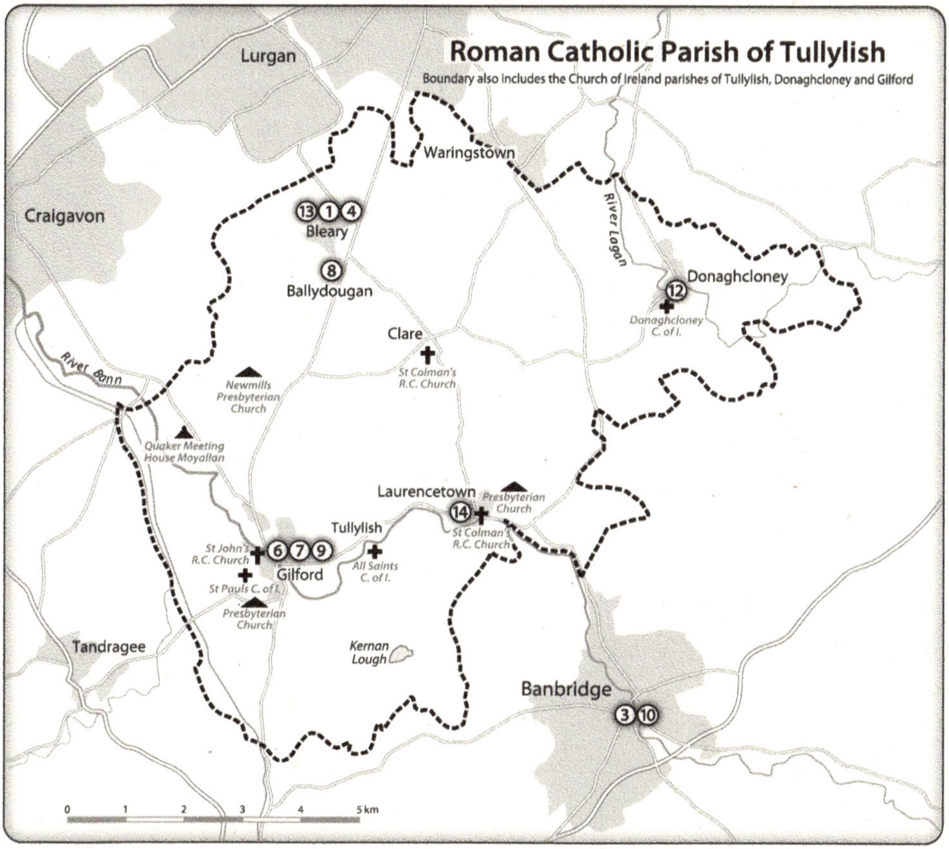

7 Richard Beattie (44), William Scott (28) and Sylvia McCullough (31), *31 December 1975*

8 Declan (19), Barry (24) and Joe O'Dowd (61), *4 January 1976*

9 Bobbie Harrison (50), *5 February 1977*

10 Alan McCrum (11), *15 March 1982*

11 Trevor May (28), *9 April 1984*

12 Pat Feeney (32), *22 February 1989*

13 Gerard (22) and Rory (18) Cairns, *28 October 1993*

14 Larry McCartan (79), *3 February 1997*

Prologue

If the River Bann was once the lifeblood of Tullylish parish, powering the linen industry that sustained its people, another body of water, Kernan Lough, symbolises the bloodshed that has stained its history.

When my brothers and sister and I were young, our parents would take us there for picnics and to feed the swans. It disturbed me to learn that this serene lake of fond childhood memories is also the site of an historic atrocity. I would later discover, however, that not everyone felt the same.

Tullylish was part of Iveagh, which had been ruled by the Gaelic Magennis clan for almost five centuries, England's northern Pale never having reached this far inland. The Plantation of Ulster in the early 1600s, a colonisation project by the British Crown to settle the north of Ireland with loyal English and Scots, created a divide that defines the region to this day.

Catholics had their churches confiscated along with their land and had to practise their faith outdoors at Mass rocks. The church at Tullylish, seized by Protestant settlers, was burned down in revenge.

In October 1641, Ulster's Catholics, led by Sir Phelim O'Neill, rose up. In Portadown, about 100 Protestants were forced into the River Bann and those who did not drown were shot. Catholics in Islandmagee and on Rathlin Island in County Antrim were massacred too.

However, what was believed to have happened became more influential than what actually happened. Modern historians estimate that 4,000 were killed and another 8,000 died of disease or exposure but contemporary historians exaggerated atrocities and death tolls for propaganda purposes, to justify violent retribution and the forcible transfer of land from a Catholic to a Protestant elite. Writers competed in their fictions, John Milton claiming 600,000 dead, Daniel Defoe '200,000 innocent betrayed Protestants'.

In the bitterly cold early spring of 1642, Sir Phelim ordered eighty or so Protestant settlers and their Irish-born children to make their way on foot from County Armagh to Clandeboye in north County Down.

As they neared Kernan Lough, a gang led by local rebel leader Captain Phelim McArt McBrian ambushed them. Rebels reportedly used their weapons to drive the refugees to their deaths in the lough, 'sparing none of them at all'. The lake's surface was so frozen that the victims could not be drowned near the edge, so the rebels allegedly threw babies as far as they could onto thinner ice, prompting their parents and other adults to try and rescue them, only to fall through the ice and perish. Their breath must have been steaming on that freezing spring day. And the prolonged sound of screaming must have carried over the nearby fields.

The story of this atrocity survives in the testimony three years later of Peter Hill, High Sheriff for County Down. His evidence was hearsay, however. His source, not even an eyewitness, told him that 'all were drowned save one man, that escaped from them wounded, and a woman, *whose names he cannot express* [my italics].'

Dr Thomas Fitzpatrick, a historian who taught at St Malachy's College, Belfast, and Blackrock College, Dublin, but whose career began at my old school, St Colman's, Laurencetown, published in 1903 *The Bloody Bridge*, a detailed examination of Trinity College Dublin's disputed 1641 Depositions, including Hill's.

Fitzpatrick questioned the accuracy of Hill's testimony. While acknowledging that fatalities may have occurred, he concluded that 'the Lough-Kernan "massacre" – if any such thing occurred there – has been prodigiously exaggerated'. However, he conceded that the incident lived on in local memory. 'I remember it well, one fine summer's evening in the year 1872, meeting on the shore of the lake an intelligent old farmer named McInerney, who lived within a stone's cast of the water. He told me how "Phellimy O'Neale drownded the people in that lough the time of the Wars of Ireland."'

My copy of *The Bloody Bridge*, borrowed from an old classmate, has that phrase underlined, with handwritten marginalia, the sectarian sentiment of which is somehow more chilling for the beautiful copperplate in which it is written: 'The more the merrier Phelim: I shall say an Ave Maria for the happy repose of your soul tho I daresay it is reposing for such a chivalrous act.'

In a twist worthy of the ghost stories of M.R. James – whose gentleman-scholar protagonists often pay dearly for disturbing the remains of the past – Fitzpatrick contracted cholera from the unfumigated papers he was handling while researching in the Four Courts, Dublin, in 1912 and died. History mishandled can be toxic.

A bejewelled brass alms dish in the chancel of All Saints' Church in Tullylish also commemorates the atrocity. The anonymous and undated gift has on the reverse this inscription: 'To the glory of God and in memory of those who died for their faith in Lough Kernan March 1641.' (The use of 1641 can be explained by the fact that until 1751 the year date changed on Lady Day, 25 March, not 1 January.)

The poet Louis MacNeice's father, Frederick, a Church of Ireland minister in County Antrim, writing in 1909, hoped 'to God we had the wisdom not only to remember but to forget. Surely there is no true wisdom in recalling year after year the story of wrongs inflicted upon Protestants in 1641.'

His prayer went unheard. In 1991, the Orange Order in Portadown produced a video likening 1641 to the Nazi Holocaust. Three years earlier, Peter Robinson, a future DUP leader and First Minister, had offered this grossly exaggerated account: 'It was on Saturday, October 23, 1641, that the Catholic Irish had commenced an evil campaign of genocide … Over 100,000 were killed in a matter of months … Among the leading butchers were those who had long been regarded as "friendly Irish", an early term equivalent of today's "moderate Catholics".'

We must familiarise ourselves with our troubled past, not least to avoid repeating its tragedies by knowing who is capable of what, what is at stake and the price of ignorance. But in this remembering, we must decommission any such weaponising of history.

Introduction

It is said you should write about what you know. To me that is just a good place to start. So I have written about my own experience of growing up during the Troubles but also about what I have since learned from my neighbours: what it was like to be a victim, not just a bystander.

This is a personal, intimate history of the Northern conflict seen through the microcosm of a single rural parish – my own. I want to tell a new generation what it was like and perhaps remind older ones just how bad it was. The scale of the suffering, more than 3,500 violent deaths over three decades, is too immense to comprehend. Perhaps narrowing the focus to the lives lost in a few square miles might make it easier to understand what communities went through. By focusing on a small community, John Healy's *No One Shouted Stop!* (*Death of an Irish Town*) captured the devastation of emigration, and Donal Ryan's *The Spinning Heart* the human cost of the Celtic Tiger's collapse. *Dirty Linen* seeks to do the same for the Troubles.

The small village in a rural parish in County Down where I grew up was the centre of the universe for me as a child, then, as a teenager, the middle of nowhere. Now, looking back as a middle-aged man, it is somewhere in between. I understand it better – its contours, its history, how it connects to the outside world – and believe it has something to teach us about the Troubles, the North, even human nature.

Laurencetown, or Lawrencetown – we can't even agree on how to spell it – sits on the River Bann, which divides the North or Northern Ireland – we can't even agree on what to call it – in two. It lies about twenty-five miles north of the border that has divided the island in two since 1922.

The village is part of the parish of Tullylish, which lies between Banbridge, Dromore, Lurgan and Portadown. Gilford is bigger and the townland of Tullylish is a couple of miles west, but I've always thought of Laurencetown as the parish capital. Our home place is the navel of the world. Even the parish is divided. The Catholic parish includes Gilford and Donaghcloney, but they are separate Church of Ireland parishes.

What makes the story of Tullylish resonate beyond its boundaries is that it formed part of two triangles, the Linen Triangle and the Murder Triangle. In the nineteenth century, the linen industry employed 80 per cent of workers in the parish.

The Bann is the North's longest river, running for eighty miles from the Mournes through Lough Neagh and out to sea near Portstewart. The softness of its water and the power of its flow made the stretch from Ballievy to Moyallan on the western edge of Tullylish ideal for the linen industry. By the early eighteenth century Tullylish was famed for its bleach greens and the Bann water for whitening linen.

In 1674, English Quaker Alexander Christy had introduced linen bleaching to Moyallan. By 1772, there were twenty-six bleach greens along the Bann, concentrated around Gilford. Samuel Law built the Bann's first spinning mill at Hazelbank in Laurencetown in 1834. The Bann Reservoir Company was formed in 1836 to increase and regulate the flow of water to power the mills along its banks. Then the six-storey Dunbar McMaster mill opened in 1841 in Gilford, whose population grew within that Famine decade from 643 to 2,814. Banbridge swelled from a village to a town to rival Lisburn and Lurgan as the linen trade transformed from a cottage industry to a factory-based one.

Seamus Heaney used the linen industry as a metaphor for the stench of sectarianism that still pollutes the North. In his poem 'Lint Water', published in the *Times Literary Supplement* on 5 August 1965, the industry's poisoning of running water symbolises a tainted land. He writes of 'flax decaying, steaming like a bog, / Wafting its heavy, nauseating fall-out', 'sheaves like half-gone carcasses'. As Roy Foster pointed out in *On Seamus Heaney*, 'Northern Irish readers would be well aware that historically, linen making was notably sectarian in its work patterns.'

The Linen Triangle stretched from Lisburn across the southern shore of Lough Neagh to Dungannon in County Tyrone and south to Newry, the heartland of a trade that was both agricultural and industrial and wove its way into the North's identity – flax is the logo of the Northern Ireland Assembly. It created great wealth for many owners and secure employment for tens of thousands, although – in the 1780s and 1790s – it became another forum for sectarian division, as Catholics, having been dispossessed of much of their land, now posed a new economic threat as self-employed weavers and suffered the consequences. After the cottage industry industrialised, Catholics would face discrimination again, excluded from higher-paying roles or expelled from employment altogether. The fields of flax from which linen was made and the huge bolts of cloth steeped in vitriol that used to be laid out to blanch on bleach greens like winding sheets or giant bandages or parchment scrolls are long gone. Many of the derelict mill buildings survive, however, like rusting hulks on wharves or the abandoned homes of murder victims. So too the cottages built for its workers and the mansions for the linen lords. The industry's decline might serve as a metaphor for the descent into communal violence. As Ciaran Carson wrote in his poem 'Turn Again': 'The linen backing is falling apart – the Falls Road hangs by a thread.'

Worn in ancient Egypt by priests, linen was a symbol of purity. The industry that produced it was a dirty one, though. It was dusty, wet, hot and humid work. One worker described Hazelbank as 'a dungeon'. In 'Strabane', poet Maureen Boyle writes of 'Byssinosis, the price the workers paid / for the privilege of a wage and a tiny street house.'

'My grandfather worked in the mill. / My mother vowed she never would, / seeing the sinister snow of scutched flax / that hid her father

when she was sent / to bring him his lunch, / making him wheeze / at night when he came home.'

In Lurgan town centre, *The Linen Bleachers*, a sculpture by artist Maurice Harron, consists of two figures holding a piece of linen, seeking to create a sense of unity in a town long divided.

Ballievy's mill became a film studio where much of the famously violent TV series *Game of Thrones* was shot. It is now a tourist attraction. A *Game of Thrones* linen tapestry, imitating Bayeux's, is displayed in the Ulster Museum. A Troubles tapestry, its cataract of atrocities artfully stitched onto damask, would be unthinkably obscene. By contrast, the Memorial Quilt of the South East Fermanagh Foundation victims' group is a tender commemoration, made of patches provided by victims' families.

The mill pond in Bessbrook – a Quaker town built on linen that had neither pub nor police station but did boast a mill that became an

army base with the busiest heliport in Europe – is now adorned with a sculpture by Alan Burke, which rises like Excalibur from the water. Wrought in stainless steel, it is a six-metre single stem of flax with a blue blossom at its apex. It was inspired by the poem, 'The Ballad of Camlough River', by James N. Richardson, the local linen lord, which celebrates his industry's power supply and observes how the river changes its tune as it flows: 'For at Camlough his ripples ring sweet "Garryowen", / While at Millvale they brattle "The Protestant Boys".'

Nine of the Protestant mill workers murdered by republicans in the Kingsmill massacre on 5 January 1976 in south Armagh were from Bessbrook – an atrocity that followed the day after murderous attacks on two Catholic families, the Reaveys nearby and the O'Dowds in my parish, which claimed six lives. It is the subject of Michael Longley's poem 'The Linen Workers': 'When they massacred the ten linen workers / There fell on the road beside them spectacles / Wallets, small change, and a set of dentures: / Blood, food particles, the bread, the wine.'

Longley's exquisite 'The Linen Industry', one of my favourite poems, is, by contrast, a celebration of love, not a dwelling on hatred:

Pulling up flax after the blue flowers have fallen
And laying our handfuls in the peaty water
To rot those grasses to the bone, or building stooks
That recall the skirts of an invisible dancer,

We become a part of the linen industry
And follow its processes to the grubby town
Where fields are compacted into window-boxes
And there is little room among the big machines.

But even in our attic under the skylight
We make love on a bleach green, the whole meadow
Draped with material turning white in the sun
As though snow reluctant to melt were our attire.

What's passion but a battering of stubborn stalks,
Then a gentle combing out of fibres like hair
And a weaving of these into christening robes,
Into garments for a marriage or funeral?

Since it's like a bereavement once the labour's done
To find ourselves last workers in a dying trade,
Let flax be our matchmaker, our undertaker,
The provider of sheets for whatever the bed –

And be shy of your breasts in the presence of death,
Say that you look more beautiful in linen
Wearing white petticoats, the bow on your bodice
A butterfly attending the embroidered flowers.

'The Ballad of William Bloat' tells of a Shankill Road man who tried to hang himself with a bedsheet after cutting his wife's throat: 'But the strangest turn of the whole concern / Is only just beginning / He went to hell, but his wife got well / And she's still alive and sinning / For the razor blade was German-made / But the rope was Belfast linen.'

The linen industry even produced its own literary set, the rhyming weavers or weaver poets, the most famous of whom is James Orr, whose verse decorates the Irish passport: 'The hedge-hauntin' blackbird, on ae fit whyles restin', / Wad fain heat the tither in storm-rufflet wing'. A Presbyterian who wrote in Ulster Scots, he was also a United Irishman, an Irish patriot who rejected the idea that Gaelic ethnicity was a precondition to this.

There is an industrial map of Ireland in the Linen Museum in Lisburn that was published in the *Belfast News Letter* around the time of partition with the purpose of highlighting the prosperity and vitality of Ulster in contrast to the moribund, agricultural South. Laurencetown features prominently, reminding me of one of those biblical cities which is now some dusty village. A similar map today would make sobering reading for the *News Letter*'s readership. One could argue that the IDA, Ireland's foreign direct investment agency, has done far more for the prospects of a reunited Ireland than the IRA.

***

The term the 'Murder Triangle' was first used in a pamphlet entitled *The Triangle of Death*, which was written by two Catholic priests, Father Denis Faul and Father Raymond Murray, during the period 1974–75. The pamphlet reported that within this triangle – the corners of which were roughly Newry, Lurgan and Dungannon – loyalist paramilitaries had carried out a murder campaign against Catholics. Away from the urban hotspots of Belfast and Derry, this was the cockpit of the Troubles, where some of the worst atrocities were perpetrated over almost three decades.

The Linen Memorial, begun in 2002 by Lycia Trouton, combines the two triangles. It is made up of 400 white Irish linen handkerchiefs, on which the names of all those Troubles victims killed between 1966 and 2006 are embroidered, intended 'as a sign of mourning, marking the pure, white cloth ... As linen has been used for centuries to shroud the dead, it highlights an emphasis upon the body and the private rituals of grief, mourning and reparation.'

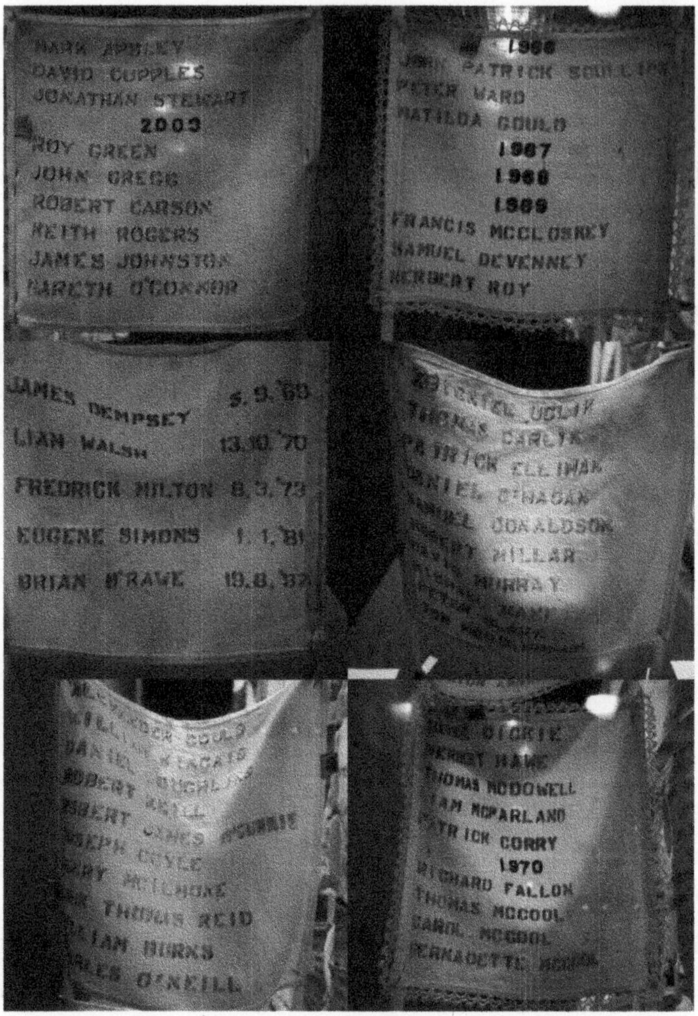

Linen, critic Jessica Hemmings pointed out, is used to stanch tears and the flow of blood. As Trouton notes, waving a handkerchief was the gesture of goodbye made by the countless individuals that became our diaspora. This 'counter-monument' was inspired by *Lost Lives: The Stories of the Men, Women and Children Who Died as a Result of the Northern Ireland Troubles* (1999), by David McKittrick, Seamus Kelters, Brian Feeney, Chris Thornton and David McVea, a work which brings home like no other the Troubles' atrocious toll.

A vital part of the North's linen heritage was itself almost destroyed in 1976 when the IRA bombed Malone House in Belfast, where the Ulster Museum's original collection of costumes and textiles was stored. Paul Muldoon wrote of it in 'Gathering Mushrooms': 'We might have been thinking of the fire-bomb / that sent Malone House sky-high / and its priceless collection of linen / sky-high.' Muldoon's father, Patrick, grew flax during the Second World War near Portadown. 'One of my very first memories was of the local linen barons, the Cowdys, riding by on their impossibly high horses,' the poet recalled in his foreword to *Cloth*, a 2007 collaboration with the artist Rita Duffy. By contrast, 'Our place was in the flax field or the flax dam,' he wrote in 'Glad Rags', which juxtaposes the politics of linen and class with sectarian violence.

After I moved away to university in Scotland in 1986 and then to London, people would occasionally ask me what it was like growing up in the Troubles. I would explain that I grew up away from the major flashpoints, and that while I had experienced sectarian abuse, I had witnessed violence only on the news, albeit in undiluted form through local bulletins that were saturated in the stuff, unlike the news from London.

It was only while researching this book that I realised more than twenty people from my parish had lost their lives in the conflict, most of them when I was a small child or after I had moved away.

As Patrick Kielty said about his father's murder in the Troubles to fellow comedian Tommy Tiernan on the latter's chat show in 2022, 'It wasn't normal but it wasn't special.'

There is a school of thought that says we wallow in our misery, and that we should all move on, forget the past, tell new, contemporary stories. My experience is the opposite. A veil of silence has been drawn over the horrors of the past, its terrors left unprocessed, details forgotten, killings happening so thick and fast that the dead were not properly memorialised. While the immediate families of victims must of course be allowed to grieve and remember their loved ones in private and as they see fit, society would benefit, I believe, from a greater understanding and appreciation of the trauma that two generations endured.

The first victim listed in *Lost Lives*, John Scullion, a 28-year-old Belfast Catholic, died on 11 June 1966, murdered by UVF founder Gusty Spence. The RUC denied he had been shot, despite eyewitness statements and loyalist claims. Only after his body was exhumed did an autopsy confirm he had been shot. Don't dig up the past, some say. Where else would you find the truth?

It is by sharing our stories that we build a ridge of common ground from which good things can grow. The Troubles were a blight on all our lives and while things are so much better now, the spores are sadly still in the air.

'What we need to do is to find within that rubble of suffering and Golgotha an unconditional love,' the writer Michael Harding told me in 1992. 'That is what literature is about, telling stories of love amid the shit.'

***

When my neighbour Pat Feeney was murdered in February 1989 for the crime of being a Catholic, set up by a Protestant colleague while working as a night-watchman at Liddell's linen mill in Donaghcloney, I was a 21-year-old student at the University of St Andrews. As this was long before the era of the mobile phone, I only found out about what had happened a few days later, when my cousin Julie came to visit for a student ball.

I keenly remember the feeling of survivor's guilt that not only had I got away, while one of those left behind had been so cruelly, pointlessly murdered, but worse, that I had been oblivious to the atrocity. As I imagined the crowd of mourners at Pat's funeral, my own black-tie event seemed obscenely frivolous.

My English girlfriend shared with me that evening the story of a school friend, Nikki, whose family had suffered a similar tragedy to the Feeneys. Strange how the world turns. In London, years later, I would meet Nikki; we would fall in love and become husband and wife. Together we would create a new family. I thought that Nikki's tragic past, which she had overcome with such resilience and courage, would magically inoculate us from future misfortune. I was wrong.

When Nikki died of cancer in November 2013, at the age of 48, leaving our three young children behind, I raged at the casual cruelty of life, but I also dimly sensed the oneness of humanity, that this was our common fate.

Bereavement in the early days is like being caught in a flood. You force yourself to float so as to cope with the knowledge of the depths below you. But as the waters over time recede, the challenge changes to one of conservation, the suddenly urgent need to construct irrigation channels to preserve the precious memories that earlier had threatened to overwhelm you.

One way I coped was to ask friends and family to write down their memories of Nikki, so that I could share them with our children to enrich their mother's legacy. I used to make spoof newspaper front pages for friends' and family members' birthdays, embellishing anecdotes into scoops and pairing them with funny photos. I had done one for our son Ruairi's thirteenth birthday, three days before Nikki died. So it occurred to me to turn the A4 pages of memories of Nikki into a half-dozen illustrated broadsheet pages.

I believe instinctively in the power of storytelling and the healing power of nurturing, not neutering, the memories of loved ones we have lost.

There is no cure for some trauma. There is only care. And often that can, must be enough.

'The people we most love do become a physical part of us, ingrained in our synapses, in the pathways where memories are created.' I love this idea, the words of a psychiatrist quoted by the American writer Meghan O'Rourke in *The Long Goodbye*, her memoir of grieving for her mother. O'Rourke writes beautifully and honestly about her loss.

'I think about my mother every day,' she writes, 'but not as concertedly as I used to. She crosses my mind like a spring cardinal that flies past the edge of your eye: startling, luminous, lovely, gone. It's not a question of getting over it or healing. No; it's a question of learning to live with this transformation … It's not an emergence from the cocoon, but a tree growing around an obstruction.'

***

The Troubles cast a long shadow over my childhood and played an important part in my first decade as a journalist in London. While I never fully moved on and switched off, it would be fair to say that the peace, however imperfect, that led to and followed the Belfast or Good Friday Agreement in 1998 afforded me the luxury of no longer dwelling so obsessively on the daily machinations and frustrations of politics in the North. There were days when I did not click on every link on Nuzhound, the website run by Irish-American John Fay, which aggregated and hyperlinked to Irish, British and international coverage of the Troubles and the peace process.

Brexit changed all that. Pursued by British politicians who cared little for its potential consequences for Northern Ireland and championed by many unionists, who seemed to positively relish its potential to destroy the common ground that the Common Market and its European Union successor had fostered, Brexit dismantled the EU framework that provided a shared European home for rival national identities. Professor Brendan O'Leary interpreted the DUP's strategy thus: 'The truth that should be spoken is that their Westminster team wanted to restore a harder land border to render reunification more difficult: no other explanation makes sense of their conduct.' Lines that had become blurred were now, in the DUP's words, blood-red again. Unionist anger over the Protocol agreed by their government with the EU to manage the North's unique position stands in stark contrast to the relish with which they pursued and then celebrated a Brexit opposed by a majority in the North.

The elite behind the Leave campaign remind me of F. Scott Fitzgerald's line in *The Great Gatsby*: 'They smashed up things and creatures and then retreated back into their money or their vast carelessness, or whatever it was that kept them together, and let other people clean up the mess they had made.' (And yes, working-class paramilitaries and soldiers were far more careless with people's lives.)

As then assistant literary editor of *The Irish Times*, I canvassed the opinions of more than twenty writers, mostly from the North, on the day in June 2016 that the referendum result was announced, and they were almost unanimous in their dismay. Group-think? More like common sense, I believe. Long before the Northern Ireland Protocol became an issue for unionists, almost all nationalists, many neutrals and some unionists had to come to terms with the destabilising effects of a decision that they had opposed.

The violent death of journalist and writer Lyra McKee on the eve of Good Friday in 2019 also sent me back to the past. Only the month before, I had featured her in an article, 'Best of Irish: 10 Rising Stars of Irish Writing': 'North Belfast is suddenly a hotbed of fiction, thanks to Man Booker winner *Milkman* by Ardoyne's Anna Burns, flanked by Paul McVeigh's *The Good Son* and David Keenan's *For the Good Times*. Next up is Lyra McKee, a 28-year-old journalist, whose debut, *The Lost Boys*, will be published by Faber next year.'

'We were the Good Friday Agreement generation, destined to never witness the horrors of war but to reap the spoils of peace. The spoils just never seemed to reach us,' she had written. Now, twenty-one Good Fridays later, she too was dead. I wrote, 'The senseless shooting dead of journalist and author Lyra McKee by dissident republicans in Derry last night feels like the worst of our past reaching out its cold, dead hand to rob us of the best of our future.

'To paraphrase L.P. Hartley, for violent extremists of whatever shade, bitter orange or bile green, the past is not a foreign country. It is the only country they know and love and they are seemingly incapable of doing things differently, i.e., living and letting live in peace. All we can do as a society is protect ourselves from them and provide a better example. Lyra McKee represented the future, another country, a better one.'

When the Belfast writer Paul McVeigh asked me to contribute to *The 32: An Anthology of Irish Working-Class Voices*, I agreed on the understanding my thesis would be that, as a Catholic growing up in the North in the 1970s and 80s, the prejudice I had faced had far more to do with my religious and ethnic identity than my class. No one ever called me a working-class bastard.

The resultant essay, 'Dirty Linen', wove a thread that linked the expulsion of my grandfather and his sister from a local linen works in 1920 to Pat Feeney's murder at a linen mill in 1989. The essay also chronicled other Troubles murders in my parish, including the killings of three members of the O'Dowd family in January 1976. Declan, who was only 19 when he was murdered along with his brother Barry and uncle Joe, had been our coalman. His father, Barney, who was also shot but had survived, had been our milkman and we all loved him.

The O'Dowd family moved South and I didn't see Barney again until 'Dirty Linen' was published in *The Irish Times* in May 2021. Barney's son Noel made contact and brought me to meet Barney and his family. It was a very moving experience and as I listened to Barney and Noel tell their remarkable stories, I felt compelled to write about them. Noel offered to show me the family farmhouse, abandoned since the murders forty-five years before, and as we drove around the parish, he pointed out the sites of other atrocities. In January 2022, to mark the anniversary of the O'Dowd murders, *The Irish Times* published my essay, 'A Ghost Estate and an Empty Grave'.

Conversations with Tullylish neighbours, sparked by my first attempts to share their loss, made me feel there was much more to be told. In the same way, perhaps, that a writer knows that their short story must be a novel as it cannot be satisfactorily told in a few thousand words, I realised that the O'Dowds' story alone and the parish's other tragedies required a longer form.

I have never walked in the funeral cortège of a Troubles victim or felt the weight of their coffin on my shoulder. But having visited the graveyard where the O'Dowds had been buried and having paid my respects at the graves of the other victims buried there, I resolved to bear in mind these dead, to attempt to celebrate their lives and record their tragic deaths, which stole not just who they were but what they could have become.

'How many years is it now?' I remember someone asking me casually about Nikki's death, as if it were a piece of trivia that might pop up one day as a quiz question. There are dates etched in the mind as surely as they are engraved on marble or slate, which divide one's life into before and after, just as Jesus's birth is the dividing line for how Christians mark time.

Victims and their families are at the heart of this book. While working on it, I was often asked whether I found the conversations and the subject matter difficult. I usually answered that I found it deeply moving rather than distressing. It was akin to attending a wake or a funeral. Any sadness I felt was as nothing compared to the lifelong grief of the neighbours who were sharing their stories. I believe that the very least I – we – owe them is our time, the time it takes to listen to what they went through and are still going through.

I wanted this to be a polyphonic work, communicating different perspectives through many voices. There are more stories I would like to have heard and shared but some people understandably decided against being in the book and others I was unable to reach. I was surprised sometimes by who responded positively – an Orangeman – and who did not engage – some politicians and clergy.

When Nikki was being buried, the celebrant invited close relatives to scatter earth upon the coffin. Her cousin Graham seemed not to know how to handle a spade, turning the blade upside down. I knew he was a city boy but this was ridiculous. I learned, however, that this was a Jewish tradition, symbolising the alien nature of the task, perhaps also the reluctance to let a loved one go. We should be similarly reluctant to bury memories of the Troubles. It might seem perverse, like writing with the reverse side of a nib, but difficult stories are often the most important ones to tell, despite or perhaps because of the pain they contain.

It is humbling for me to contemplate as an adult that people I knew as neighbours when I was growing up had been afflicted by such terrible loss and bore it with such dignity. I have tried to record the toll the Troubles took on my parish, and the long tail of trauma it has left behind.

I have stood in graveyards and watched the love poured out towards the lost by those left behind, who tend the grass, replace the flowers, polish the gravestones and change the gravel. I have witnessed the bereaved keep vigil. And no, we are not unique. My heart breaks for the Ukrainian soldier's wife in Donetsk Oblast, widowed by Putin's cruel war, who said as she arranged her husband's grave, 'Please cover this black earth with flowers for it to be Eden. Let it be like heaven, for you have witnessed hell.'

I intersperse these emotionally powerful stories with my own account of growing up during the Troubles, and of the community of which I was part, conveying the texture of ordinary life, drawing on my own family history to give a sense of the before times as well as putting events in their broader historical and cultural context.

I have sought where possible not to inject humour, but rather not to exclude it, because it is what makes us human, it is how we cope. The people I grew up with are not dour. They are yarn-spinners who love nothing more than a good story.

At a family funeral in 2021 a cousin was wearing a cap, which someone compared to the one our grandfather Arthur Pat always wore, reminding us how he used to place it on the kneeler at church. Was this for padding, I wondered, or to protect the knees of his trousers from wear and tear? The latter, it was decided, to extend the life of this already ancient garment. It is funny how memories stir like sediment after a storm.

My bereaved cousin's brother-in-law paid a moving, affectionate tribute from the altar, with that saving grace of humour that draws the sting of death if even for a moment when we need it most – 'he treated everyone the same; gave the same bad manners to everyone' – and I wonder later whether a eulogist at the funeral of a Troubles murder victim would have had such licence. I doubt it. Another small comfort that would have been denied those grieving.

Hilary Mantel's great-grandmother Catherine O'Shea grew up in an Irish Quaker mill village, Portlaw. When the mill closed, she emigrated to Lancashire and two brothers left for America, never to be heard of again. For her first Reith lecture in 2017, Mantel wrote, 'Saint Augustine says, the dead are invisible, they are not absent. You needn't believe in ghosts to see that's true. We carry the genes and the culture of our ancestors, and what we think about them shapes what we think of ourselves, and how we make sense of our time and place.'

Benedict Anderson, the Anglo-Irish author of *Imagined Communities*, wrote, 'The dead, far from being gone, remain as a powerful part of the community. How we think about the dead, and the stories we tell about the relationship between the dead and the living, are central to imagining new forms of community and /or narratives of nationhood.'

Memories can be both precious and painful, like walking barefoot on diamonds. But to be forgotten is to die a second time. 'No one is finally dead until the ripples they cause in the world die away,' wrote Terry Pratchett. 'The span of someone's life is only the core of their actual existence.'

As the Jewish prayer goes, may their memory be a blessing.

One

Brothers Murdered on a Birthday

The final two murders in the parish of Tullylish, less than a year before the ceasefires, were two of the most shocking.

The photograph at the end of birthday celebrations, complete with cards, candles and cake, is a treasured souvenir for every family, a snapshot of a special moment in time. But a photograph of Róisín Cairns's eleventh birthday, taken by her mother Sheila, is charged with an unspeakable sense of tragedy.

The birthday girl is flanked by her brothers Gerard (22) and Rory (18), and they in turn by her dad, Eamon, and her youngest brother Liam (14). Someone – I can't quite tell whether it is Rory, who is grinning

broadly, or Liam, who seems to be suppressing a smile – is holding up two fingers behind Gerard's head, giving him bunny ears.

It's just after 7 p.m. on Thursday, 28 October 1993, in the kitchen of the family home in Bleary. The candles have been blown out, the cake cut and the cards put up on the mantelpiece. Sheila and Eamon leave for their weekly Irish-language class a few miles away in Lurgan. Liam goes to visit a friend who lives nearby. Gerard and Rory are watching television in the living room.

Róisín is still in the kitchen when, at about 8 p.m., the back door opens and two men enter wearing navy-blue boiler suits and black balaclavas. At first she thinks it must be her brothers' friends playing a Halloween prank. One goes through to the living room while the other stares at Róisín and raises a finger to his lips, signalling for her to keep quiet. He then joins his accomplice, they produce weapons and they shoot Gerard and Rory. All Róisín hears is the sound of things smashing and breaking glass. As the gunmen run off, Róisín goes into the living room and sees Rory slouched on the chair with his eyes closed. Gerard's eyes are open so, not realising they are both dead, Róisín asks him what is wrong with Rory. She then runs screaming to Liam's friend's house to raise the alarm.

Eamon and Sheila return about an hour later and are stopped at a police checkpoint. The RUC man, on learning their surname, walks off. Eamon now sees that his home is surrounded by soldiers and policemen. His distraught sister-in-law tells them Gerard and Rory have been shot. Eamon asks if the ambulance has come. She answers no, and he knows.

Eamon and Sheila's eldest daughter, Paula (21), is at university in Luton, but they are in such a state of shock they cannot remember where she lives or her phone number. They are allowed into the kitchen to find their address book. The forensics team do not want them to go into the living room, but Eamon insists they will see their sons. A police officer says it would not be pleasant. Sheila replies that Gerard and Rory are her sons and they would never be hard to look at. After a lot of persistence, permission is given. After spending some time in their presence, deafened by the silence and mystified by the lack of movement of their sons who were always so full of life, Eamon closes Gerard's eyes. Then he and Sheila hug and kiss their boys goodbye.

The brothers 'never had a bitter word or a cross word to say of anyone,' a neighbour told the *Lurgan Mail*. 'I grew up with them, spent every day of the last twenty years with them. I can't believe it has come to this. It's small comfort to the family but the people who did this will have to answer to God.'

Father Des Loughran, in his sermon at the boys' funeral Mass, said, 'Evil always self-destructs and these evil people have self-destructed. They are on the road to Hell because they have flouted the word of God, which states "Thou shalt not kill." Cruel, evil people have decided to deal out death and our little community here in Clare [townland] has been devastated once again with the death of Gerard and Rory, two fine young men. Murder was committed by nameless, faceless men but they are that only to us – not to God. He knows who they are.'

Almost thirty years later, what sticks in Father Loughran's mind from that day is catching sight of the double grave for the first time, its shocking size bringing home the enormity of what had happened. 'It just was a massive wide hole. I froze.' His white handkerchief fell onto one coffin. 'It was then I realised, oh my God, there's two of them.'

Three decades on, and no one has ever been charged with the murders. To those who might ask why you would want to reopen old wounds, the answer might be that some wounds have never been allowed to heal. Instead, they have been contaminated at every turn.

***

My grandfather Arthur Pat made up a rhyme when I was young: Martin Arthur William Doyle, Native of the Soil. In truth, my fingers have seen far more ink than soil, whereas Eamon Cairns, who greets me in his back garden, has worked hard in fields all his life. Today he has been pulling weeds with his bare hands, which are covered in scratches.

'It's great therapy, the weeding, rooting out everything under the sun that grows that shouldn't be growing,' he says. Would he not wear gloves, I wonder? 'No, that would spoil it. Something that's hard to pull out, you need your bare hands to get a closer grip.'

He shows me his impressive vegetable garden. 'The half-acre is the key to everything because you can produce the spuds and the vegetables and that's a powerful saving of money.' Sheila points out a plant which my parents gave them a few years ago and is still thriving. (Gerard and my brother Shane were in the same class at primary school; Rory and my brother Garry too.) I spot a Famine pot, which he salvaged from a local farm. If that is a reminder of our tragic past, the outdoor hot tub belonging to his daughter Paula, who lives next door, is a welcome symbol of a brighter present.

Sheila is a Haughian from Derrytrasna near Lough Neagh. 'Lord Lurgan chased the Catholics from the Lurgan area down into the bogs of Derrytrasna,' says Eamon. Her father was a lorry driver and her mother worked in a stitching factory, as she would later.

Eamon's grandfather was a weaver from Ballydougan, just up the road from Bleary. Family lore has it that when he was 16, he brought the first web of cloth he had woven to the nearest factory, Blane's (where my mother had her first job), and, unhappy with the 'seven white shillings' he was offered, put it on his shoulder and walked seven miles to Ferguson's big house, now part of Banbridge Academy, and then to another linen lord, but couldn't better the price. So he emigrated to Scotland before returning home to marry a local woman.

Their son Seamus married Kathleen Greene from Bleary, who stitched linen handkerchiefs for Blane's. Seamus was a labourer who worked on the roads and building sites. Every year he also took ground that was overgrown, cleaned it up and planted potatoes. Eamon was one of their sixteen children, eight boys and eight girls, so Seamus had a ready-made workforce.

'Our winters were spent cutting hedges, digging shores, draining a field and putting it into shape for spuds. The farmers would lend the field free of charge and in return be happy to get it back in shape.

'We were a big family and were in demand the whole year round by local farmers. We knew all the farmers round here because we'd ate in their houses, well treated. I'd be talking to a lot of Protestants over the years, people my own age, going up in the train to Dublin. And we all come to the same conclusion, we'd all love to get back to the 50s. Because we worked into each other's hands: you'd give them a lock of days' work at harvest time and they'd have lent you their machine. That's what communities are built on.

'My ma lived till she was 98. She thriv' on it! She was a great grafter and my da was similar. They still went out for their social drink every weekend to Molly's in Hall's Mill, they always liked the sing-song. My da loved to sing "The Galway Shawl" and "Boolavogue".' Rory, too, was a singer. His party piece was 'Seven Drunken Nights'.

Eamon and his siblings attended the State primary school at Ballydougan until the parish priest insisted all Catholic children switch to the nearest Catholic school, a three-and-a-half-mile walk away. In their youth Eamon and his brothers sometimes went to dances in Orange halls. 'Now the Catholics in Lurgan or Portadown wouldn't have knew what a Protestant was. But us out in the country? When you're 17 or 18, sure you don't fear anything. You're out for the craic.'

Eamon and Sheila met at a dance at the Lurgan Catholic Association and were married in 1969. Their first child, Andrea, died at birth in 1970. Gerard was born in '71, Paula in '72, Rory in '75, Liam in '79 and Róisín in '82.

What were Gerard and Rory like?

'Well, they were fairly different,' says Eamon. 'Gerard was that quiet, gentle, neat and tidy. Did everything as soon as you asked him.

He was a very easy child to rear. Whereas Rory, he was the opposite. Couldn't have cared less, always untidy. You got him to do any household chores, such as washing the dinner spuds or chopping a few sticks for the fire, it was always the minimum type of thing. So, I was never off his back. That was hard to live with. Oh, Jesus, the tears I shed over that. Thank God, by the time he reached 16, he cracked it. He would have done anything for me without hesitation, but I can tell you it took some work and discipline. Rory took his time coming into this world. He was ten days overdue but kept growing and arrived to tip the scales at 10lb 9oz. I was so proud of Sheila for giving us such a big, strong son.

'But Gerard was just a real pleasure. He would have washed the car, kept everything shipshape. If somebody had to be brought to the train station or down to the airport, it was Gerard. [He had been driving a tractor since he was 12.] We had just got to the stage in life, me and Sheila, we were pulling back. We were 48 years of age when they were murdered.'

The back garden back then was a sports pitch. 'It was non-stop rugby and football, hurling, you name it, two big goalposts, a big high fence to keep the ball from going over the road, all that craic. It's only in latter years that you realise how good children they were, because you hear people talking about them. It's so important, it's such a relief, it's such a joy to hear people remembering your children. It's the most important thing of all. I hear the slightest wee tidbit, somebody saying, "I went to school with your Gerard," or this, that and the other. That's just heaven. It sort of brings them back to life again.

'You miss them all the time because Paula's children are hurling for Ballyvarley, so we're never off the road. So, Gerard, Rory probably would have been married, they'd have had cousins playing with them, you know what I mean? The pain, the loss is unbearable.'

***

Eamon and Sheila have lived in this labourer's cottage since 1972 and bought it off the council a decade later. 'God bless Maggie Thatcher's policy,' says Eamon. The local area is predominantly Protestant but the Cairnses always got along well with their neighbours. The Douglases next door have passed away but 'we miss them a terror. They were genuine people. I would have made their hay, I cut the hedge for them, this, that and the other. She'd have reached over a plate of ham and tomatoes, everything and anything. She was a great baker. My father had Protestant neighbours that he depended on and trusted. And I would be the same.' Eamon traces the spike in anti-Catholicism locally back to the vitriol of Ian Paisley preaching in the Orange hall beside Clare chapel in 1966.

'Paisley brought hatred into the community. People were enraged with temper against us. Some started shunning us. A lot of the Protestant people held their common sense for a good number of years and still were friendly enough, but then when the IRA murdered cops, that done the harm. The decent ones then couldn't trust us or have anything to do with us. But our family never really accepted the breakdown. We still stayed friendly.'

While Eamon, like Sheila, is a practising Catholic, he is critical of the Church, which he sees as part of the establishment. He, like his father before him, is a socialist, with a strong, practical sense of community.

'Catholicism breeds a sort of slave mentality into people that they can't think for themselves. We always had our socialism to keep up on another pad. We wouldn't be rushing to the chapel every day of the week. For some people, that's their life, they don't realise how narrow-minded it makes them. I call them upper-room Catholics. The people in Jesus Christ's time when he was murdered, they went and they hid in the upper room. Well, there's that much fear in the Catholics in the North, their safe haven in their upper room is their chapel.'

Eamon believes that centuries of subjugation have taught many Catholics to seek to assimilate, to distance themselves from expressions of Irish identity, from Gaelic games to the Irish language and traditional music.

Jesus's example means you should take the risk, says Eamon, maintain contact with Protestant neighbours, not retreat into a cocoon. 'Christianity's a very lovely, wide thing, you know?'

***

Eamon and Sheila attended the first Northern Ireland Civil Rights Association march in 1968, from Coalisland to Dungannon. He remembers Austin Currie and Gerry Fitt speaking and Paisley's crowd screaming. Eamon believes his involvement in the civil rights movement made him a marked man but also that any demonstration of an Irish identity was enough to make you a target, be it the sound of traditional music coming from your home or the colours of the Down football team on a flag in your garden put up by your sons after their county won the All-Ireland senior football final. Guilty of being Irish. Convicted of being Catholic.

Nine people, including local UVF leaders Billy Wright and Robin Jackson, known respectively as King Rat and the Jackal, were arrested within days of Gerard's and Rory's murders. But no one was charged. The usual suspects had been rounded up, with the usual consequences. Wright was a British agent, working for 'both the police and military', senior security sources told the BBC's *Spotlight* investigation team, which made a documentary about the murders in 2019.

The killers had tried to destroy evidence by setting fire to their getaway vehicle, containing the balaclavas and boiler suits they had worn, but it failed to properly ignite. Despite this, no forensic evidence was recovered. Police would later lose other evidence while transferring it from Lisburn to Lurgan.

The RUC conducted door-to-door enquiries the day after the murders, asking if anyone had seen anything suspicious, which was rather awkward as the stand-out thing that neighbours and parishioners attending Clare chapel did notice earlier on the day of the shooting was an unusually high security presence. 'There were a lot of roadblocks the night the Cairnses were shot,' recalls Catherine McEvoy, a local historian. 'A number of people were late for the novena in Clare chapel, yet [the killers] were able to get through.'

Two nights before the shooting, Father Loughran told me, someone had stuffed potatoes up the exhaust pipes of cars parked outside Clare chapel. On his way home that night, he'd had to stop the car to remove potato sacks that had been soaked in petrol and were on fire in the middle of the road. He reported both incidents to Lurgan RUC station, and was told the potatoes sounded like a prank, but the burning sacks seemed sinister. He asked for a police car to be parked outside the chapel the following night.

On the day of the shooting, an army helicopter droned overhead for hours and Father Loughran was stopped en route to Gilford by the British Army. 'I was up to high doh. I was full sure they [loyalists] were going to hit the chapel.' That evening, he went through two security-force checkpoints between Laurencetown and Clare. 'No sooner was Mass over than the squealing started. The Cairnses had been shot.' When he got to the house, an RUC man said, 'You were the one called us out.' 'I said, "Now you know why." I find it hard to believe that the Police Ombudsman found there was no collusion.'

A neighbour said to Eamon that an officer had told him an attack had been expected, just not so soon. Sheila and Eamon recalled seeing a stranger acting suspiciously outside a neighbour's house late one night a few weeks previously and a car parked on an empty stretch of road overlooking the back of their house.

An RUC detective on a follow-up visit randomly started discussing the informer system and how successful it was. At the end of the conversation, he asked Eamon directly what he thought of the informer system. Eamon wonders now whether it was an attempt to recruit him. One might also question how the security forces defined success, given the likely involvement of at least three informers or agents in carrying out the murders of Gerard and Rory.

Almost two months after the murders, Eamon asked for an update on the case. A detective told him two men arrested in Lisburn with loaded weapons in their car, one of whom matched the description of the purchaser of the getaway vehicle, were the chief suspects. The detective told them that the UVF locally was split into two factions led by Wright and Jackson. Both 'travelled on these roads most days', but when an attack was taking place, they would drive to a checkpoint to have their whereabouts recorded to secure an alibi.

Gerard and Rory were killed twenty years almost to the day after Down Shoes' shop steward Pat Campbell was murdered in Banbridge, the first of Robin Jackson's many victims. And the brothers' murders came five days after an IRA bomber killed nine Protestants and himself in a fishmonger's on the Shankill Road. Two days after their deaths, loyalists killed seven people in the Rising Sun pub in Greysteel, County Derry. However, while Gerard and Rory's murders appeared to be part of a loyalist backlash, the BBC's *Spotlight* documentary revealed that loyalists had planned to kill every male member of the Cairns family the previous year.

Laurence Maguire, the first person in Northern Ireland convicted of directing terrorism, said in the documentary that he, Billy Wright and Robin Jackson had been part of a four-man team who took part in an aborted plan to 'murder any male occupant' of the Cairns household in 1992. Despite Wright and Jackson being agents or informers, the Cairns family was never informed of this threat to their lives. Maguire was in prison when Gerard and Rory were murdered the following year.

Less than three weeks after Gerard and Rory were murdered, Jack Charlton's Ireland team played Billy Bingham's Northern Ireland team in a vital World Cup qualifier in Belfast's Windsor Park. The visceral sectarian hatred of many home supporters shocked the visiting reporters from Dublin, but what prompted Marie Jones, a playwright from working-class Protestant east Belfast, to write a play – *A Night in November* – about it was the 'sure, what did you expect?' complacency of locals. In the original production, Dan Gordon played Kenneth, a middle-class Protestant, whose childhood friend Norman became a loyalist paramilitary. 'We all believed the same as Norman but we couldn't dirty our hands killing Fenians,' says Kenneth. Gordon told me in an interview in 1995, 'My best friend at school was a Catholic and we called him the big Taig, almost as if to say it's OK. I'm not doing this Protestant guilt thing that we're all guilty, but there is a certain responsibility that has to be shouldered and shared.'

Detective Chief Inspector Dave Hoare examined some murders that had been carried out by the Mid-Ulster UVF for the Historical Enquiries Team (HET), a unit of the PSNI set up to review and investigate the more than 3,000 unsolved murders of the Troubles. Pondering why so many remained unsolved, he remarked, 'it raises the question, did the RUC not try hard enough or were they just not good enough to deal with the Mid-Ulster UVF? Well, I don't buy the argument that they weren't good enough, they were certainly good enough.'

Eamon Cairns said, 'The significance of these comments brings into sharp focus the very reasons why the RUC investigation into the murders of Gerard and Rory failed to bring to account those responsible. It was to protect agents and their handlers.'

In 2007, Nuala O'Loan, then Police Ombudsman, published her report into the murders. She found no evidence of collusion but said that the RUC investigation had been 'unacceptably flawed'. Special Branch had withheld relevant intelligence and police had failed to conduct a thorough investigation. After the *Spotlight* programme, O'Loan said that if she were still Ombudsman, she would reopen the investigation. 'If that evidence had been available to me, it would have changed a lot of things.'

'Supposedly rigorous investigations were deliberately flawed and collusive,' Eamon said. 'At least three agents, including Jackson and

Wright, were involved in the murders of my sons, including the conspiracy the previous year. The third agent, one of the actual gunmen who shot Gerard and Rory, was Alan Oliver, who is responsible for up to fifteen murders.'

In a civil action in May 2021, Oliver was found liable in the High Court for the murders of Katrina Rennie (16), Eileen Duffy (19) and Brian Frizzell (29) at a mobile shop in Craigavon in March 1991. However, he has never been prosecuted for any terrorist activity. Having become a born-again Christian, he has worked for a Protestant church, which praised his 'record of over 20 years' exemplary service in the church and serving the wider community'. The comment distressed the many families who believe he killed their relatives.

'We are appalled that Alan Oliver has risen to a trusted position in this church given his background,' Paula Cairns said.

In 2021, after Eamon failed in a legal bid to compel the British Secretary of State for Northern Ireland to hold a public inquiry, he declared that he had no faith in police ability or willingness to investigate his sons' killings. He said, 'It is both shameful and inhumane that no officer of the PSNI has come to explain to my family what steps it has taken to investigate the admissions made by Laurence Maguire [in the 2019 *Spotlight* documentary] ... that he conspired with others to murder me and my sons, based on information supplied by the security forces.'

Eamon and Sheila feel they have been let down repeatedly by the security forces and the State. The initial RUC investigation was a failure. The HET report was a 'whitewash', says Sheila. When Nuala O'Loan was conducting her investigation, Eamon kept challenging her on her remit. 'But, Nuala,' he'd say to her, 'where your remit ends is where our case starts.' Eamon believed Special Branch had the answers in its files. 'Why do they tell us that we were in nothing, which we weren't, there was never any case against us? What's in the files then?' He asked if he could sit down with her – and the police if needs be – and go through the files together, but this was refused.

'I lost the head with her sometimes,' says Eamon. 'I seen her walking out of the room. I seen her turn white. I seen her bouncing her pens off the table because I was getting to her, because I would tell her, "Look, the job you have, you're supposed to get us the truth."' When the report was published, its finding that there was no evidence of collusion undermined the entire enterprise for the Cairnses.

Eamon is convinced that the police were deeply implicated in his sons' murders. 'I would be convinced the police organised most of it, knew what was going on. They [Gerard and Rory] were particularly targeted. I would say that much. Loyalists get their up-to-date information, the inside track, from the police. They know more about you than anybody because they're constantly stopping you, asking you questions all the time.

'The police never come near us to say how well the case was going forward or nothing. The cruelty of that. People don't want to know or wouldn't understand the cruelty that imposes on us. You're looking for justice, a wee bit of hope. So, we're stuck in this silence and everybody else is getting on with life.'

***

I ask Eamon how he has changed. How has he come to terms with the terrible loss, the wrong done to him and his family?

'Well, it might seem strange, but it shouldn't seem strange really,' says Eamon. 'But I'd say most people wouldn't grasp how important hatred is to me. It's a practical human thing to be full of hate, especially for what society, the police force and Church has done do me, to our family.

'But it's how to discipline it, how to keep it from destroying you. So, I have preached all my life to my children that the number-one thing is to get back to the type of person you were before it happened. I want to be the jolly, talkative Eamon Cairns, getting drunk, ball of craic that always was … carefree. At any job I was ever on, the time flew because you're slagging and craicing. That's me, type of thing. And I have lost that.

'I made a deal with myself that I'd get drunk once a month and that's what I've done. I used to get out of taxis there, drunk, and I'd fall into the hedge, that bank down there, and cry and cry and cry and talk to myself, and then I'd come up here and go to bed and cry a bit more.' His brothers took him to GAA matches, but he would lose himself in the crowd.

'But a great saviour for me too was the All-Ireland Fleadh. They were murdered in '93, so Enniscorthy in '96 was the first Fleadh I was at after. And I have been at them ever since.

'I'd find a quiet corner up the street somewhere, round the back of a house, have a good cry and that was me ready for the fleadh, because I'd squared it with Gerard and Rory. The key thing is keep asking your loved ones when you're in a difficult situation for their help. "What do you think I should do, Rory?"

'I'd have been travelling to different things, meeting families like ourselves – that M1 was a big saviour to me. I have been blinded and got red with anger and frustrations. And that's what helped to keep my sanity. Getting drunk occasionally is a damned good thing for relieving stress. I'm perpetually suffering from that post-traumatic stress, so my health's up and down.

'Sheila would certainly be more religious than me. She was brought up in a very Catholic house, whereas I was brought up more open-minded, radical, call it whatever you like. I see the Catholic Church in the same division as I see the British government. Britain couldn't have done what she done in Ireland without the willing compliance of the Catholic Church. And my experience in dealing with them, also, proves it, you know, that it's part of the establishment.'

I'm reminded of James Joyce's verse: 'Ireland my first and only love, where Christ and Caesar are hand in glove.'

***

Eamon wanted to put up a memorial in Clare chapel's graveyard to all the victims of the Troubles buried there. 'I went round all the houses, expressing what I'd like to do, put up a cross, and all the families were all on for it at the start and then some dropped out for different reasons. I couldn't understand all their reasons and I certainly wasn't going to press them. I was putting this thing up for only myself, to tell you the truth. I was commemorating my children regardless.'

The parish priest said he would call to discuss it. Eamon already felt very disappointed in him as he had come only three times to his house in the first year after Gerard and Rory were murdered and never actually crossed the threshold. Eamon was advised to take the matter up with the bishop. The parish priest's successor invited the congregation to give their views and told Eamon the proposal needed over 90 per cent support, which was not forthcoming as some parishioners feared loyalists might vandalise it and other headstones. Eamon was unperturbed. 'I just said straight to him, "Father, this is going up with or without your blessing," and I never was as happy in my life to tell him that.'

The memorial is a simple Celtic cross engraved with the words, 'This cross was erected in memory of those who were murdered in the Bleary and Ballydougan townlands between the years 1969–2006. We remember them in their youth, middle age and old age. That we may bear witness to and draw strength from the goodness of their ordinary yet exceptional lives.' On the other side is written, 'Injustice anywhere is a threat to justice everywhere' and 'The native Irishman has paid with his life for the deeds of foreign empires'.

One of the memorial stones below it remembers the victims of the bingo bus shooting: Joe Toland, James Marks ('A gentle man and a gentleman. We love you more each day') and Rose McConville ('For a mother we never got to know, who was taken away from her five sons'). Chris remembers her brother Joe Toman, murdered in the Bleary Darts Club. And the Cairnses write of Gerard and Rory, 'In memory of our sons & brothers. Their spirit in life gives us strength and courage on our journey to freedom. *Beidh an La Libh, agus Saoirse ag an Fhirinne*.' (This is inspired by Terence MacSwiney's rallying cry: 'It is not those who can inflict the most but those who can endure the most who will conquer.')

A few yards away stand the gravestones of Joe, Barry and Declan O'Dowd, friends and neighbours of the Cairnses, who were murdered in the family farmhouse just a few hundred yards away from the Cairnses' home, seventeen years before Gerard and Rory.

Eamon's birthday is Remembrance Day, the eleventh of the eleventh. He turned 77 in November 2022.

'Society bombards you to let go and move on. But you can't tell parents that. I see people mourning their dead every year in the month of November from the First World War, a hundred years ago, and I've shed tears with them people watching them on TV because I can relate to it so well, people whose grandparents were shot in the First World War, still shedding tears, and they're expecting me to move on and forget about my children. The ignorance of people, the cruelty of people is unbelievable, boy. But we weren't supposed to have any pain. It was only a UDR or policeman's family had pain.

'And I'm saying, but my children were totally innocent, they're Irish, they're going to be forgot about. We are all going to be forgot about because Church and State are telling me to move on, leave the thing behind. I don't feel right about that there. I want my children remembered when I'm long gone. I want my grandchildren to know who their uncles were, find out as much about them as possible.'

A few years after Rory and Gerard were murdered, the family published a pamphlet. Sheila wrote of how their birthdays are hard. Where once they would have had a party, 'Now all I have is going to Mass and down to their grave and lighting a candle. But I am proud of my sons and I know their short life on this earth was a happy one.'

Róisín wrote, 'Before the murders of my brothers Gerard and Rory, I think I had a carefree life. I emphasise this because the last three years or so seem like 303 years.' She recounted having flashbacks in class. 'I could see black balaclavas and guns roaring and I got really nervous and panicky. I started to tap my pen and sweat a lot. I felt a bit numbed and started to scratch my hands really hard. They went red but I couldn't feel anything.

'Another [flashback] in school was when I had a substitute teacher. He did not know anything about my situation. He asked the class to write about a special occasion such as a birthday. I started to write and I came to the part about eating sweets and the like and suddenly I was hearing the sounds of guns and the sight of the clock which was sitting on the mantelpiece being shot up with pieces of glass falling …

'I always have an image in my mind. I see the murderers in the living room and then leaving. Then I see Rory lying over the seat with blood pouring from his head and the noise of the dripping terrifies me. At night-time I can't go into the kitchen to get a drink, for example, if no one else is there. I am scared to look out the window.'

She told the BBC in 2019, 'When Gerard and Rory were buried, I wanted my birthday cake to go in with the coffins. Just the childlike mind, isn't it? I have Gerard's birthday card and there's a bullet hole in it and wee specks of blood. I still have the card. There's no words for the pain and how harrowing that felt.'

Two

'It was a really scary time'

One day when I was very young, maybe eight years old, my mother told me that an elderly neighbour who lived a few doors down from us had died. 'Who shot her?' I asked. The idea that an old woman might have died of natural causes did not even occur to me.

Growing up in a quiet village in a rural parish we were not, to the naked eye, on the front line of the conflict. Peace walls and security checkpoints were not part of our street furniture. The only time I remember seeing British soldiers in the village was in the aftermath of the Maze prison escape in 1983, when it was rumoured that IRA fugitives might follow rivers such as the Bann to evade roadblocks.

And yet the Troubles saturated our lives, in the same way that the Covid-19 pandemic dominated politics, hogged headlines, transformed society and delivered a daily toll of deaths and hospitalisations. Except the pandemic lasted a few years; the Troubles, decades.

Trauma was piled on trauma, like a dangerous double concussion for a rugby player or a boxer sustaining blows to the head in quick succession.

When our parents went shopping in Banbridge, our job as children was to stay in the car. Every high street back then was a Control Zone where, to deter car-bombers, vehicles could not be left unattended. The longer we were left, the more I began to suspect that my parents might be bombers and my siblings and I become sacrificial lambs. It was a strange time. I had a warped imagination. And trust issues.

If my parents went for a night out and were late back, I wondered whether they would ever come home.

When I tried to visualise what I might become when I grew up, I often pictured myself behind bars. It is said you can only be what you can see and on the nightly news I saw a steady stream of mostly working-class Catholics being sent to jail. Growing up in the North during the Troubles, this was just another prospect to be internalised, like being murdered or unemployed.

To be aware of your mortality is part of the human condition. To be conscious that you might be murdered is a mutant variation in a conflict society such as the North was back then.

My parents opened a clothes shop in Banbridge in 1978. I vividly recall the newsflashes announcing that an incendiary device had gone off in a commercial premises in the town and that key-holders were requested to return to their shops and search for devices, which always struck me as a rather unfair burden. Lending a hand is one thing; sacrificing one is quite another.

I was talking to my cousin outside my uncle's filling station in Laurencetown one day when the windows wobbled from the blast of a bomb ten miles away, news from elsewhere.

***

My mother was pregnant with me when Banbridge Council started building a housing estate in Laurencetown. Discrimination in housing allocation was one of the triggers for the civil rights movement, but it was less of an issue in council areas such as Banbridge. It had a comfortable unionist majority, so allocating Catholics comfortable council houses didn't pose an existential threat.

The estate was named Millar Park after a local unionist councillor in what seems at this remove like a spectacular if small-scale example of proprietorial political vanity. (Locard Park in nearby Tullylish, developed at the same time, was named after another councillor.) While these men undoubtedly had some role in their creation, it was not as if they had funded the estates out of their own pockets.

Council houses are the subject of snobbery in some circles, but Millar Park's were a big step up for most of the new residents. To secure a house there, you had to be living in a place condemned as unfit for habitation. While my parents' home in Hall's Mill undoubtedly qualified, it had not officially been declared as such, so they moved strategically to a similarly dilapidated mill cottage on Barrack Hill. The rent was 10 shillings, or 50p. By contrast, the rent on a council house in Millar Park in 1967 was £2.50. At the time, you could have bought a mill cottage for £50 but renting a new council house with an indoor toilet was more attractive. Millar Park would have been described in the jargon of the time as 'predominantly Catholic'. That it was exclusively working class was unspoken – a given.

My mother told me recently that when I was born Granda Byrne had said I was his most handsome grandchild yet 'with his little white face and red hair'. Overhearing this, my daughter Isobel piped up, 'And now it's reversed!'

Our postal address was so long, it appealed to my sense of the ridiculous to make it even longer – 59 Millar Park, Laurencetown, Gilford, Craigavon, County Armagh, N. Ireland, BT63 6DX, United Kingdom, Europe, Earth, the Milky Way, the Solar System, the Universe.

It later struck me that the place names, and the other places we lived before and after – Hall's Mill, Barrack Hill and Holymount Road – were redolent of the history of the locality and even of the North as a whole.

As well as Millar Park, named for the unionist councillor, Holymount Road – although pronounced Holly-mount – is named after a Mass rock, where the local priest said Mass for local Catholics in Penal times, when England's rulers outlawed the practice of the faith. Barrack Hill is named after a military garrison established in the late 1700s to protect local Catholics from sectarian attacks by the Orange Boys, an agrarian secret society.

Laurencetown and Gilford are named after relatives of Cromwellian army officers who acquired lands confiscated from the local Gaelic chieftains, the Magennises, after the 1641 Rebellion – a Colonel Richard Laurence and John Magill (Magill's ford being a crossing of the River Bann). Craigavon, a planned but never completed new city, was named after Lord Craigavon or James Craig, the North's first prime minister, who notoriously boasted, 'We are a Protestant Parliament and a Protestant State.' Armagh is from the Irish *Ard Macha*, or Macha's Height, named after a sovereignty goddess of ancient Ireland.

Similarly, the names of many of the townlands of the parish harked back to an older, Irish-speaking, Gaelic Ireland, rolling off the tongue like a litany in a Brian Friel play: Drumnascamph, Tullyrain, Lenaderg, Ballylough, Lisnafiffy, Drumhorc, Coose, Tullylish, Kernan, Drummiller, Mullabrack, Drumaran, Loughans, Knocknagore, Ballymacanallen, Moyallan, Ballynagarrick, Ballydougan, Bleary and Clare. Drumnascamph, the name of the road heading north towards the Clare crossroads, sounded comical, exotic even to me as a monoglot, anglophone child, but it is of course a transliteration from the Irish, preserving the sound but obliterating the meaning: Ridge of the Ferns.

Our most famous neighbour in Millar Park was Maggie Barry, a singer from a Travelling background who once shared a bill with Bob Dylan at the Newport Folk Festival. Her legacy is not officially recognised. Have you ever seen a blue plaque on pebbledash? Her grandson Paddy Barry, however, runs the Margaret Barry folk club in a cross-community centre based in our old primary school.

The houses weren't big. The parish priest once pronounced that one should sit eight feet back from the TV set. Doing so would have meant moving the settee to the front step. It was a close-knit place, with many large families going back generations. We were in and out of each other's houses all the time. When we locked ourselves out, a regular occurrence, my cousin Julie was called on to stick her skinny arm through the letter box and twist her hand up to open the lock.

There was a real sense of community, centred round the parish and the GAA. I was an altar boy. Perks included 50p for a funeral; £1 for a wedding; and, unofficially, all the communion hosts we could eat (unconsecrated – we weren't monsters) and all the altar wine we could drink when the safe was left open (putting me off sherry for life).

Three altar boys per Mass was over-manning as the workload was not arduous. But as with a chorus line, our numbers added to the sense of ceremony. The priest had the second-biggest house in the village and one of the best cars. The biggest house belonged to a builder who religiously sat in the front pew.

My parents, wanting the opportunities for us that they did not have, brought us to the library every week as faithfully as to Mass – literature and liturgy.

Standing guard at my sister Andrea's First Holy Communion with our parents, John and Marie.

We were members in Banbridge and Gilford, plus the mobile library in summer. Books were accessible in a way theatre, galleries, even cinema were not. Living on the periphery is a disadvantage too. A lot of culture is urban based. Books were a form of escapism and would ultimately provide a means of escape.

The books I read as a child were the gateway to the genres I loved as an adult.

If the Famous Five, Alfred Hitchcock and the Three Investigators, the Hardy Boys and Nancy Drew were my gateway drugs to crime fiction then Anthony Buckeridge's *Jennings* series and Richmal Crompton's *Just William* stories were a foretaste of Gary Shteyngart, Martin Amis and Lisa McInerney.

In the literature of the working class, the rural experience is the poor relation, so in its absence I loved urban working-class writers such as Christy Brown, Alan Sillitoe, David Storey and Keith Waterhouse. The latter's Billy Liar, another Northerner like me, albeit an English one, with notions of escaping to the bright lights down south, memorably said, 'I turn over a new leaf every day. But the blots show through.' Books connected me to a more benign Britain than the benighted regimes that misruled the North.

Irishness and Catholicism were the active ingredients in my identity then, class the unconsidered filler. I took Graham Greene, Evelyn Waugh and David Lodge for the Catholicism; and digested pretty much every Irish fiction title in the local library, from Joan Lingard to Brian Moore, Jennifer Johnston and Frank O'Connor, running into a brick wall only with Breandán Ó hEithir's *Willie the Plain Pint agus An Pápa*, which turned out to be *in* Irish, a bridge too far. (I could and did study French, German, Spanish and even Latin at school, but not my ancestral language.)

Most cars back then needed a push-start in winter and some at other times of the year – I can still hear cries of 'Put the choke in!' as some banger bucked when the ignition caught. The roads were bad, North and

South, with loose chippings like shrapnel. The route to my grandparents in Wexford was a dot-to-dot puzzle of accident black spots, signs that told motorists: this bend is lethal but we can't afford to fix it. The black spot's association with death and danger dates to Robert Louis Stevenson's *Treasure Island* (1883), perhaps inspired by the Caribbean pirate tradition of giving an Ace of Spaces to a suspected traitor. The one given to Long John Silver was torn from the last page of the Book of Revelation. I imagine a Troubles map of Tullylish, dotted with a black spot for every murder.

Our coalman was Declan O'Dowd – my parents were so fond of him, they gave my brother Shane the middle name Declan. I used to love the sound of the coal being poured into the bunker in the backyard, as if we had our own personal coal butler. Declan wore a leather tabard, like something medieval, to protect his back and his clothes, I suppose, as he lugged the bag off the lorry by its ears and slung it over his shoulder. Our milkman was Declan's father, Barney – we called our rocking horse after him. ('*My* rocking horse,' my sister Andrea corrects me.) I was fascinated by his big leather satchel full of coins, like a pot of gold. Declan's murder, along with his brother Barry and uncle Joe, and Barney being shot brought the bloodshed to our doorstep.

My mother worked as a dinner lady at my primary school, which was a win when it came to second helpings. My father worked in Goodyear – we had a lifetime's supply of clingfilm and a glass ashtray with a rubber tyre around the rim. Daddy also brought home an ugly chunk of untreated rubber, like a hunk of raw meat gouged from an animal. It felt colonial. Goodyear bailed, of course, as multinationals do.

Every letter my father opened from his fretting mother in County Wexford in the 1970s and 80s contained a newspaper clipping of an advertisement for a job somewhere, anywhere, south of the border, out of harm's way. How would you feel, I remember my mother asking us, about moving to Dublin? Conflicted and anxious is what I felt, I think, whatever about what I said. Children tend to be conservative, siding with the status quo, however bad that might be, wary of change.

'He went for different interviews but it just wasn't to be,' my mother said. 'We lived in fear.' One day my mother was out cleaning the windows when Mrs Byrne came over and said, 'Marie, they shot someone going into Goodyear this morning.' My mother burst out crying. 'Every night in life, you'd be sitting watching the six o'clock news and it never went over without you hearing of somebody dying that day.'

Samuel Gardiner, a 26-year-old Protestant from Lurgan, was a passenger in a car driven by a fellow Goodyear employee, who was also a UDR soldier, when IRA gunmen opened fire as it left the plant on 24 June 1976. He died in hospital on 6 July. His fellow workers marched to Lurgan town centre in protest.

The violence meant that many neighbours considered leaving. My mother says, 'We were going to go to Australia at that time. Your daddy had an interview in Galway for a job shortly after the O'Dowds were shot. Garry [my parents' fourth child] took his first steps that weekend too. Everyone was terrified. Sally McAleavey said to me, "I've my family allowance book and any papers of any importance in my handbag, so if we have to get out I'm ready to go."'

My uncle Tony lived in Millar Park too and had worked on the same production line in Down Shoes as Pat Campbell when Pat was murdered. After that, my mother said that if anyone came to Tony's house 'he didn't answer the door, he went round the side of the house with a crowbar. It was a really scary time.' If someone knocked at our door, Mammy would always go. Magical thinking, as if that would have saved Daddy.

When a neighbour, Gerard McEvoy, got married in the 1970s, he bought a house from a Protestant neighbour, Jack Jones. He moved in on a Thursday and it was burned on the Sunday. He had to jump out of the bedroom window. It was set on a fire a second time, and then the third time, it was burned to a shell. In the end, he sold it back to Mr Jones, who was good enough to offer the same for it as he had been paid.

Two books were published in 2021 about the burning of Ireland's big houses. Perhaps more attention should be paid to the burning of small houses.

***

I had started at Bann Primary School in Laurencetown in September 1972, three weeks before my fifth birthday. I loved school to begin with. I can picture my first classroom, its play area with a raised container filled with water and a sandpit. My earliest memory is of drawing a brown and yellow dog, which I coloured in with those fat, blunt crayons.

I could not draw a straight line with a ruler, but otherwise I was a fast learner so it was agreed that I would skip second class and go straight into primary three. My new teacher and I did not hit it off.

My mother tells me that if I didn't get enough pages to read, I would write my own homework assignment in big, scrawly writing. 'You near put your teacher mad, telling her she was spelling words wrong. She said you were getting too much attention at home.'

The only two things I remember from that year are feeling left out when I wasn't picked for the class choir – to be fair, I can't hit a note – and getting into trouble with the teacher for not wanting to go to a classmate's father's funeral. My mother explained to her that my uncle Willie had just been killed in a road accident and that I had been very upset. She also reminded her that I was only six years old. 'I have only ever taught one other child as clever as Martin,' my teacher replied, 'and he ended up in jail as a matter of fact.' I have yet to receive a greater back-handed compliment.

My cousin Julie was in my new class and a line from one of her compositions, which she recited proudly to her mother, Una, has entered family folklore. 'Sometimes my mammy gets very cross and beats us all with the brush, and sometimes she goes hysterical and puts us to bed without any supper, and the next day we would be very hungry.'

Aunt Una said, 'You did not write that, for you don't know how to spell hysterical.' Julie replied, 'No, but the teacher does and she wrote it right across the blackboard, and she roared with laughter.'

What's that? What did *I* write? 'My mammy has a lovely face with brown hair and curls at the back. My daddy loves her. He gives her lots of hugs and kisses.' Uncle Sean said to Julie, 'Why could you not write a story like that?'

Mammy was very house-proud. I was happy to help, using the same cloth to clean the hearth, then the doors, then the horizontal blades of venetian blinds. In my memory she was always bleaching the front step, a rough grey cement, turning it briefly bluey-white with detergent, Vim or Flash, and a scrubbing brush that would skin your knuckles if you weren't careful.

There weren't many amenities in the village. Millar Park was built around a green, but it was years before the council thought to put in a playground. At the risk of being prolier than thou, the play area between the school and Millar Park was called the Dirt Track. Still, my childhood was also Heaneyesque: blackberry-picking in the autumn; playing football all year round till the fading light turned the ball into a blur; putting slack on the fire; peeling potatoes either side of a pot.

I remember nature walks at primary school, on which we would learn to distinguish trees by their leaves: sycamore, oak, chestnut, ash. Now I can just about tell the difference between a conker and an acorn. Prising loose bits of pebbledash off the wall of our house felt like scratching a scab or worrying at a loose milk tooth with my tongue. We played under the chestnut tree in the school playground and in the barley field behind it, a sea of straw you could lose yourself in.

Less idyllically, we played *Space Invaders*, an early computer game, at the back of the local shop. I was fascinated by the dangerous-looking bacon-slicer with its blade like a circular saw. After a wipe with a damp cloth, it could also slice crumbed ham.

What else did we eat back then? Scotch broth, Irish stew, fried mince and brown stew. Sausages, pork but also beef. Vegetable roll, so named because the sausage meat was flecked with parsley, was fried with the plastic wrapping on – it became like white lace and we removed it before eating. I marvel at the memory of Marvel powdered milk and Smash dehydrated potato, food fit for catastrophic times. Uncle Sean's chipmaker forced a potato through a guillotine-sharp grille before the chips were dropped into boiling oil. Danger was everywhere in the 1970s.

A lot of neighbours had side hustles in their back sheds. Uncle Tony mended shoes. Mrs Agnew made jam – as she paid by the pail, blackberry-picking became a competitive sport for the month of September. Geordie Berry cut hair in such a distinctively take-no-prisoners fashion that his victims could be spotted at fifty yards. My brother Shane was once so traumatised by a haircut that he wore a woollen hat for a week, indoors and out. Finally persuaded that the worst was over, he was coaxed into taking it off, only for an unwarned Aunt Una to visit and admire his 'Geordie Berry special'. Back on went the hat.

Once we found bloody bandages in a sheugh, or ditch, between two fields and thought we had stumbled on an IRA field hospital or some kind of criminal hideout. A teenager had been beaten up and had got himself cleaned up there before facing the music at home.

Almost everyone had a nickname. I hadn't seen John O'Dowd, the former Sinn Féin education minister and a cousin of Declan and Barry, since primary school, but when we met in 2022 he still remembered the nickname I gave him. 'Was it Rowdy Dowdy? Or Cloud?' It was the latter and it never stuck, but Colm Campbell is still known as Flea, thanks to me. My old classmate Paddy Barry used to be called Dusty. 'It was originally Dustin Hoffman, I looked a wee bit like him,' he says. 'That's a lie,' says his wife, Donna. 'There was a programme on called *3–2–1*, with Dusty Bin.' I knew Paddy's brother Kevin as Spook, but he is also known as Lovely Ball, Paddy says. 'We'd have been playing football and he'd say, "Lovely ball, lovely ball."'

Daddy was involved with Laurencetown Swifts and wrote the match reports for the *Banbridge Chronicle* under the byline Coubray, the name of the field where they played. I use the term advisedly as they shared the pitch with a herd of cattle, which meant you were lucky if you finished a match covered only in mud. The goalkeeper once gave the linesman his false teeth to mind. He wrapped them up in his hanky, which also served as his flag. Waving for a throw-in, the teeth went flying and were lost for good, ruining the goalie's prospects for Saturday night.

I hunted in vain in the archive for Daddy's match report with the headline 'Unlucky to lose' after a plucky 7–0 defeat for the Swifts. He claims the sub-editor garbled a line from the intro to the effect that they were unlucky to have lost by so many goals. But when you're explaining, you're losing. 7–0, in this case.

I became Coubray Junior and got a taste for journalism, as did my brother Garry. My dad kept a scrapbook of his clippings, which I read as enthusiastically as my comics. (I kept clippings for my kids and they call me a hoarder.)

I founded my own newspaper, 'The Doyles Weekly Herald'. The only surviving copy (in truth, the only copy) is dated 16 April 1978. The title's political leanings can be gleaned from a centre spread on Margaret Thatcher, still over a year away from becoming prime minster. There is no actual text – writing is hard – but the illustrations under the subheading 'Her favourite photographs' include Willie Whitelaw, Enoch Powell, piles of banknotes and coins, Jack the Ripper and Al Capone, plus a portrait of Thatcher with a pirate's eyepatch and horns.

Three

Bigotry on the Bann

Working-class politics and activism seemed ineffectual. Trade union leaders called in vain for peace, but the inspirational solidarity of striking miners in Britain or Dunnes Stores workers in Dublin in the 1980s was sadly lacking. People from all sides and classes had come together in the civil rights movement in the late 1960s and the Peace People protests in the mid-1970s, but these organisations were overpowered by the forces of reaction and violence.

But for me, the most formidable, if regrettable, display of the power of organised labour was the Ulster Workers' Council strike in May 1974, when pickets, given muscle by loyalist paramilitaries, brought down a power-sharing government and delayed peace by a generation.

During the strike, local loyalists drove into Millar Park, shouting threats that they would be back that night to burn us out. For one of our neighbours, this was history threatening to repeat itself, my mother says.

'May McAlinden, who lived opposite us, used to live in Lisburn and they were burned out in 1920. She used to say, never count anything that you own for you could lose it all in the blink of an eye. They were burned out totally other than the clothes they stood up in. They came here to live and opened a shop in Chapel Row. She was very ladylike. She had an old aunt lived in Cross Row who wasn't able to look after herself.' My mother has never forgotten the terrible condition of the mill cottage the aunt lived in. 'The house was black and windows were so dirty with soot you couldn't see out. Her hair was yellow and her face was black from the smoke of the fire.'

There were other historical echoes. When my mother was young, every 12 July, Orangemen would march from the Orange hall past the chapel to the crossroads. 'I remember them drumming outside the chapel and Father Lennon coming out and telling them to go about their business. They did the same at Lisnagade Chapel once. This boyo banged and banged the drum till he had himself blue in the face and was exhausted, and he left the drum down on the ground. My mammy's aunt, Annie McKay, got up on the ditch and jumped down on it and bust it. They christened her Annie the Rattler.'

At the time of the strike, I was about to make my First Holy Communion along with the rest of the pupils in my year, a big milestone for Catholic children. But there was no electricity and no one could get to work, so my parents decided to bring us to stay with our grandparents in County Wexford. My mother asked if I could make my Holy Communion in Gorey and was reassured that I could make it anywhere. 'So we went to Gorey and took your Holy Communion suit with you. We thought we might have to stay indefinitely.' We did, in fact, make it back in time.

Mammy has her own Holy Communion story. Her father was a part-time undertaker. 'The shrouds were all in a big brown chest upstairs. I came down the stairs one day in this cream shroud and said to my mother, "Wouldn't this be a lovely dress for my Holy Communion?" "Oh my God," she says, "get that off at once."' Mammy's brother Artie had died a few years earlier along with another child when they drank poisoned water from a stream.

The first person I ever interviewed, for the *Banbridge Chronicle* in August 1990, was an impeccably middle-class Catholic senior public servant, Patrick Manson, who had defied those loyalist strikers and kept the lights on and the telephone lines open. A hero in pinstripes.

Manson was a Dubliner who had lived in England for thirty years. While serving with the Royal Irish Fusiliers during the Second World War, he had survived being blown up by a mine in Italy and been awarded the Military Cross. As director of the Post Office in Northern Ireland and chairman of the Postal and Telecommunications Board, whose buildings and services were a prime target for paramilitaries, he had been appointed CBE. He spoke with pride of having always maintained priority telephone services even when, at one stage, one-third of all exchanges had been put out of action. During the strike in 1974 he'd had portable generators flown in from England to outmanoeuvre a loyalist embargo on the electricity supply.

But class consciousness was not really a thing for me, perhaps because reality belied any notion of class solidarity surpassing the religious divide. In our low-level civil war, sectarian trumped proletarian; belligerents on both sides were largely drawn from the working class, divided by a common rung.

Certainly, there were class-based divisions within unionism and nationalism. Sinn Féin dismissed the SDLP as a party of schoolteachers and solicitors. The DUP painted the Ulster Unionists as out-of-touch elitists, the fur-coat brigade. But these differences were understood to be secondary concerns.

***

I could absorb a lot of British cultural influences without ever feeling British. I devoured comics. *Tiger and Scorcher* – I remember feeling somehow short-changed by the merger of the once independent titles – *The Dandy*, *Beano*, *Whizzer and Chips*, *The Hotspur*, *Warlord*, *Victor*, *Wizard*, *Roy of the Rovers*, *Battle*, *Action*. For a young Irish boy, these picture stories celebrating the derring-do of the British Army should perhaps have gone against the grain, given the depredations that men in the same uniform were committing in my country, but in the comics their enemy was Hitler's Germany or Hirohito's Japan, so that was all right.

Daddy was concerned about the effect all this comic-reading was having on my vocabulary – Kerpow! Yikes! Donner und Blitzen! – and threatened to cut off the supply lines, but peace was somehow restored. When we visited our Doyle grandparents in Gorey, County Wexford, one of the highlights was that Granny would have saved all my cousins' comics for us. So what if they were *Mandy*, *Bunty* and *Jinty*. A good story is a good story. And I was as much as a fan of Enid Blyton's Malory Towers and St Clare's as the Famous Five and the Secret Seven. So I got a kick when I discovered decades later that Darrell Rivers was, like me, an alumnus of the University of St Andrews. Twins!

Our home and other houses in the village had tall aerials and signal boosters too, antennae seeking to pick up a signal, however attenuated, from an RTÉ transmitter south of the border. I can't remember what we watched, other than the GAA, and strange ads for farming products dealing with unfamiliar ailments such as fluke and ringworm. But the voice of commentator Micheál Ó hEithir narrating the All-Ireland football or hurling final seemed the quintessence of Irishness to me.

If Daddy had doubts about my comics, I had grave reservations about his *Sunday Express*, which he bought for its coverage of our team, Manchester City. Its editor, John Junor, was censured by the Press Council in 1985 for his racist remark: 'Wouldn't you rather admit to being a pig than be Irish?' We switched papers.

My sense of Irishness was uncomplicated, I think, partly because half of my relations lived in the South and they were no different to us. Well, I say that. Granny and Granda Doyle didn't have UTV, they had HTV, with programmes in Welsh.

Granda Doyle's pride and joy was his greenhouse – the heady smell of ripening tomatoes is my madeleine. He also had several rows of strawberries, a fruit that is part of Wexford's DNA. Doyle in Irish is Ó Dubhghaill, meaning dark foreigner, i.e., Danish Viking. This strawberry-blond (now sadly strawberry-bald) raider from the North on his summer holidays went through those rows like a locust.

The term Free State is sometimes used as an insult, but often its use comes from a natural attachment to an old term, like calling a Snickers bar a Marathon, or a five-pence piece a shilling. The South did represent freedom, though, from bigotry but mostly from fear. I felt freer south of the border. Who wouldn't want to be in a free state, a state of freedom?

My aunt Peggy is the Doyle family historian, author of a book on the Coolgreaney evictions in 1887, when sixty County Wexford families, including a branch of our own, were crowbarred from their homes during the Plan of Campaign. She unearthed in Collins Barracks a photograph of my great-uncle, John O'Donohoe, marching with fellow Irish Volunteers with Mausers from the *Asgard* in Howth in July 1914. (It's not a war crime but John has my father's ears.) Peggy also showed us the bullet hole in the wall that marked the spot where District Inspector Percival Lea-Wilson was shot dead in Gorey on 15 June 1920. After the rebels surrendered in 1916, Michael Collins had witnessed him humiliating Tom Clarke, one of the signatories of the Proclamation, by having him stripped naked, and had ordered that he should be killed. (Lea-Wilson's widow, Marie, gave a painting, later identified as Caravaggio's *The Taking of Christ*, to the Jesuits in gratitude for their support after her husband was killed on Collins's orders.)

But all that was in the past. Uncle Ray in Galway assured me the South wanted nothing to do with the North. Uncle George in Gorey wasn't so sure, however. There was plenty of republican sympathy in this heartland of the 1798 Rebellion. As editor of *The Irish Post*, I interviewed the Gorey-born Irish ambassador to Britain, Ted Barrington, who skipped the revolutionary generation to cite as his heroes Parnell and O'Connell, 'people who used constitutional methods to achieve real change and benefits for people'. But sure enough, on 18 February 1996, nine days after the Docklands bombing broke the 1994 IRA ceasefire, 21-year-old Ed O'Brien from Gorey was blown up by the bomb he was carrying on a London bus, which also injured several other passengers.

Identities in Ireland can be complex. My namesake, Martin Doyle from New Ross, County Wexford, won the Victoria Cross fighting in the Royal Munster Fusiliers in the First World War before joining the IRA and winning a War of Independence medal fighting against his former comrades. A descendant, London-born David Cooney, became Ireland's ambassador to Britain. George Mitchell called him one of the two 'unsung heroes of the peace process'.

***

Mammy's family had moved within Laurencetown in 1953, from Chapel Row to School Road. The new houses had bathrooms, whereas the two-up two-downs on Chapel Row had only a dry toilet at the end of the garden. A neighbour's son said to one of my uncles, 'Isn't this great? All you have to do is sit well down into the toilet and pull the chain and you get your bum washed and you'll not need to get bathed.'

Mammy left school at 14, having learned very little, she says. The teacher sat in front of the fire reading books all day. If anyone asked to do the eleven-plus, he said, 'Who told you you had brains?' An inspector once told the teacher that my mother was bright and asked, 'Is anything being done with her?' But her father wouldn't hear tell of her sitting the technical school entrance exam. 'Sure a Catholic would never get anything anyway.'

'What Daddy was saying was the truth. A Catholic wouldn't have got a job. People had seven or eight children and couldn't afford to keep them at school. Even some who got the eleven-plus left school at 16 to start earning. I've no regrets, but I would have loved learning. I really enjoy reading history. But it just wasn't to be.'

Mammy's first pay was £2 from Blane's where she made handkerchiefs. She took a bus to Gilford, then another bus, then she cycled. Next, still only 14, she got a job in the shoe factory in Banbridge and cycled there as well. There weren't as many cars on the roads then. Granda had an old banger and used to buy second-hand engine oil, which made the engine smoke. One day he collected her from work. 'Look, here comes Puffing Billy,' said her friend, not realising who it was. The shoe factory was the Rolls-Royce of jobs. Mammy earned more than her eldest brother, Paul, who was a motor mechanic. 'I hated it, though, sitting with your head down the whole time, feeding leather into the machine all day. That's why you all had a good education. I used to say, whatever you do, work hard at school and don't end up in the shoe factory.'

The money was good, but they didn't get to keep it. 'Ma took it off us and gave us ten shillings a week.'

She went to London for a year in March 1962 to train as a nurse. Back then a primary school education was the sole requirement. But she came home because she was homesick. 'I loved nursing but had a fear I wouldn't pass the exams. Every letter from my da was saying, "Maybe you'll think of coming home, it's not such a bad place."' Her friend Agnes's letters said, 'Work hard, we'll be so proud of you.'

Her father got her a job in Laurencetown filling station to make sure she wouldn't go back. People would fill up their own cars and would sometimes ask if they could wash their hands afterwards. 'The owner was so mingy she wouldn't buy a bar of soap but kept a box of Tide washing powder beside the basin instead.'

By the time she came home, my mother, Marie, had met my father in the Gresham in 1962 – not the smart hotel on Dublin's O'Connell Street but the ballroom on London's Holloway Road, a meeting place and a melting pot for so many working-class Irish of their generation. Brendan Bowyer was playing with the Royal Showband. Thirty years later, my mother queued for his autograph at the Rose of Tralee Festival. She got him to inscribe on a card, to my father's amusement, 'Woe the day!'

My parents got married in 1965, when Mammy was 24 and Daddy was 23, settling first in Summerhill in Dublin's north inner city. 'John hasn't just brought you to one of the worst areas in Dublin,' his best man, a garda, said cheerfully to my mother. 'He's brought you to *the* worst area.'

Actually, the neighbours could not have been kinder and it was with mixed feelings that – after my sister Andrea was born in 1966 in Dublin's Rotunda Hospital – my parents moved north to make a life in Laurencetown.

Their first home was in my great-grandmother Bessie McKay's old two-up two-down house, complete with outside or off-suite toilet, in Hall's Mill, an adjoining hamlet.

Bessie was originally from Greenock in Scotland. Still in her teens, she got a job as a maid in the mansion of a wealthy linen manufacturer called Sinton in Tullylish. My great-grandfather, Owen McKay, whose family had a farm at Lisnagade, near Banbridge, worked across the road, driving a linen cart for Sinton. A generation later, Barney O'Dowd, our milkman, would meet his wife, a housekeeper, there too. The Big House – where love stories begin.

Bessie was a Presbyterian and Owen a Catholic. They were married in St Patrick's Catholic Church in Banbridge and set up home on Clare Street in Hall's Mill. Mixed marriages were frowned upon by all sides. Bessie's first child, named Owen after his father, was born with spina bifida. Father Doyle announced that if mothers came to the parochial house they would be given a voucher for free boots for their children. When Bessie went, however, Father Doyle grabbed her by the shoulder and said, 'There'll be no boots for you or yours.' Catholic charity was only for Catholic mothers, it seemed, even if Bessie's children were being raised as Catholics.

***

My mother's father, Arthur Pat, was a big influence and a great storyteller. As his day job was selling insurance, I smiled when a character in one

My grandfather Arthur Pat Byrne, third left, back row, c.1914.

of his play scripts made a big speech about the importance of being well insured. Guerrilla marketing or evangelism – either way, it tickled me.

Visiting him, however, was a form of Vatican roulette. If you were lucky, you got a fireside story, a mug of cocoa and a soda farl with butter and jam. If you were not so blessed, you got five decades of the Rosary with all the trimmings.

I used to earn pocket money collecting my grandparents' laundry. Granny usually paid in silver coins but once it was Arthur Pat, who paid in coppers, prompting me to ask Mammy plaintively whether he understood decimal currency.

The violence that was visited upon my community when I was young was initially shocking but quickly became the norm. It would, however, have been very familiar to my grandfather's generation, for their youth was tarnished by similar events. It tore Arthur Pat's family apart.

The war memorials in Gilford and Banbridge reflect the devastating effect of the First World War. Scores of young men, mostly Protestants but many Catholics too, a Doyle among them, had sacrificed their lives in that imperial conflict. Violence locally, however, was only beginning.

A series of killings in 1920 ensured that communities in Banbridge and Gilford and every village in between would be divided as surely as Ireland would be partitioned.

On 17 July 1920, Lieutenant Colonel Gerald Brice Ferguson Smyth, divisional commissioner of the RIC in Munster, was shot dead by the IRA in Cork. Smyth, 34, had been born in the Punjab, where his father, George, was British High Commissioner, but both his parents were from Banbridge's linen aristocracy and his family had strong links to the UVF. His mother, Helen, was the daughter of Thomas Ferguson of Edenderry House. A British Army veteran, Smyth had been wounded six times, and had had to have his left forearm amputated.

On 19 June 1920, Smyth had addressed RIC officers in Listowel, County Kerry, informing them that martial law would be introduced and 'a policeman is perfectly justified in shooting any man who he has good reason to believe is carrying arms and who does not immediately throw up his hands when ordered'. If innocent people were shot, that could not be helped and no policeman would have to answer for such an eventuality. In what became known as the Listowel mutiny, the RIC men rejected their new orders. More than a thousand RIC men resigned from an already depleted force.

Smyth's coffin was borne from Banbridge train station to the family home, Clonaslee House, by employees of Ferguson's linen mill. Every linen factory closed as a mark of respect for the funeral, as did most shops.

Protestant workers at the Banbridge Weaving Company demanded the removal of Sinn Féin workers, i.e., Catholics, from the factory. Mill workers pledged not to work alongside Catholics who refused to take an oath that they would not associate with Sinn Féin. A mob looted, burned and smashed up Catholic pubs and shops. When the Monaghan family home and furniture business on Scarva Street was attacked by a loyalist mob, the Monaghans opened fire. Three people were injured and William Sterritt (17) was shot dead. He is commemorated to this day in Banbridge by the William Sterritt Memorial Flute Band.

On 22 August 1920, Detective Inspector Oswald Swanzy, the alleged ringleader in the assassination that 20 March of Tomás Mac Curtain, the Lord Mayor of Cork, was himself assassinated by the IRA in Lisburn, County Antrim, twenty miles away from Laurencetown. In the ensuing riots, many Catholic homes and businesses were looted and burned, and most Catholics fled to nearby Belfast. Pearse Lawlor's *The Burnings* gives a detailed account of the orgy of violence against Catholics in Lisburn, Banbridge and Dromore: ethnic, sectarian cleansing that Catholics labelled pogroms. Loyalists expelled thousands of Catholics from the shipyards and other workplaces. Almost 500 people were killed in Belfast alone between July 1920 and October 1922, more than half of them Catholic, despite Catholics making up only a quarter of the population of the city.

On 3 September 1920, William McDowell, who was driving a cashier back to Gilford Mill with the week's wages, was shot dead in an armed robbery. William 'Yankee' Conlon, a local hoodlum home from the US, and two accomplices were sentenced by a court martial to death, commuted to life imprisonment.

Choosing to treat this crime as politically motivated, which it almost certainly wasn't, Protestant workers held a meeting in Gilford's Orange hall the next day. There they resolved that every linen mill and bleach green owner and their Protestant workers would turn away any Catholic who refused to sign the Banbridge oath: 'I … hereby declare I am not a Sinn Feiner nor have any sympathy with Sinn Fein and do declare I am loyal to King and country.'

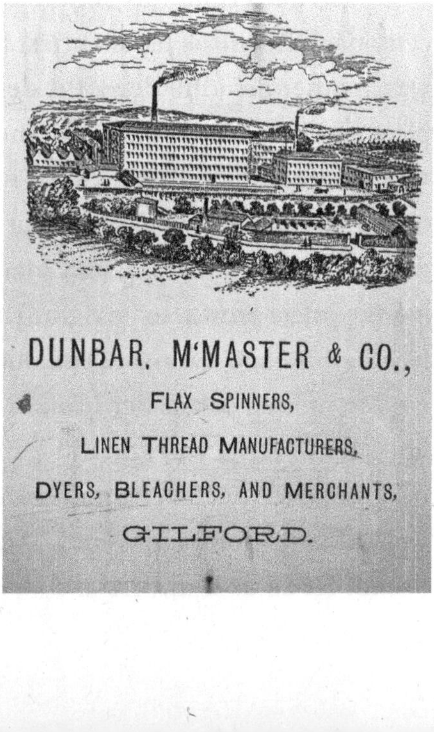

My grandfather Arthur Pat and his sister Lizzie, who had both worked at Uprichard's Bleach Green in Hall's Mill since they had left school, were among the vast majority of Catholics who refused to sign. Deprived of income, Arthur Pat had no choice but to return to his uncles' farm near Rostrevor to work for his keep. Lizzie emigrated, first to Canada and then to New York. They never saw each other again. Arthur Pat couldn't bear the prospect of having to say goodbye once more.

Under the headline 'Bigotry on the Bann', on 18 September 1920 *The Irish News* reported on 'the infamous pogrom': 'The Catholic workers refuse to sign and even though long weeks have passed they still loll aimlessly about the streets, outcasts of society, men and women whom the children of the "elect" pass with a shudder. They are outcasts in every sense of the term with scarcely a nod of recognition from former friends of the workshop … The dinner horn sounded and a stream of workers marched up the avenue for their midday meal. Do they ever give a thought as workers of the world to their former comrades, perhaps without a dinner and they the cause?'

'A terrible crime was committed last week: the murder of an innocent man,' Tullylish's parish priest told his congregation. 'And then there was another dreadful deed, the denial of hundreds of Catholics to their place of work.' He prophesied, 'The grass will grow green over their factory chimneys and there will be work for neither Catholic nor Protestant. I might not live to see it but some of you will.' As speeches go, it was not exactly on a par with Martin Luther King's 'I have a dream …' but the priest proved to be right. The work did run out, but one thing the North of Ireland has never run out of is dirty linen.

My mother asked her brother Joe if he remembered the story too. 'Joe says, "Marie, you and me were reared on that story." My da told it over and over, he never got over the hurt of what happened. People you worked with from you were 13 years of age and regarded as your best friend. He said, "I understand that they had no choice because if they had objected, they'd have sacked them as well, but they were still there blocking the way."

'My father said they were two of the saddest years of his life, both his parents dead and his only sister away to Canada and the cousins he was so close to away to Scotland. A neighbour became a maid and said, "I never in all my life met such aul' gorbs. They hadn't their breakfast et till they're telling you what they want for their lunch." That's where my father got the ideas for his plays.'

Granda was a leading light in local amateur dramatics. He staged Dion Boucicault plays and formed the Laurencetown comedy club in 1919. The footlights were candles on tin. 'Then the Troubles started in 1920 and there was none for a good time when I was with my uncles in Warrenpoint.' Granny dusted her arms, which were red from washing laundry, with flour before going on stage.

He got scripts at a penny a piece from Dick's of London, but 'there was a lot of talk complaining about plays making fun of the Irish' so he began writing his own. One play won a cup in the County Louth Drama Festival in Dundalk. He got a letter explaining that protocols would delay sending it across the border.

During the Famine the local elite had been shamed by the local

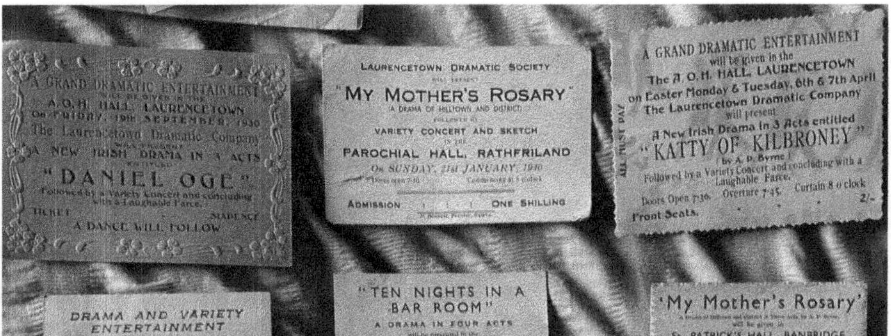

Tickets to some of my grandfather Arthur Pat Byrne's stage productions.

Church of Ireland minister Reverend William Butler Yeats – grandfather of his namesake, the Nobel Prize-winning poet – into saving the lives of the starving. Now Catholics, deprived of their livelihoods by that same elite, had to rely on the charity of Irish-Americans to survive. More than £400 was raised, mostly in Irish America, to support Laurencetown's expelled Catholics in 1922 alone.

Armed with the foreknowledge of what was to come, the manoeuvres of the West Down Battalion of John Redmond's National Volunteers, as reported in *The Irish News* on 4 November 1914, two months after Britain had declared war on Germany, seem tragically naive. 'The parade was led by the Laurencetown Flute Band, rendering National airs and headed by a flag bearer with a beautiful silk flag which was a combination of the Union Jack and the Irish flag which was sent from America.' Arthur Pat, who turned 20 later that month, was a member and future leader of the Laurencetown Flute Band, so he was most likely on that march.

The Home Rule Act had become law that September, but Redmond, leader of the Irish Parliamentary Party, had accepted its suspension for the duration of the war, which was only expected to last a few months. That same month, the party and the Irish Volunteers, formed to add military muscle to the fight for Irish self-determination, had been split by Redmond's call for its members to enlist in Britain's war. Ulster's unionists, meanwhile, backed by their own militia, the Ulster Volunteer Force, had decided to embrace their own, Rome-free version of Home Rule in Down and five other northern counties, which they felt they could comfortably control.

I discovered while researching this book that Arthur Pat had given a series of taped interviews in 1988, just before he died aged 94, to a local teacher, Kathleen McFlynn.

He talks of a world that is gone: blacksmiths and beetlers and tramp hackers. The fate of a friend who died in the First World War is mentioned in a matter-of-fact way: 'Larry went to war and was killed.'

There used to be dances and band practices in the Orange hall near the Bannville Hotel, whose members were 'all very nice fellas, I knew them all'. He wore clogs to work in the bleach green and saved a shilling a fortnight for a pair of boots. He doesn't talk in any detail about the time he was put out of work, describing it as 'the time he went away to live with his uncles'.

Arthur Pat was a member and later the local head of the Ancient Order of Hibernians (AOH), which had a hall in Hall's Mill and others in Gilford, Bleary and Ballydougan, and whose banner featured Allen, Larkin and O'Brien, the Manchester Martyrs, members of the Irish Republican Brotherhood executed in 1867. He marched from Warrenpoint to Rostrevor with the AOH, the Irish National Foresters and the United Ireland League, who 'all had the same way of thinking', he said. The Hibs was a moderate Catholic nationalist organisation under the sway of Belfast politician Joe Devlin, who was allied to John Redmond's Irish Parliamentary Party. Some on both sides of the religious divide saw it as a sectarian mirror image of the Orange Order.

'It was Catholic but no bigotry,' Granda told Mrs McFlynn. 'Unity, friendship and true Christian charity. But then Sinn Féin took a lot away. If they had just followed that we wouldn't be in the awful fix we are now because people can be quite agreeable. There was a flute band up at the Presbyterian church and if we were short of a flute we'd exchange with one another. There was no such thing as throwing stones at one another. One would have gone to hear the other play. Most of them played the same marches.'

***

Seamus Monaghan, who had led an IRA squad that burned down the abandoned Laurencetown RIC station in April 1920, was born in Banbridge in 1896, a couple of years after my grandfather. I suspect he would have found Arthur Pat's brand of nationalism a little too pale green. At least three AOH members were killed and several halls destroyed by Sinn Féiners in this period.

Monaghan had served in the Banbridge Battalion of the Irish Volunteers but quit over Redmond's acceptance of partition and support for Volunteers joining the British Army. According to his Irish military pension record, he formed the hundred-strong Banbridge Battalion in May 1920, 'some time before the pogrom … In that area, we would only have about one in 10 of a nationalist population.'

'Practically everyone of the Protestant population of the area was an enemy,' he wrote in his pension application, whose references were impeccable: Frank Aiken, then the Minister of Defence, and Dr Mick O'Hanlon of St Bricin's Hospital. 'Even the Catholics and the nationalists, they were different to the nationalists in other parts of the country. They were mostly hostile also. They had a British outlook, and were sympathetic with the British systems. Therefore the difficulties of recruiting were great.'

After William Sterritt was shot in the attack on the Monaghans, Seamus, his father, Dan, and brother, Daniel O'Connell Monaghan, were charged with murder. While in Belfast jail awaiting trial, on 1 September, Seamus wrote in Irish to Joseph Dolan, a fellow Sinn Féin supporter and Irish-language enthusiast in Ardee, County Louth. 'We'll be charged with killing Sterritt and injuring two others,' he wrote. 'We'll be hanged after that, I suppose, and then we won't have to do the three years.'

The murder charges were dropped and he was sentenced to twelve months in Worcester prison for arms offences, serving only six. On release, he spent three weeks on holiday with an aunt in Liverpool, whose home was a meeting place for the IRA. While there, he took part in setting fire to twenty farms in March 1921. He became Officer Commanding of the IRA's 2 Brigade, 4th Northern Division under Frank Aiken but was captured a month later and imprisoned at Peterhead prison, Scotland, until January 1926. He lived above his furniture shop in Dublin until his death in 1974.

Rory O'Hanlon, a former Fianna Fáil minister for health and father of the actor and comedian Ardal O'Hanlon, grew up in Mullaghbawn in south Armagh and knew Seamus Monaghan well. Rory's father, Mick, had served with him and Frank Aiken in the War of Independence and they became great pals, he says.

'I would have known Seamus through my father primarily but also he was a patient in the Mater while I was a houseman there in 1959–60. I used to go and sit with him. He was a great raconteur. He cycled twice a week from Banbridge to Dublin to attend Irish lessons. He told me once he was cycling down the quays and he saw a woollen Union Jack hanging from a pole. He climbed up and took it down and used it as a blanket for all the time he was in Dublin.'

The Military Services Pension Collection file on the 4th Northern Division's 2 Brigade 3rd Battalion lists forty-two members in Banbridge, twenty-two in Ballela, thirty-nine in Laurencetown, twenty-eight in Knock, thirty-nine in Loughbrickland, ten in Tullyorier, ten in Lisnagade and twelve in Gilford. By the Truce, of those who were on active service in Laurencetown, one had left for Canada, one for Australia and two for the US while their captain, Jim Smyth, was in prison.

Plunkett Campbell, whose own father was interned on the *Argenta* for IRA membership in the 1920s, remembers Smyth, who was jailed for membership of the Laurencetown Battalion. 'He got thirteen lashes from the cat in Wormwood Scrubs. He swam in the Bann and you could have seen the lash marks. He went to swim where no one could recognise him.'

Sean O'Rourke was one of Monaghan's successors as OC of the Banbridge Battalion of the Old IRA. In his witness statement to the Bureau of Military History documenting their modest record, he wrote: 'Only for our little activities the district would be comparatively quiet.'

One detail stands out. In December 1920, in preparation for an attack on the British Army in Newry – during which a hand grenade went off prematurely, killing an IRA volunteer – he and Shevlin, the

Warrenpoint OC, hired a car and driver from a unionist-owned garage in Newry. Shevlin was armed and was supposed to use the threat of force to steal the car but did not go through with it, saying 'he wouldn't mind shooting a policeman or a soldier but he wouldn't shoot an Orangeman'.

Such scruples were not universal, given IRA atrocities such as Altnaveigh and UVF ones such as Weaver Street. There would be even fewer when the Troubles re-erupted in 1969.

Lessons were learned in the 1920s, but by the 1970s they had been forgotten. IRA attacks led to loyalist atrocities, 'the Catholics of Belfast being punished for the sins of their brethren elsewhere', in the words of Bishop MacRory of Down and Connor. A 1924 IRA report said of Northern nationalists, 'They regard Republicans as attempting the impossible and as a menace to their peace.'

Irish nationalism had failed to imaginatively embrace a dual Protestant, British identity, and Southern nationalists had prioritised their own independence over Irish unity. 'We have been abandoned to [James] Craig's mercy,' said Cahir Healy, a Northern nationalist.

Anti-partition parties won 41 per cent of the vote in the 1920 local elections in the six counties which would form Northern Ireland; outright majorities of seats in Counties Tyrone and Fermanagh; and almost half in County Armagh, as well as in the urban centres of Derry and Newry. But no local plebiscites were held. The boundary therefore did not fairly or accurately encompass the two nations. It was a lie on a map, not just a line, 'manifestly unjust in relation to conceptions of self-determination', in the words of political scientist Brendan O'Leary.

Unionism did not even try to assimilate or accommodate its Catholic minority, relying on coercive control to secure compliance. Catholics, although only 35 per cent of the population, represented 60 per cent of emigrants, among them many potential leaders. When a new generation emerged in the 1960s, demanding equal rights, the backlash they provoked would show that the Troubles had not ended, but instead had been stored up.

Four

A Booby-trapped Playhouse

There is a hole in the hedge on Cranny Road in Bleary with a recessed gate across a laneway so overgrown it is like a grassy moat between the two neighbouring fields. Only locals would remember that a house once stood at its end. Only a slightly wider circle of people, with the families of the victims at its centre, will remember that the first three Troubles killings in the parish of Tullylish occurred there, on a Sunday afternoon, on 18 June 1972.

The house in question was the home of Seán Moore. Moore was born in Gilford, County Down, in 1945 and although christened William John had used Seán as his first name from his early youth. He had married Nuala McKerr in Lurgan in 1967. She had been raised in a republican family and soon Seán became active as well. After the 1969/70 split, he joined the Provisional IRA, according to academic Dieter Reinisch of the University of Galway, who interviewed him in 2015. By August 1971, Seán and Nuala had two children, a daughter, Dara, two, and son, Seán Óg, one. Moore had been working for Sinton's of Tandragee for eight years as a foreman joiner and was part of a team building an abattoir in Lurgan.

At 4.10 a.m. on Monday, 9 August 1971, British soldiers broke into his home as part of Operation Demetrius. Brian Faulkner, prime minister and minister for home affairs, had introduced internment, detention without trial, almost exclusively targeting Catholics, many without any paramilitary or even republican connections. Moore was one of 342 whose names were on the State's arrest list. Designed to curb violence and crush the IRA, internment did the opposite. Twenty-three people were killed in the next forty-eight hours, including ten victims in the Parachute Regiment's Ballymurphy Massacre in west Belfast. Of the 171 killings in 1971, almost 150 occurred after 8 August. Almost 500 people were killed in 1972, the worst year of the Troubles.

The British Army, brought in to restore order in August 1969, had initially been welcomed in Catholic areas. Soon, however, led by decorated veterans of colonial wars such as Frank Kitson, it was applying violent tactics learned in Malaya, Kenya, Cyprus and Aden to target not only the IRA but the Catholic population, deliberately poisoning the sea in which republican paramilitaries swam. 'If a fish has got to be destroyed,' Kitson observed, 'it can be attacked directly by rod or net ... But if rod and net cannot succeed by themselves [polluting the water] may be necessary.'

Moore was met at his bedroom door by a soldier, who poked his rifle into his neck. Still in his pyjamas, he was taken to the living room where he was told he was being arrested under the Special Powers Act 1922. He was allowed to dress, but hurriedly; shoes but no socks, trousers but no underpants. He was allowed to see his children, who were asleep in bed, and he said goodbye to his wife. Two soldiers each grabbed him by a shoulder and made him run down the lane to the road.

He was first taken to a factory in Lurgan – where he recognised a few other men, including his brother-in-law Gerry McKerr – and then to Ballykinler army camp. Moore later made a record of being subjected to hours of exhausting exercises before being interrogated. He and the other internees were fed a mixture that Moore 'could only compare to dog food' and given hardly any water. Moore ended up falling unconscious and came to lying in the doctor's room. A military policeman 'had a sheath knife in his hand and he started to push it into the front of my throat. He said, "I'll cut your fucking popehead fucking throat.'" The doctor arrived and dragged him off, complaining about being got out of bed 'because of all these boys conking out'.

Later, Moore was interviewed by a detective he knew from Lurgan. 'At that stage I was completely exhausted,' he wrote. 'My nerves had gone and I was trembling all over. He never once asked me what happened me. I was completely filthy with sweat and dust.'

The detective told him he was only there because of his brothers-in-law. (Barra McKerr had been detained as well as Gerry. Gerry McKerr was one of the fourteen men who were chosen for 'special treatment' and were taken to a secret interrogation centre where they were tortured. They became known as the Hooded Men.) Could Moore tell him what his brothers-in-law were in? Moore said, 'It's like this. I took my in-laws as outlaws,' and the detective smiled. He was asked if his house was used as an arms dump and whether his car was used 'to run stuff'. He was told soldiers had taken his wife 'and you know what soldiers are'. Then he was told his wife and sister-in-law were in Armagh jail and his children were in a home.

He began to vomit but was only retching with nothing coming up and a soldier said, 'Don't you fucking vomit, you're only going to waste good army food.'

After another day of abuse, Moore and the other men who were being held at Ballykinler were herded into helicopters and flown to the *Maidstone* prison ship, which was moored in Belfast Lough and on which 120 men were interned from August 1971 until April 1972.

'I was almost hysterical and very nervous,' Moore wrote. The food on the ship looked better but he could not eat. His lips were cracked, his tongue swollen and his mouth parched. The morning after their arrival he could hardly move and needed his brother-in-law Barra to massage his muscles before half-carrying him to the shower. 'I undressed and I discovered that my backside was in raw flesh and blistered and that I had what appeared to be a cigarette burn underneath my left arm.' While on the prison ship he suffered from nausea and insomnia and developed a stutter.

Moore was released on 24 August and left the North for good four days later, smuggled out on a boat to Omeath by his solicitor, the father of novelist Eoin McNamee. 'I wasn't too long getting involved again,' Moore told Reinisch. He became a close associate of Provisional IRA leader Seán MacStiofáin.

Moore successfully sued the chief constable of the RUC and the British Ministry of Defence for wrongful arrest, detention and assault. McNamee was in the public gallery when, on 28 February 1972, Judge Rory Conaghan ruled in Moore's favour, awarding him the maximum damages of £300, and was sharply critical of the treatment of detainees. He said the men had been detained in primitive circumstances, which were 'deliberate, unlawful and harsh,' and that he believed three British Army witnesses had lied in their evidence about how the physical exercises had started. He referred to a 'deafening silence' from the RUC and a senior army officer; an army doctor had 'shut his eyes' to what was happening; and the military police officer in charge of eighty-nine detainees had 'abandoned responsibility' to his NCOs.

Two days later, *The Times* wrote that the case 'brought into question the legal status of the Stormont's Government internment policy.' A 'source close to the Stormont Cabinet' commented that the judge's decision was 'potentially disastrous' and that hundreds of internees could demand compensation. However, such fears proved unjustified. Internment continued until December 1975. Of the more than 1,900 people interned, only about 100 were loyalists.

***

Despite having a flair for languages, I have a tin ear for accents and can't sing a note. I digest information much more easily in written form. So, aged about 11 or 12, when I wanted to learn the lyrics to the protest song about internment, 'The Men Behind the Wire', I got a friend to write them down.

'Armoured cars and tanks and guns / Came to take away our sons / But every man will stand behind / The men behind the wire.'

Appropriately enough, this exchange took place either side of the wire fence that separated our backyard in Millar Park from the green behind. I then secreted the lyrics within the pages of a book and forgot about them till my mother found them and gave me another history lesson on the dangers of being seduced by militant republicanism.

'The Men Behind the Wire' was written by Paddy Joe McGuigan of The Barleycorn and it topped the Irish charts in 1972. In a case of life imitating art, McGuigan was then interned on the *Maidstone* prison ship. In an interview I commissioned as editor of *The Irish Post*, he told how he had won the Larry Adler Trophy in the All-Britain Harmonica Championships at 19, before being commissioned to write a protest song by the Civil Resistance Committee, 'a fairly non-violent bunch [most of whom went on to form the SDLP]. I wrote it as a non-violent song – based pretty much on the sentiment of "We Shall Overcome".' A balladeer was interned while loyalist killers were not.

***

Once Seán Moore had fled south of the border, where he was reunited with his family, his old home lay abandoned. It proved too great a temptation for the local children to resist, particularly after a storm had invitingly dislodged some slates on the roof. Imelda Campbell, who lived in Cranny Terrace, a couple of hundred yards away on the other side of the road, recalled, 'We used to play in it but we daren't have told anyone. There must have been a storm and the slates moved. Gary Toman in his wisdom decided to make a ladder. And we climbed up the ladder and got in through the roof. If we had broken a window in a house we would have been killed [by our parents]. We were in practically every other night. We made a wee hut in that attic, we would have gone up and sat in it, especially on a bad night when there was nowhere else to go.'

The children's days in their life-size playhouse were numbered, however. Three days before the summer solstice, on 18 June, following a telephone tip-off, a ten-man patrol of Gordon Highlanders was searching Seán Moore's home. At about 7 p.m., a booby-trap bomb containing 20–50lb of gelignite, concealed under the living-room floor, exploded, set off either by remote control or contact of some type completing the circuit. The initial search party had gone through the building and found nothing. Two more soldiers were called in from outside and one may have triggered the booby trap.

The subsequent explosion destroyed half the building. Two soldiers were killed instantly: Sergeant Ian Mutch, a 31-year-old married man with two children living in Nairn but originally from Aberdeen; and Lance Corporal Colin Leslie, a 26-year-old single man from Kirkwall on Orkney, who was survived by his father, brother and sister. A third died two hours later in hospital: Sergeant Major Arthur McMillan, who had just returned to duty after attending the funeral of his mother, Lilley. The 37-year-old, married with two children, was preparing to retire from the army, having joined as a 15-year-old, and had recently bought a new bungalow in Hull. Five more soldiers were injured. The three fatalities brought the number of soldiers killed that year to eighty.

An army spokesman said, 'This was obviously a booby trap designed to kill soldiers but the most horrific thing is that anyone could have come along and been killed. Children, especially, are always playing around empty houses. Whoever planned this murder had no regard for anyone else's safety.'

After the blast, neighbours who ran to the scene met two soldiers carrying the dead body of a third, reported the *Press and Journal*, the regiment's local newspaper in Aberdeen. An unnamed Bleary woman who was first on the scene told a reporter, 'I'll never forget to my dying day the scene of devastation on the street. One soldier was crying and another was shouting for blankets and told me two of his mates had been killed and others were lying badly mutilated.' Neighbours brought blankets before an army helicopter airlifted some of the injured to Lurgan Hospital.

Julia Campbell, Imelda's sister, was putting stuff away in the store, a brick shed at the back of their house, when she heard the bang. 'I thought one of my sisters had shut the door on me. By the time I got out, Mummy and Betty Toman and my aunt May had brought up blankets and water. They said to the soldiers, "If there's anything you need …"'

Imelda said, 'The night they blew the soldiers up there was a crowd up on Cranny Brae hill. They were threatening to come down and burn us out. We had to go to our Jim's [her brother's].'

Imelda and Julia's nephew Philip added, 'There was never anyone down here involved in anything. But sure you're always guilty by association.'

Women wept as thousands lined the streets in Aberdeen for Sergeant Mutch's funeral. Scores of wreaths including many from Northern Ireland and one from Bleary were piled on the Land Rover that pulled the gun carriage bearing his coffin through the streets. Among the mourners was Sergeant Kenneth Nicol, who had been injured in the blast. As news came through of another three soldiers killed in County Derry, Reverend G.D. Gouldie said, 'We commend to Thee all his comrades and all those who serve in Northern Ireland. Guard them in the dangers of their task, sustain them in temptation and make them strong to defend right.' Reverend James Bruce-Hannah, vicar of St Nicholas' Church, Beverley, who conducted Sergeant Major McMillan's funeral, condemned the killers as 'cowards and beasts'.

Two months later, the local Presbyterian minister from Newmills, Reverend James Campbell, handed over a cheque for £317 from his church and the local Church of Ireland parish, Knocknamuckley, to the battalion's commanding officer, Lieutenant Colonel J.R.A. MacMillan, to pass on to the dead soldiers' families. 'Other people, representing all shades of opinion, also contributed,' he said.

Six months after the bombing, on 8 February 1973 and again on 20 February, shots were fired at Cranny Terrace from a passing car, the *Belfast Telegraph* reported. Although some bullets struck walls and doors, no one was injured.

In June 1973, June McMillan, one of two women widowed in the explosion, was awarded £7,000 and her son Kevin £500.

The coroner for South Down, A.D. Orr, commented on the gallantry of the soldiers at the inquest. 'Someone has to do the job and one can only pay tribute to the bravery of these men.' RUC Inspector W.J. Crowe said, 'Despite inquiries, appeals through the press, radio and television, the perpetrators of this horrible crime have not been traced.'

In 2010, Sergeant Major Arthur McMillan's name was added to the war memorial in Beverley, Yorkshire. On 8 October 2013, a short service was held in St Magnus Cathedral in Kirkwall, Orkney, to dedicate a new panel added to Kirkwall War Memorial commemorating the death of Lance Corporal Colin Leslie of the Gordon Highlanders. Colin's brother Robert and his sister Yvonne (now Nicholson) joined a delegation from Kirkwall Royal British Legion. Piper Brian Findlay opened proceedings by playing the regiment's quick march, 'Cock O' the North'. Eddy Ross read a short account of how his friend had died. Reverend Jack Muir delivered a short sermon and prayer on the theme of family love before Royal British Legion president Bryan Taylor laid a wreath and Brian Findlay closed with a lament on the pipes.

Eddy Ross of Kirkwall Royal British Legion, who had known Lance Corporal Leslie, approached his family on my behalf with my invitation to talk about their brother and the impact of his death, but in the end they decided not to participate. 'This has been with them for many years and will be for the remainder of their days,' Eddy Ross told me. 'The Orkney people are a laid-back lot and like to keep in the background and prefer to keep out of the limelight if possible.'

Eddy was happy, however, to talk about his other former colleague. 'I first met Corporal Mutch in 1969, at the Scottish Infantry Depot, Bridge of Don Barracks, Aberdeen,' he said. 'He and three other corporals and a sergeant were responsible for the training of our squad. The sergeant was from the Black Watch Regiment and the other corporals were from the Argyll and Sutherland Highlanders Regiment, The Queen's Own Highlanders Regiment and the Black Watch. I found him to be the best instructor out of all the corporals. He was a natural as one would say. He explained things in the simplest of forms, which made it easy for everyone to understand. He was also an exceptionally nice individual and easy to get on with. I was serving in the Black Watch Regiment at that time. I remember being upset when notified by my father of the bomb explosion and that two of those killed were people I knew personally. Sad times for all in those days.'

***

Judge Rory Conaghan cropped up again in the story of Tullylish and the Troubles when he awarded £35,000 in compensation to Christine Fegan, whose husband Joe was the first person from the parish to be killed. (Shamefully, the award was reduced to £28,000 by Judge McGonigal after an appeal by the State.)

Conaghan, a Catholic from Derry who had to surmount many obstacles to attain a position where he could apply the law fairly, was murdered by the IRA on 16 September 1974, in his home, in front of his nine-year-old daughter Deirdre. In a coordinated attack, the IRA murdered another magistrate, Martin McBirney, minutes before.

In a statement shortly after the attacks, the Irish Republican Publicity Bureau in Dublin said the men had been killed for being 'willing agents of a most corrupt, rotten and evil judicial system'. In fact, according to the report, both Conaghan and McBirney were viewed as 'moderate and humane' members of the judiciary.

In October 2011, Rory Conaghan's daughter Mary approached *The Irish Times* to speak publicly for the first time about the murder of her father. The previous month, on the thirty-seventh anniversary of the murder, she had heard the news that Martin McGuinness would be a candidate for the Irish presidency. Her main motivation for speaking out, she told Róisín Ingle, was McGuinness's repeated assertion during the campaign that the media were guilty of 'stirring up' the feelings of victims.

'The media don't need to stir up our feelings,' said Mary, who lives in Dublin, where she works part-time as a bereavement counsellor. 'The victim's feelings are there all the time. It may all be in the past for the perpetrators, but this is our present. I want to speak for my father, to honour his memory. He was a good man. A man who lived for the rule of law and for justice.

'I suppose I'd like the perspective to be aired that the war was not just waged by the IRA on the British and Protestants but on Catholics or anyone who got in the way of their project.

'There is this duplicity the whole time with Sinn Féin and the IRA. They want everyone else to be accountable, but they don't want to be accountable themselves. They don't, for example, give information to the Historical Enquiries Team. If somebody was caught and tried for my father's murder, they would be let out under the Belfast Agreement. I could live with that. What I am most interested in is the truth. I wouldn't wish the kind of suffering we as a family went through on anybody. You literally take a shattered life and spend the rest of your life reconstructing a new one. You learn to live with it, but it never goes away.'

***

Seán Moore remained active in the republican movement throughout the conflict. He died on 10 November 2020 in Monaghan.

His son Seán Óg was convicted in May 1995, with Republican Sinn Féin general secretary Josephine Hayden and four other men, of having guns and ammunition in Tallaght, and sentenced to five years in prison.

Another son, Fergal, is a former vice-president of Republican Sinn Féin. In 2010, he delivered the oration at a commemoration in Lurgan of Tom Harte, an IRA man from the town who had been executed in Mountjoy jail in September 1940 along with Paddy McGrath, a veteran of the Easter Rising in 1916. Harte and McGrath had been convicted of shooting dead two gardaí, Richard Hyland and Patrick McKeown.

'The torch of Irish freedom was carried by Paddy McGrath and the men and women of 1916,' he said. 'They passed it on to Tom Harte and it burned brightly in his hands. Now the torch is in our hands. We must not only ensure that it is passed to a succeeding generation but while it is in our hands we must use it to set a fire in the hearts of all Irish men and women and burn the forces of oppression and corruption from our land.'

Republican Sinn Féin is linked to the Continuity IRA, the organisation responsible for the murder of Constable Stephen Carroll, the first PSNI officer to be killed, in Craigavon in 2009, a couple of miles away from Lurgan. Carroll, a Catholic, lived in Banbridge. Another soul consigned to earth scorched by the fanatic's flame. His widow, Kate, said, 'A good husband has been taken away from me, and my life has been destroyed and what for? A piece of land that my husband is only going to get six feet of.'

Five

A Bomb at the Border

There is a house belonging to the Catholic Church in the graveyard of Clare chapel that Tullylish parish has traditionally rented to a newly married couple. By the time the Troubles ended, nine of its victims would be buried in that graveyard.

In 1972, that house was the home of Joe and Christine Fegan and their children: Kieran, the eldest, who was six years old, Mary, Joanne and Denise, the baby of the family, just six months old.

When Joe and Christine had married on 2 August 1965, there was no inkling that the North was on the brink of thirty years of violence. Yet when they celebrated their seventh wedding anniversary on 2 August 1972, almost 100 people had died violently in the previous month alone, the worst month of violence in the worst year of the Troubles (a death toll of 496, of whom 258 are categorised as civilians in *Lost Lives*).

Less than three weeks later, on the morning of Tuesday 22 August, Joe set off for work, leaving Christine and the children behind to make the most of the last days of summer before the eldest two went back to school.

Joe had been working as a lorry driver for a plant hire company in Hillsborough for more than six years and was so well thought of by his employer that he was trusted to arrange his own work schedule. That day's load would require him to cross the border, so his first port of call was Newry Customs Clearance Centre, just off the main Belfast to Dublin road, where he would fill in the required paperwork and have it signed.

He was waiting beside another lorry driver, Jack McCann from Inniskeen, County Monaghan, at about 9.45 a.m., when three IRA men entered the office. They were armed with a sub-machine gun and a revolver, and one of them was carrying a 50lb bomb. A fourth IRA man waited outside in a getaway car, a black Austin A35. The IRA men ordered people out, shouting that they had a bomb. A customs officer would later tell the inquest that he was at his desk when he heard someone shout, 'Get out, get out.' He then heard an alarm bell ring for about five seconds before the bomb exploded. It seems likely that a customs officer had pressed an alarm button as he evacuated the building and that the bomber dropped the device in panic. The getaway driver also panicked, crashing into a lorry as he drove off before escaping across the border on foot. He was never caught.

The aftermath of the Newry Customs Clearance Centre bombing. © Victor Patterson

Christopher Daly, 26, the customs clearance manager, told reporters that everybody was trying to get out of the building when the bomb exploded. 'Some people almost ran into the explosion but if we had had another five seconds we would probably have been across the yard. There was a lot of smoke and rubble and everyone was in a panic. We didn't know if anybody had been killed at first, but when we started counting it got worse. Some people were missing and then we started finding the bodies.'

Joe Fegan and Jack McCann were killed instantly along with four customs officials and the three IRA bombers – the premature explosion reduced the customs post to rubble. Six other customs officials inside the building were injured, one seriously. It was the single biggest loss of life involving customs and excise officials during the thirty-year history of the Troubles.

One of the customs officers was Frankie Quinn, a 30-year-old single man from Hilltown, who had just moved to the border checkpoint the day before, having previously been stationed in Belfast. 'He said to me he was going to buy himself a brand new Hillman Hunter car,' said Conor McConville, his colleague and best friend. The others were Michael Gilleece, a 32-year-old single man from Newry; Patrick Murphy, a 41-year-old married father of four from Newtownhamilton; and Marshall Craig Lawrence, a 33-year-old father of five, including twin three-year-old boys. He and his wife had just sold their home in Newry and were set to move to his native Scotland just a few days later. He had a daughter with disabilities who 'adored him', Conor McConville told *The Irish Times*.

The three dead IRA men, all from Newry, were Oliver Plunkett Rowntree, 22, who, according to death notices, was OC of the Provisional IRA in Newry (his twin brother, Colman, a member of the Official IRA, died in a premature explosion two years later); Noel Madden, a single 18-year-old; and Patrick Hughes, a 41-year-old married man with six children. His wife wept as she told an inquest she had no idea he was in the IRA until a death notice appeared in a newspaper claiming he was on active service as a captain in the IRA. A stranger had handed her Patrick's driving licence, saying it had been found in debris at the customs post. Later, she identified fragments of torn material taken from the scene as belonging to a pair of her husband's trousers: she recognised the material and her stitching where she had turned the trousers up. Two years later, their son Michael, also an IRA member, was shot dead by the British Army as he tried to hijack a bus in the Derrybeg estate where they lived.

***

Joe Fegan was from a well-known family in Tullylish. His father, John, was a farmer in Kernan. His brothers, John, Hugh and Martin, and sister, Patsy, all lived locally too. 'Joe was such a popular man with a young family,' recalls Catherine McEvoy. 'He was in our house every night of the week for a crate of milk, parked his big lorry across the road. Country people like their milk.'

Norman Kerr was best friends with Hugh Fegan. 'Hugh used to come up every Sunday morning and say, "I was at prayers last night in the Clare and I prayed for all sinners and you pair [Norman and his wife] were at the top of my list." Joe would have pulled your leg, the same as Hugh.'

When Norman heard the news about Joe, he had been filling in and ploughing over an old linen hole or retting dam in the corner of one of his fields in Drumnascamph, consigning to history another tract of the district's once dominant industry just as Ireland's violent history had erupted again fifteen miles south. Ploughshares turned back into swords once more, cratering countless lives, the bomb blast's ripples of harm and hurt and horror radiating for miles and decades. 'The digger driver was in bringing stones and I was levelling the stones in a flax hole, and that was his first words: "Joe Fegan has got blew up",' recalls Norman.

Mary was in my class at primary school, Kieran the year above me in

Full Range of LADIES' Autumn Fashions NOW ON SHOW at O'HARE & CO. 11 Newry Street, Banbridge. Phone 3429

BANBRIDGE CHRONICLE

Also Circulating in DROMORE, RATHFRILAND, GILFORD, POYNTZPASS, SCARVA, TANDRAGEE and Districts

FRIDAY, AUGUST 25, 1972

YOUNG CLARE MAN BLAST VICTIM

"It really brings it all home to you"—just one of the many sad comments locally that mirrored the shock and deep regret that followed the news that amongst those killed in Tuesday morning's bomb blast at the Customs Station, Dublin Road, Newry, was Mr. Joseph Fegan, a young man very well-known and very popular here in Banbridge.

Mr. Fegan, who resided at Clare—his home was just beside Clare Chapel—was in his late 20s. He drove a lorry for Lilburn Plant Hire, of Newport, Hillsborough, and it was while waiting for customs clearance at the Dublin Road Station that he, another lorry driver, Mr. Frank Quinn, Hilltown, four Customs officers, and the two bombers themselves, were caught in the premature blast of the 50 lb bomb.

Young Mr. Fegan, who had been a playing member of Laurencetown GFC, leaves his wife, Mrs. Christine Fegan, and four children; his parents, Mr. and Mrs. John Patrick Fegan, Kernan, Gilford, and brothers and sisters—and to them and to his many friends we offer sincerest sympathy in this, their tragic loss.

EMPLOYER'S TRIBUTE

In a telephone call to the "Chronicle" office on Wednesday afternoon, the managing director of Lilburn Plant Hire, Mr. T. C. Lilburn, said words failed him to express the deep sorrow felt by the management and deceased's fellow-employees at the appalling circumstances under which Mr Fegan had met his untimely death.

Mr. Fegan, he said, had been with the firm for over six years, and the management, staff and employees had come not only to know him but also to respect him.

He was, said Mr. Lilburn, a completely trustworthy man. So much confidence did the firm repose in him that he had been allowed to arrange his own programme of work.

FUNERAL TO LAURENCETOWN

The remains were removed from the residence of his parents on Thursday morning at 10.30 for Requiem Mass in St. Colman's Church, Laurencetown, at 11 a.m., after which the interment took place in the adjoining cemetery.

The funeral arrangements were entrusted to the firm of Messrs. T. L. Keenan, Church Square, Banbridge.

my sister Andrea's year. Joe's brother Hugh lived opposite us. I knew his brother John from our shared, long-suffering membership of the Gilford branch of the Manchester City Supporters' Club. This was in the 1980s, when the club was owned by a local butcher, not petrobillionaires in the Middle East; their biggest celebrity fan was Eddie Large, not the Gallagher brothers; and the stadium was Maine Road in Moss Side, not the City of Manchester Stadium. For years the team laboured in the old Second Division, so we tended to go to games against another fallen giant, Newcastle United, so that we could pretend we were still in the big league.

John once gave up his bunk when I was sick on the Belfast to Liverpool overnight ferry. I was 'seasick' officially – I was bunking on the cabin floor – although three underage pints of cider cannot have helped. These trips as a teenager to matches were like being allowed backstage at the theatre, listening in to the grown-ups' banter and realising that the adults in the room, solid citizens though they might be, were at one level just big kids, teasing each other like siblings or schoolmates. But talking briefly to John fifty years on about what happened to his brother,

I realised that adults must also often mask a world of pain, putting a brave or stoic face on unfathomable loss.

After Joe's death, Christine and her children moved to Lenaderg. Doreen Feeney and her family moved in next door after her husband, John Michael, was murdered by loyalist paramilitaries, leaving eight children without a father, the youngest only three. Twelve children left fatherless in two terraced houses, two terrorised homes.

Christine, still in her twenties when her husband was killed, never remarried and five decades on, the wounds are still too raw to talk about.

***

In 2018, Mary Casey, the daughter of Jack McCann, the other lorry driver killed in the customs post explosion, had given an interview to my *Irish Times* colleague Simon Carswell. She recalled how Jack used to bring home tubes of Rolo chocolates and leave them under her pillow, right up until he was killed when she was 21.

Simon introduced me to Mary and her husband, Pearse, and we met in their home village of Inniskeen, County Monaghan, six miles from the border. Inniskeen is the birthplace of the writer Patrick Kavanagh, who is commemorated in an impressive visitor centre. Kavanagh was peripherally involved in the anti-Treaty IRA in his youth but became bitterly disillusioned. The ten hunger strikers who died in 1981 are also commemorated in a memorial at the T-junction in the centre of the village. 'Daddy's fifty years dead this year, but they don't want to know round here.'

I knew from Simon's interview that Mary and her family hate the description of Jack as 'an innocent victim of his country's Troubles' and the 'awful habit' people have of saying he was in the wrong place at the wrong time. 'He was in the right place at the right time,' Mary's husband, Pearse, told Simon. 'He was doing his job, earning his pay, making a living.'

Jack was born in Philadelphia in 1912 but was still a baby when the family moved home to Derrylaughan, County Tyrone. His mother was from Magheracloone, County Monaghan, and while visiting relatives there he met his wife, Mary Ann. They moved to Inniskeen with Mary and her sister Kathleen in 1957.

'He was Daddy to me, Jack to most people but he was Johnny in Tyrone,' says Mary. 'He loved his Gaelic football. Tyrone would be his passion.' His brother drove a coal lorry too, so they would meet up at Newry docks. 'If he had a loose load there'd be room for a passenger and I loved going with him.'

The day he was killed he was covering for another man who was going to a wedding. 'Daddy had an awful fear,' says Mary, 'that when picking up loads in the North his lorry would be hijacked.' Jack had worked for the same employer, M.J. O'Rourke & Co., coal merchants in Dundalk, for more than twenty years and his employer took his death very badly, according to Mary.

Mary was 21 and working in Dunnes Stores in Dundalk when her father was killed. 'That weekend I'd been out dancing and come home late, so in the days leading up to his murder our paths hadn't crossed. I never did get to say goodbye.

'Daddy was identified by the braces of his trousers and because he was black with the coal dust,' Mary says. 'The inquest form was all blacked out but they found every part of him except his brain – so that will give you an idea. Him and the other lorry driver would have got the main force of the bomb.

'Mummy was sedated most of the time. She didn't get to the funeral. We had no corpse anyhow. A plastic bag. Daddy was buried in Tyrone. He used to tell us if we didn't bury him in Tyrone he would haunt us. People sympathised at that funeral but I'm sure there was some that knew exactly what happened.

'Mammy had had cancer but she had got over it. When Daddy was murdered it brought it all back. She had nothing to live for. She had a relapse and she died in December 1973. Two parents dead within fifteen months. The following year I got married. I lived in a cocoon. I didn't talk to anybody. Living in the South I was on my own. Nobody in the Irish government wanted to know.'

Simon Carswell's feature on the customs post bombing, illustrating the risk of a return to a hard border post-Brexit, made the front page of *The Irish Times*. 'When Leo Varadkar went to Brussels he took twenty-six copies of the paper with him,' says Mary. 'When the European leaders finished their dinner he passed the interview around. It helped secure the backstop. My father had been remembered.

'The one killer who got away, I would like to meet him. Nothing will ever come out of it, but I just want to look into his eyes and see what kind of life he had. I just want somebody to say sorry. No one has ever come and said sorry.'

Simon Carswell also interviewed Kate O'Hanlon, whose father, Vincie Trainor, had been a worker at Daisy Hill Hospital in Newry. He had volunteered at the scene of the bombing, joining firefighters and ambulance workers who donned rubber gloves for the grim task of gathering body parts and placing them into polythene bags. What he saw 'left him speechless and disturbed for a long time. This stoical, hard man who thought he had seen everything. He did not talk a great deal about it, but he did describe finding pieces of human remains scattered right across the road, over the surrounding fields and hanging from the electricity wires. He himself found a human head on top of a nearby greenhouse.'

I hesitate to include such gruesome details, but on the day I write this, a LucidTalk opinion poll published in the *Belfast Telegraph* found that 69 per cent of Northern nationalists and republicans agreed with Sinn Féin's Northern leader and NI First Minister designate, Michelle O'Neill, that 'violent resistance to British rule during the Troubles' was the only option. The glorification of 'physical force republicanism' is enabled if you allow a new generation to ignore the gore in which it is steeped.

The Provisional IRA accepted responsibility for the blast and said in a statement that 'the unintended loss of life was regrettable'. But this was never enough for McCann's family. 'I never had closure,' says Mary.

Nobody was ever arrested over the attack. Mary still has trouble trusting people she meets.

'Daddy was Fianna Fáil,' Mary says. 'When the Troubles started a few of my friends were selling *An Phoblacht*, the republican newspaper, and I remember coming home and saying I was going to start selling it too. He just said, "Is that right, Mary? So where do you intend to sleep tonight?"' In other words, she would not be doing it while she was living under his roof.

***

In 2018, Mary participated in *Blood Red Lines*, a piece of verbatim theatre – a form of documentary in which plays are constructed from the precise words of the people at the heart of the story – devised and directed by Robert Rae. Paul Reavey, three of whose brothers were killed by the Glenanne gang the same night as the O'Dowds, also took part. (The Glenanne gang was a group made up of loyalist paramilitaries and serving and former members of the security forces that is believed to have carried out more than a hundred killings. The 'Glenanne' series of incidents is so named after the findings of an Independent International Panel (Centre for Civil and Human Rights, Notre Dame Law School) report in 2006. This report concluded that security force personnel and loyalist paramilitaries jointly carried out many murders and terrorist attacks from a farm in Glenanne in south Armagh. Many such incidents occurred between July 1972 and June 1978, around the towns of Armagh, Portadown and Dungannon, and their immediate surrounding areas.)

Jon Boutcher – a former chief constable and head of Operation Kenova, which is investigating Troubles crimes and the role of the State – saw the play and sent all sixty members of his investigating team to see it. 'By going to see the play it builds trust and confidence with the families,' he said. 'I want them to see that for my investigators, this is vocational. It will be therapeutic for everyone.'

'I became involved in this project to make sure my father is never forgotten,' Mary said. 'I never want the horror of the past to repeat itself. It is important to me that the next generation learn from my story.'

There were 484 attacks on customs posts along the border between 1969 and 1992. The Newry customs office was attacked twenty-seven times. Only three customs posts were attacked more.

Unionist politicians and loyalist paramilitaries have accused the Irish government of exploiting the threat of republican violence to divert the inevitable post-Brexit customs frontier between the EU and the UK from the land border to the Irish Sea between Britain and the North.

Mary and her family, however, were warning of the risk of violence based on bitter personal experience, not threatening its use, fearing that the return of a hard border might mean a return of the Troubles. Mary is particularly concerned about the reaction of those not old enough to remember the conflict. Her son Sean shares her view and is worried too that the border youth have a romanticised view of the IRA, that they don't remember what she can't forget.

***

Newry is sixteen miles south of Laurencetown, but the two places are closely connected. Most Catholics from the village who passed their eleven-plus exam went to grammar school in the town.

Daddy used to have a stall at Jonesborough market, just south of Newry and right on the border. The setting gave it a bit of an edge, but it was a fascinating if windswept place to wander around, when I wasn't helping to assemble or disassemble the stall's metal frame like an incompetent scaffolder, or assisting Dad in selling the duffel coats that seemed to be more uniform than fashion back in the 1980s.

Newry has always been a predominantly nationalist town – since 2003 a city – but unlike Derry at the other end of the border, its majority was so huge that it could not be gerrymandered, so it has always had a nationalist council.

John Lynch from Newry played the eponymous Cal in the film adaptation of Bernard MacLaverty's novel. Paying tribute to Bernard at the Hennessy New Irish Writing Awards in Dublin, I reminisced about seeing *Cal* with a Protestant girlfriend. Given that the plot revolves around an IRA man's affair with the widow of an RUC man, in whose murder he was complicit, I ad-libbed, 'A great novel, a fine film but a terrible date movie.'

Born in Newry and reared in Dundalk, the poet and novelist Conor O'Callaghan has a border sensibility. Like Joe Fegan and Jack McCann, he learned to drive a lorry and holds a HGV licence.

O'Callaghan's first novel, *Nothing on Earth*, is a Gothic ghost story set on a ghost estate. Set in the hinterland of Dundalk after the Celtic Tiger tide went out, its cast's gradual disappearance from their half-finished homes is emblematic of the way society's cast-offs can fall through the cracks but also calls to mind the Disappeared – the IRA's guilty little secrets that have come back to haunt them.

His second novel, *We Are Not of this World*, is an exquisite exploration of loss and grief. 'Characters are there and then are not. I never understood why that was considered unrealistic or fantastical. It happens all the time. Our loved ones just disappear. They were in the same room as us yesterday, and now they're gone, and we have to circumnavigate their ever-diminishing absences. We try to rationalise it with biology. We construct a grammar around it. We call it death. But the truth is we have no idea what just happened, where they went to and if we'll ever see them again.'

Six

Dreadful Symmetry

When I ask Donna Barry what memories she has of her father, Pat Campbell, the preface to her answer has a painful poignancy: 'The good memories …'

'He used to say God should have given him three knees, because I had one knee and the two boys [her brothers Paddy and Stephen] had to share his other knee when he came in from work. He was very loving and very gentle, you know. We would have been all excited to see him. We'd have brought his slippers. The boys would have brought a slipper each and I would have took his white coat.'

The bad memory, the one that has never faded and may never fade, is the night in 1973 when he was murdered.

'I still remember that night as if it was … as if it happened last night,' says Donna, who was only ten years old at the time. Paddy was eleven, Stephen just seven. Donna and her brothers were all in bed when there was knocking at the door.

Donna's family lived in a bungalow on Cline Walk in Banbridge, County Down. Her bedroom door was down the hallway, directly in line with the front door, where her father had been standing when two gunmen shot him dead.

'I run out into the hall and … it was just carnage. There was a wee half-moon hall table and a wee brass gong used to sit on it. Daddy would have banged it – "Dinner's ready!" you know, carrying on – and we would have all been running then. And it was in smithereens and the glass of the front door was everywhere.

'And Mummy says to me, "Get down, get down on your knees. Right, hold your daddy's head, hold his head still." And I wasn't allowed to let him move. I asked why and she said she didn't want his face cut. And when I looked, I couldn't understand why she didn't want his face cut. Well, there was just a massive hole, a massive hole, that's what it was.'

***

Pat Campbell worked on the production line in Down Shoes, the shoe factory that was by far the biggest employer in Banbridge since the linen industry collapsed in the 1950s; hence the white coat, which Donna helped him to take off every night. One day, she put her hand into the pocket and found a scrap of fur, which he had clipped from a pair of slippers he'd been working on and absent-mindedly put in his pocket.

Pat Campbell and his daughter Donna.

'It was only a wee tiny piece of fur, but I got so excited,' Donna recalls, 'I just loved the feel of it and so every so often then, he would have took home only a wee tiny piece. And I used to keep them in a shoebox and when I was going to bed at night, Mummy says I had the fur all out. I don't really remember, you know, I was only four or five years old … and they would have waited till I was sleeping and then took the fur and put it in the box under the bed. And that was the ritual every night.'

In about 2007, when the HET was re-investigating her father's murder, Donna was going through a very hard time. She was happily married to Paddy Barry, an old primary school classmate of mine from Laurencetown, and had three of her own children but was suffering from depression. 'I always had depression, you know, as a teenager and all, and just never connected it to my daddy's death. But I remember it was a Saturday night and the boys was in bed and Paddy saying to me – and he wasn't being nasty – "Donna, you're going to have to pull together or you're going to end up in the ETU [Emergency Treatment Unit]. And them three children is depending on you."

'And I took the huff and I went up to bed and I pulled the quilt over me, and I says, think of something else, think of something else. I got a photograph of my dad and me lodged in my head but I couldn't find it. All I could think about was I must leave that coat into the cleaners because I can't wash it in the machine with the fur on it. And the fur! This come into my head and such a feeling I got. I could feel my daddy's arms round me and I could see this box of fur and the comfort that I got from that box of fur and before this Mummy had been telling me, "Donna, talk to your daddy and he'll answer you. Talk to your daddy and you'll get peace."

'I phoned Mummy the next morning and I didn't even get the words out. She says, "Your daddy spoke to you last night," and I said, "It's not that he spoke to me, Mummy, he was with me." And she asked me about it and she says to me, "Do you remember the box of fur?" And I says, "No, Mummy, but the feeling I got from this box of fur," I says, "I never, ever had such a feeling of peace ..." so she told me about it.'

Donna's mascara is running and as she dabs her eyes with a hanky her tears are black.

***

Pat Campbell had joined Down Shoes straight after he left St Patrick's secondary school in 1953. He was a keen amateur boxer, a teetotaller who didn't smoke but loved to socialise. And although not involved in party politics, he was an active trade unionist. He had become shop steward in the factory and president of the Northern Ireland branch of the National Union of Footwear, Leather and Allied Trades.

When Pat and Margaret were first married, they rented an old mill cottage on Barrack Hill in Laurencetown. 'Pat Campbell was a lovely fella, always smiling,' my mother says. 'His wife was very, very good-looking. I worked in the shoe factory with her sister Brid.'

The shoe factory opened in Banbridge in 1947 on the site of an old brewery and bleachworks, before moving to a purpose-built factory on Yellow Hill. In 1967, Down Shoes opened a second factory on the Scarva Road, bringing its workforce to over a thousand. It also established a social club and formed numerous sports teams, including a Gaelic football team, underlining its cross-community credentials.

As the factory was part of the British Lotus company, it was largely free of the discriminatory practices that had plagued indigenous companies in the North, but it was still not always a comfortable place for Catholics to work.

When my mother worked in Down Shoes in the 1950s and 60s, she thought it was very modern, with music from the radio playing over the speakers. She remembers hearing in this way of the Munich air disaster and the Suez crisis. In another way, though, the factory culture was stuck in the past. She remembers little Union Jacks hanging from many of her fellow workers' machines. She and a Catholic colleague would sit having lunch with a Protestant colleague at her machine, with her Union Jack flapping over their heads. 'You didn't like it but you accepted it. They didn't see it as if they were doing anything wrong.' When a Catholic friend's machine broke down and she was asked to transfer to a machine with a Union flag on it, she claimed she had a migraine and went home. Another sabotaged the machine rather than work on it.

The factory shut for the July fortnight, either side of the 12 July Orange celebrations, the peak of the marching season. Many Catholics who could afford to take a holiday crossed the border to escape the parades and the associated tensions; de facto, their holidays were dictated to them. Other than public holidays, the July fortnight constituted the bulk of the workers' entire annual holiday allowance. So if a Catholic wanted to celebrate the Feast of the Assumption on 15 August, which was marked by parades and celebrations in towns such as Warrenpoint, they had no choice other than to take a sick day. My mother recalls how Protestant workers reported her friend for doing so.

The message to the Irish Catholics who worked in the shoe factory was: this is a Protestant, British place; you just live in it. Such practices were not outlawed until the Fair Employment and Treatment (Northern Ireland) Order of 1998 prohibited discrimination and harassment on the grounds of religious belief or political opinion by employers. The Fair Employment Code of Practice stated that to promote equality of opportunity 'you should … promote a good and harmonious working environment and atmosphere in which no worker feels under threat or intimidated because of his or her religious belief or political opinion, e.g. prohibit the display of flags, emblems, posters … which are likely to give offence or cause apprehension among particular groups of employees'.

Pat Campbell was murdered twenty-five years before the enactment of this legislation. He did, however, strive to keep politics off the factory floor.

When Royal Highland Fusiliers John and Joseph McCaig and Dougal McCaughey were brutally murdered in March 1971 in Belfast, some Protestant workers wanted the machines stopped as a mark of respect but Pat as shop steward refused. He took the same line after Bloody Sunday, when some Catholic workers wanted a stoppage.

When Princess Margaret and Lord Snowdon visited Down Shoes in May 1967, Pat as senior shop steward was one of only three of the 900 employees to be formally presented to the royal couple. According to the *Banbridge Chronicle*, he spoke positively about industrial relations in the factory and showed the dignitaries a consignment of shoes that was part of a £1m order for the Russian market.

Pat did not discuss politics at home, Donna says. His view was: 'You had your beliefs and you kept them to yourself.' Banbridge, unlike Lurgan and Portadown, was not segregated along sectarian lines. Protestants outnumbered Catholics two to one, but they lived side by side.

'My dad used to take us down on the Twelfth for the parades. One of his best friends was in the Orange Order and a UDR man. He was a wee thin man and my daddy was a big man and when you saw the two together it was like Laurel and Hardy – he used to run over and put the bowler hat on my daddy's head and they would have had a laugh, you know? He died recently and there was a write-up. His children told the minister that he had left the Orange Order because he had a friend died in the Troubles.'

***

In March 1969, as the civil rights movement was raising awareness in Britain and further afield of the discrimination Catholics faced in Northern Ireland, Down Shoes held its annual dinner dance in the Ardmore Hotel in Newry. After a five-course dinner and a toast to Queen Elizabeth II and another to Down Shoes, James Bostock, chairman of the Lotus Group, recalled how over twenty years before they had struggled to find premises for a factory in Banbridge, eventually taking over an old brewery, adding amidst laughter that 'ideas are like babies, easily conceived but difficult to deliver'.

The group's insurance broker, F.J. McGibben from Belfast, joked that 'Our English visitors must be aware that we have been having some stirring times recently and the cry has gone out for "one man, one vote". You will all be relieved to know that this matter has now been settled – I'm he [laughter], I am the one man with the one vote – a vote of thanks to the directors of Down Shoes and all concerned in making this such a happy occasion.'

The Ardmore Hotel would be destroyed in July 1979 as part of an IRA bombing campaign. A heavily fortified RUC station was built on the site, which made approaching Newry from Banbridge feel like entering a war zone.

Just over a month after the dinner dance, on 28 April 1969, Terence O'Neill, the reforming unionist prime minister, resigned – undermined by hardliners in his own party, and harried by his rising rival, Reverend Ian Paisley, and a bombing campaign by loyalist paramilitaries targeting public utilities. (The paramilitaries had bombed water and electricity installations, hoping the IRA would be blamed and the civil rights movement discredited. The truth was exposed when Thomas McDowell, 45, a member of the UVF and UPV, electrocuted himself while planting a bomb at a power station near Ballyshannon, County Donegal.)

In an interview with the *Belfast Telegraph*, this putatively progressive, non-sectarian unionist leader argued, 'It is frightfully hard to explain to Protestants that if you give Roman Catholics a good job and a good house they will live like Protestants because they will see neighbours with cars and television sets; they will refuse to have eighteen children. But if a Roman Catholic is jobless, and lives in the most ghastly hovel he will rear eighteen children on National Assistance. If you treat Roman Catholics with due consideration and kindness they will live like Protestants in spite of the authoritative [*sic*] nature of their Church.'

In March 1970, Robin Jackson, a 21-year-old Protestant from Donaghmore, a village near Newry, and a Catholic colleague were dismissed from Down Shoes for fighting.

In July 1970, the factory had to be evacuated after a bomb made of gelignite was discovered in a flower bed next to the offices. An RUC spokesman said, 'This is an obvious attempt by some evilly-disposed person to disrupt a community where both Protestants and Catholics live peacefully together.'

The following week, Ian Paisley addressed 5,000 locals at an open-air meeting in the town's Ballymoney Hill area, at which £450 was raised to build a Free Presbyterian Church in Banbridge.

In October 1970, the town's power station was bombed.

Banbridge's Free Presbyterian Church opened in June 1971 and was gutted in an arson attack two months later, on the first day of internment.

The UDR was such a regular advertiser that it got its own column in the *Banbridge Chronicle*, under the byline 'Decoy'. D Company was so busy that men had to be called away from their work. The column paid tribute to employers who willingly released staff for emergency UDR duties, singling out Down Shoes for praise for its public-spirited attitude in not only releasing key personnel but also generously ensuring that no one was out of pocket. Thus 'it will be understood why Down Shoes Ltd has a special place in the thoughts of D Company'.

The army began to use the shoe factory canteen, which meant workers on their breaks could not get a seat or found there was no food left. Pat objected. 'That didn't go down too well,' says Donna.

On 8 March 1972, Joseph Jardine, a 44-year-old Banbridge man, married with two sons and living in Newry, was marking cattle at Middletown customs post when three men drove across the border and shot him dead. A lance-corporal in the UDR, he also worked as a veterinary inspector for the Ministry of Agriculture. The *Banbridge Chronicle* observed that his murder 'will strike local people with more than just usual regret that another victim has been claimed in the present Troubles, his tragic death being especially felt here for he was one of our own, a Banbridge man'.

That same month, a car bomb containing around 50lb of explosives detonated on the town's main shopping street, damaging sixty premises. 'Whoever was responsible for this lunatic act,' the *Chronicle* editorialised, 'there can be little doubt that one of their main aims was to stir up sectarian tension in Banbridge, or at least to create a state of high tension – but within minutes of the blast they got a right poke in the eye, for if anything it drew the residents of the town closer together, and in a marvellous demonstration of the "Dunkirk spirit", everybody – shopkeepers, public, friends, strangers – joined in to clear up the mess and carry out whatever on-the-spot repairs they could.'

Gilbert Honeyford, urban council chairman, commented that his first reaction was 'Father, forgive them, for they know not what they do.' He was sure this would be the attitude of local people generally and that they would leave the matter in the hands of the security forces. 'This is not an inside job,' he said. 'I know the people of Banbridge.' He had spent months sounding out local opinion 'and could confidently state that local people, whether moderate or militant, wanted nothing to do with violence, and he had too much faith in Banbridge people to believe that there would be any sort of recriminations as a result of the explosion'.

Later that month, at a special meeting of the local council, which had to be held by candlelight, the town centre was declared 'a designated zone wherein no vehicles may be left waiting or parked, except when attended by a person over 15'.

O'Hare's held an explosion sale. 'Bomb-damaged stock must be cleared – £23.50 ladies coats for £5. We ask you to cash in on our misfortune.'

On 28 March 1972, fifty years of one-party unionist rule of Northern Ireland came to an end when Stormont was prorogued after Brian Faulkner refused to accept British Prime Minister Edward Heath's decision that security policy would be transferred to Westminster. Banbridge Workers' Unionist Association held a protest rally at the war memorial over Westminster's decision 'to deny Ulster its democratic rights'. John Dobson, the local unionist MP, said that 'half a million malcontents have been temporarily quietened and one million new vociferous protesters have been created'.

To mark the event, a UDR man and an ex-serviceman placed a wreath of red and white carnations and red tulips at the war memorial, which bore the inscription, 'In remembrance of those members of the

Army, UDR and RUC who have given their lives. From the Loyalists of Banbridge.'

On 19 April 1972, James Elliott, a 37-year-old UDR corporal from Rathfriland, a market town near Banbridge, who was married with three children and a fourth on the way, had just driven his delivery lorry across the border into the North when he was abducted and taken back into the South to be killed. His body was found near Newtownhamilton in south Armagh. His commanding officer described the murder as 'a bestial act comparable to the tactics of the Mau Mau'.

When James Elliott's body was returned to his family, it appeared mutilated. This led to claims, amplified by unionist politicians, that he had been tortured, but these were emphatically denied by the RUC, which issued a statement to that effect to be read from the pulpits of local churches. A 600lb bomb was found in milk churns in a culvert near the body and, suspecting a booby trap, soldiers had had to drag the corpse from where it lay using a grappling hook. At the inquest the State pathologist declared that he had found no evidence of torture. One of the bullets that killed James Elliott could have caused a broken nose. However, a brother-in-law who identified the body in the hospital mortuary still thought he had been tortured.

When news of his killing broke, youths in Rathfriland smashed windows in Catholic-owned premises in the town. There was an arson attack on the parochial house and a Catholic family's new home in Gilford was gutted by fire.

Four men were charged with possessing a homemade incendiary device made of industrial bleach and sulphuric acid. One admitted planting one such device in a dance band's van outside the Castle Ballroom. One had stolen the sulphuric acid from his linen works and got the powder from the Ulster Defence Association (UDA) hut in Banbridge. A petrol bomb and gun attack on a Catholic home in Gilford on 22 August 1973 had also been planned at the UDA club.

***

It was against this backdrop that on Monday, 29 October 1973, at about 9 p.m., a silver Ford, either a Cortina or an Escort, with four men inside pulled up outside the Criterion Bar in Edward Street, Lurgan. It was also known as News's pub, after its owner, Hugh News, a Catholic SDLP councillor. A hand grenade was thrown into the bar, injuring a barman's legs. As the car drove off towards Banbridge, a passenger shot a teenage passer-by, hitting him in the chest and arm.

Pat Campbell was at home with his wife, Margaret, in Banbridge, about ten miles away. Just after 10 p.m. there was a knock at the front door. When Margaret answered, two men whom she had never seen before asked to speak to Pat. The light was on in the hallway and there was another light at the end of the path so she was able to get a good look at them. She paid particular attention to the one 'who did all the talking', noting his moustache and big, bright eyes.

When Pat went to the door, Margaret heard a voice say, 'You had better come with us,' and Pat replied, 'Anything you have to ask me, you can ask me here.' Margaret heard what sounded like feet being dragged along the path and returned to the hallway where she saw Pat wrestling with the two men on the path.

Pat, who had been an amateur boxer, was able to resist and had made it back inside the house when one of the two strangers produced a handgun and fired a shot. Pat cried, 'My God, not this!', then the second man produced a Sterling sub-machine gun, hitting him at least nine times in the chest and trunk, and shattering the glass in the doorway. One bullet hit the headboard of the bed where Donna had been sleeping. Margaret narrowly escaped being hit herself.

This was when Margaret called for Donna to hold her father's head still while she ran to her neighbour, Thomas McCabe, for help.

McCabe, who had just returned home after collecting his wife and two other neighbours from their shift at the shoe factory, had heard the shots followed by footsteps running down the path beside his house. He and Margaret ran back to her house, where he found Pat lying face down, semi-conscious but unable to speak. Pat lifted his head once and looked at his wife.

Donna remembers McCabe carrying her, Stephen and Patrick out of the house and handing them over to his wife to look after, while he waited with Pat until the ambulance arrived.

'He had me under one arm and the two boys under the other arm.'

I am struck by the dreadful symmetry of Pat needing three knees for his three children to sit on, and his friend and neighbour who could have done with three arms to carry them away from the house where Pat now lay dying.

At 10.25 p.m., a four-man RUC mobile patrol was on the scene of the shooting. Sergeant Francis Hewitt found Pat lying face down in the hallway, covered with a blanket, with his wife Margaret kneeling by his head in great distress. Ten spent 9mm cartridge cases were recovered from the scene. At 10.30 p.m., a local GP, Dr Ben Moran, arrived. He found Pat to be deeply unconscious and could not find a pulse. He cut open Pat's clothing and found bullet wounds to the right side of his chest. Pat was taken by ambulance to Craigavon Area Hospital, where he was pronounced dead on arrival at 11.10 p.m.

An RUC patrol found the getaway car abandoned three-quarters of a mile away at 10.45 p.m. It had been stolen earlier that evening in Banbridge.

The next morning, 30 October, at 10.30 a.m., two RUC men interviewed Margaret at the home of her sister-in-law Rita Magennis. She described the first gunman to the police as about 5ft 9in to 5ft 10in tall with a moustache and very prominent, staring eyes. The second gunman, she said, was at least 6ft tall, clean shaven with short, fair hair.

That afternoon, at 3.15 p.m., an anonymous phone call to the *Lurgan Mail* claimed responsibility for Pat's murder – falsely alleging that he was an IRA man – as well as for the attack on the bar in Lurgan. The caller said that the same weapon had been used in both incidents, a claim confirmed by ballistics analysis. Both were in retaliation for the wounding of an RUC man in a gun attack in Lurgan the previous week, said the caller, who claimed to represent the Ulster Freedom Fighters, a cover name for the legal UDA. Despite being responsible for hundreds of murders, bombings and other crimes over two decades, the UDA was not proscribed by the British government until August 1992. The State was implicitly declaring that Catholics were second-class victims.

Pat's murder dominated the front page of that week's *Chronicle*, which editorialised, 'At this tragic and brutal time, this small corner of a small island has need of big-hearted men like Pat Campbell – but though the unthinking and the callous have taken him from us, the example he set us all is still there … Of a man who lived for others – the memory of a man for whom tolerance, friendship, decency and togetherness were not abstracts, but realities.'

The newspaper highlighted that Pat had been a founder member of the Banbridge Tenants' and Community Association and had been supporting a project to form a Citizens Advice Bureau.

'It could be said that for years now his own home had become an unofficial Advice Bureau … No matter how late or inconvenient it was, Pat was invariably ready and willing to give what help he could – and the grim irony of his death is that in going to meet his assassins he was going, as always, to offer help and friendship where it might be needed.'

The same front page which reported Pat's murder and burial featured in the bottom right-hand corner a photograph of Ian Paisley being presented with a spade – a souvenir of the sod-turning ceremony for his new church in the town.

Speaking at Pat's Requiem Mass in St Patrick's Church, Father O'Rourke said that he had been an ideal family man and always took pride in Banbridge, where he carried out valuable community work. 'The murder of Mr Campbell has put a terrible stain on the good name of Banbridge, a town where community relations have always been good.' He added that the wheels of justice grind slowly but they grind exceedingly small. In fact, they ground to a halt within weeks.

Years later, Donna asked for a photocopy of the *Chronicle*'s coverage of her father's murder but was told that issue was not available. 'I did feel like saying something till them, that if it had have been a UDR man or whatever was killed, you'd have got it then.' (While researching this chapter in Belfast's Newspaper Library, I photocopied every page I could find about Pat and sent them all to Donna. I remembered how touched I had been whenever a friend or relation sent me a photograph that included my late wife. Every pixel is precious.)

Similarly, when I showed Donna the epigraph – 'To live in hearts we leave behind is not to die' – on a gravestone in Moyallan's Quaker cemetery, and told her that it was from a poem, Thomas Campbell's 'Hallowed Ground', which I had quoted from in my eulogy for Nikki, she expressed an interest in it and I sent her a copy.

Every murder is traumatic, but when it happens at home, the desecration of what should be a safe space and the association of a hallway or a living room with the most awful of memories often means that the loss of a loved one is swiftly followed by the abandonment of the family home.

'We couldn't live in the house after it,' Donna says, 'because if we had to go to the toilet, we had to step over where my daddy was lying. The four of us slept in the one bed. If one went to the toilet, we all went to the toilet. We were just afeared. Daddy died on the Monday night and he was buried on the Thursday. I would say by the following weekend we were out.'

They moved in with Margaret's sister and brother-in-law for three months until a house was found for them nearby, where Margaret still lives.

What was it like afterwards, in Banbridge, I wonder? Were people kind or did they almost pretend it never happened? 'As a child, you hear people saying "there's no smoke without fire" or "he didn't get it for nothing", Donna says, 'and I didn't know what they were talking about but I do know now.'

Banbridge is regarded as a relatively moderate town. The political commentator Newton Emerson observed to me, perhaps a little tongue-in-cheek, that when he was growing up in Portadown he regarded Banbridge as 'a shining city on a hill' but Donna experienced 'a lot of bigotry'.

At a Remembrance Day service a fortnight after Pat's murder, the Church of Ireland's Canon Noble Hamilton said that he regretted and resented a statement by the leader of Ireland's Catholics the week before. Cardinal William Conway had highlighted the disproportionate number of Catholic civilians murdered in the Troubles. While Canon Hamilton acknowledged that this was true, he felt it unhelpful to point it out and unfair that the cardinal had not mentioned that a number of those had in fact been killed by the IRA and fellow Catholics.

Before Pat was killed, Margaret had worked in Down Shoes' Scarva Road factory. She returned to work a year or two after Pat's murder. 'And she'd have seen some of the workmen in their coats and having their guns on a strap, part-time UDR or police,' says Donna. 'And that terrified her. Sure they intimidated her. She had to leave.'

Seven

Protecting a Killer

No one has ever been convicted of Pat Campbell's murder but the chief suspect, a UDR man, was identified almost straight away. Pat is believed to have been his first victim but, protected by members of the RUC's Special Branch, he went on to kill more than fifty others.

Robin Jackson was born in Donaghmore, a village near Newry, on 27 September 1948, and had worked at the Down Shoes factory from 29 November 1965 to 13 March 1970, when he was dismissed for fighting. Jackson had often got into scrapes. He and a colleague were reported to management for deliberately skidding a car on ice in the factory car park. His colleague admitted it, but Jackson brazenly denied it. Another worker caught Jackson cleaning his shoes on a hand towel in the men's toilets and kicked him up the backside for his disregard for hygiene.

On 21 August 1973, just over two months before Pat Campbell's murder, Jackson, by now a 25-year-old unemployed lorry driver, had joined the UDR, part of the British Army, as a part-time private, service number 242289963, attached to D Company, based at Scarva Road Barracks in Banbridge.

The week before Pat's murder, on Tuesday 23 October, an armed gang, claiming to be the UVF, raided Fort Seagoe, the UDR's E Company armoury in Portadown, and stole weapons and ammunition.

'There were grounds to suspect that those responsible were assisted by members of the UDR,' a police report states.

Curiously, there had also been a huge raid on the UDR armoury in nearby Lurgan exactly one year before, on 23 October 1972. Coincidence? Perhaps. But 23 October is a key date in the loyalist calendar, once as celebrated as 12 July. It marks the start of the 1641 Rebellion, in which thousands of Protestants were killed by Irish Catholic insurgents, most notoriously in Portadown. A massacre was also alleged to have taken place in Jackson's native Donaghmore.

In one of several search-and-arrest operations by security forces against the UDA and UVF after the Fort Seagoe raid, explosives, arms and 5,000 rounds of ammunition were found in a house near Portadown on 25 October 1973. The occupant was arrested and, when questioned, told police that he had been forced to store the material by Robin Jackson, Roy Metcalfe (Jackson's brother-in-law, who would be killed by the IRA in 1989) and an RUC man (who would be shot dead by the IRA in 1975).

Jackson, a serving UDR soldier, had been named by a man in custody over a major arms seizure as one of three men responsible for the haul four days before Pat Campbell was murdered, yet he was arrested only on 7 November, nine days after the killing. His home in Lurgan was searched and detectives found seventy-nine rounds of 7.62mm calibre ammunition (forty-nine rounds more than he was allowed to have at home as a part-time member of the UDR). He was taken to Castlereagh Police Station in Belfast.

When questioning started, the sole focus was Pat's murder. Asked whether he knew Pat, Jackson said they had worked together at Down Shoes. He denied that he had ever had an argument with Pat.

Jackson also said his wife's family home was just off the Old Newry Road in Banbridge so he was familiar with the area. He could not account for his movements on the night of the murder but guessed that he had been at home watching TV.

The suspect, asked if he knew why Pat had been killed, speculated that 'some time ago, three young Scottish soldiers were murdered and Pat had refused to stop work in sympathy'. DCI Meenahan informed Jackson that Pat did not believe political gestures were appropriate in the workplace and that he had also declined to stop work when similarly requested to do so after Bloody Sunday in January 1972. Jackson said that he was unaware of that.

The following day, Jackson was interviewed about general crimes in the Lurgan area and a UVF group operating in Lurgan, Portadown and Banbridge. Jackson denied membership of the UVF but said that he had been a member of the UDA.

Jackson agreed to take part in an identification parade along with eight other men of similar age and appearance.

Margaret Campbell was the Crown's best hope of securing a conviction for her husband's murder. She should have been treated with sensitivity, offered every emotional support possible and prepared mentally for the ordeal of having to face again the man who had killed her husband. But she wasn't.

Two RUC officers called to her sister-in-law Rita's house and told her to come with them to an identity parade. Donna takes up the story. 'And she said, "But I need to get my shoes on." "Get your shoes on, you're coming with us." Rita says, "Can I go with her?" "No." And she says, "Well, hold on till I ring Pat's brother Joe to go ..." "There's nobody going, only her." They took her, they put her in the back of a car, never spoke till her and the same coming home. Intimidated her.'

Margaret was brought into the room by an Inspector Quinn and asked to put her hand on the shoulder of anyone she recognised as one of her husband's killers. She began at Jackson's end of the line, halting momentarily in front of him, then walked the length of it and back, stopping in front of Jackson. Asked if she recognised anyone, she replied, 'I'm not sure', before bursting into tears and becoming distraught. She left the room for a few minutes to compose herself.

On her return she began again at Jackson's end, walked halfway along the line and then walked back to within two feet of Jackson and said to Inspector Quinn, 'That's him.' Asked to put her hand on Jackson's shoulder, she did so before becoming distraught again.

Margaret gave a witness statement, describing the man she had just identified as 'the one who did the talking and first produced the handgun. He had a moustache and his eyes were bright and big. I went back inside and had a good look at him and within reason I am satisfied this was the man concerned. This was the only person in the room who even remotely resembled the man who came to my door on 30 October. The moustache seemed somewhat different but the other facial expressions were quite similar.'

As two detectives accompanied Jackson back to Banbridge that evening, he was in a distressed state and crying. They recorded that he made the unsolicited comment, 'I am in trouble now because Mrs Campbell would remember the colour of every hair on the man's head who had been at her door and shot her husband.'

Back in Banbridge RUC station, he was asked again if he'd ever had a row with Pat. 'I don't know how you asked me that,' said Jackson. 'It doesn't say if you argued with a man you'd go out and plug him.'

He claimed that he had last seen the Campbells about three weeks before in Down Shoes social club. Jackson was also questioned about when he first heard about Pat's murder. According to Inspector Stewart, Jackson replied, 'Richard Carswell, a fellow I work with, told me the next day.' Only at this stage was he asked to account for his possession of the extra forty-nine rounds of ammunition.

Jackson was kept in custody overnight at Banbridge Police Station. Following a visit from his wife the next morning, Jackson told police, 'Mrs Campbell knows me well. My wife told me that. She spoke to me on several occasions and called me Robin.' He even claimed that after he came back from a period spent living in Australia, the Campbells had come over to Jackson and his wife and welcomed them home.

Margaret told the HET she was never asked by police whether she knew Jackson or had seen him before the incident. Had she recognised Jackson she would have told Pat that 'someone from the factory was at the door'.

Later that day, Inspector Stewart formally charged Jackson, who, when asked if he had anything to say, replied, 'Nothing, I just can't believe it.' He was remanded into custody until 4 January 1974.

When he was charged with Pat's murder, Jackson was described in the media as an 'unemployed lorry driver', not a serving UDR soldier, a much more significant and newsworthy fact. This cover-up was most likely a security forces decision.

Inspector Stewart carried out further investigations to try to find additional evidence to support the case. Richard Carswell, the local farmer who had employed Jackson, contradicted Jackson's account about who had first raised Pat's murder. The morning after the killing, Jackson brought up Pat's murder with him by asking, 'What about the job last night?' When the farmer enquired what he was referring to, Jackson replied, 'Wasn't there a fellow murdered in the town last night?'

A friend of Pat's who worked at Down Shoes told police that at 11 p.m. on the Saturday two days before Pat's murder, he was in Down Shoes social club and saw Pat and Jackson talking in the toilets. Both accounts challenged Jackson's honesty.

In his report Inspector Stewart highlighted that: Jackson had not explained where he was on the night of Pat's murder; he had not put forward any witness who could account for his whereabouts; Mrs Campbell was a reasonable witness, although her identification of Jackson was weakened by her leaving the room before returning and making a positive identification; what took place in the short time Mrs Campbell was out of the room could be the subject of negative conjecture by the defence; allowances should be given to the distress caused to Mrs Campbell and her reaction when initially confronted with the person who murdered her husband. 'After careful consideration of all the facts and the meagre amount of evidence', the question of whether or not the sole evidence of identification was sufficient should be considered by a court.

Two senior officers supported Inspector Stewart's recommendation that Jackson be prosecuted for murder but a superior officer at headquarters overruled them on several grounds, including that only two in the line-up had moustaches and also that 'although Mrs Campbell did not mention it in her statement, the "divisional police" had confirmed that she was in the company of her husband on the night of 27 October. Therefore, "could she have recognised Jackson's face as a result of seeing him in the social club and in her emotional state picked him out in the identification parade as someone she associated with Banbridge?"'

There is nothing in the case papers to support this claim that Margaret was in the social club on 27 October and she is adamant she was not there.

On 3 January 1974, a case conference was held at the offices of the Director of Public Prosecutions between the DPP, Superintendent Crawford and Inspector Stewart. The decision was made that there was insufficient evidence to support the charge of murder and that the charge should be withdrawn. It was also decided not to prosecute Jackson with the charge of unlawful possession of ammunition.

Incredibly, the Campbell family was not informed by the RUC that the murder charge had been dropped and learned about it only from the media.

'Mummy blamed herself for a long, long time that she let my daddy down and she let us down,' says Donna. In truth, the RUC had let them down.

Jackson was discharged from the UDR two months later, on 4 March 1974.

In June 1974, according to journalist Anne Cadwallader, Colin Wallace, then a British Army military intelligence officer, sent a list of loyalists his unit wished to target to A.H. Holman at British Army HQ in Lisburn, asking which of them were already working for military intelligence. Next to Jackson's name, Wallace's handwritten note states, 'Robin Jackson was charged with the murder of Patrick Campbell in October last year. Charges were dropped following RUC SB [Special Branch] intervention.'

The same 9mm Sterling sub-machine gun used to kill Pat Campbell and in the attack on the Criterion Bar the same night has also been linked by ballistic tests to a gun attack on 19 August 1973 at St Patrick's Club, Portadown, County Armagh, when twenty-four shots were fired, injuring three men (unsolved); and the attempted murder of Marion Rafferty and Thomas Mitchell on 11 February 1974, near Dungannon, County Tyrone, for which a serving UDR private was sentenced to life in May 1981. The weapon has never been recovered.

***

While the HET, which re-examined the police investigation, believed that local police were immensely keen to solve the case, and had suspicions about Jackson that would prove to be well founded, the evidence available would not have met the required standards, and so their wish that Jackson should be prosecuted in these circumstances was unrealistic. The report was more critical of the way that the family was treated – especially the way that Margaret was taken to the identity parade, and the failure by the police to keep the family informed and updated.

'None of this seems fair from the family perspective, and Mrs Campbell did everything she could have done in the circumstances. Pat's murder was a sickening, scarcely imaginable horror for the family to endure. At the same time, it traumatised a close-knit and relatively settled community; if this could happen to Pat, then who was safe?'

The failure to convict Robin Jackson of Pat's murder was not just a tragedy for the Campbell family, denying them justice and some sort of closure. It would also have devastating consequences for dozens of other families because Jackson has been credibly linked to more than fifty other murders, including the Dublin and Monaghan bombings in 1974, the Miami Showband massacre and the Bleary Darts Club murders in 1975, the O'Dowd murders in 1976 and the Cairns brothers' murders in 1993.

Equally credible are allegations by fellow paramilitaries and former members of the security forces that he was an agent working for and protected by either or both the RUC Special Branch and the British Army.

Jackson died from natural causes on 30 May 1998, eight days after voters in referendums north and south of the border approved the Good Friday Agreement that had been signed the month before.

***

There are many threads that connect Donna to other local victims' families. Mr McCabe, the neighbour who had carried her and her brothers from their house the night her father was shot, told police that the week before he had collected his wife from what was called the housewife's shift at Down Shoes but couldn't get into his usual parking space as another car was parked there. Inside he recognised Jackson and another neighbour, who would be jailed a couple of years later for armed robbery and UVF membership. There is no record, however, that Pat's UVF neighbour was questioned by police about Pat's murder either at the time or after his conviction. The UVF man's son would in turn be convicted of the murder in 1989 of Pat Feeney, one of whose sisters is married to one of Pat Campbell's brothers.

Donna visits Róisín Cairns, whose brothers Gerard and Rory were murdered in 1993, for complementary therapies. 'Róisín's place is called the Little House of Calm. And do you know what, the girl has a healing touch.'

Donna was at school with Maria Feeney, whose father, John Michael, was murdered in 1975. Her brother Stephen was married to a great-granddaughter of Joe Toland, who was shot dead on the Bleary bingo bus.

The loss of a parent hits home hard on big occasions. It cast a shadow over Donna's wedding day. Without her father to walk her down the aisle, Donna's instinct was to downsize her big day to a small one.

'I didn't want a big wedding. Even though I had two brothers… my daddy wasn't there. There was nobody there, only me and Paddy and two witnesses.'

Donna's husband, Paddy, is the grandson of Margaret Barry, the renowned ballad singer and banjo player. Donna and Paddy's son Marty studied traditional music at the University of Limerick and is gaining a reputation as a traditional musician.

Inspired by his mother's story, he composed an instrumental tune called 'The Box of Fur'. Another of his tunes is on the soundtrack of *Unquiet Graves*, a documentary film about loyalist murders in Mid-Ulster. It plays as the film lists all the people who were killed, including his grandfather, Pat.

Marty is part of a new generation of victims' relatives who have been encouraged by the Pat Finucane Centre to fight the British government bill that threatens to defund legacy investigations into cases such as Pat's.

When Sean Murray was making *Unquiet Graves*, Donna was to stand in for Margaret, who did not feel up to talking on camera. But at the last minute Margaret changed her mind, telling Donna, 'Your daddy, when I got into bed last night, told me, "It'll be the last thing you ever do for me."' In the end Donna froze and could not speak, and Margaret did it on her own. It is one of the most compelling moments of the documentary.

'Mummy has told her story now and the truth is out,' says Donna. 'That's her done. God forbid anything happens her, but she wants me to keep on fighting, to try and get some form of justice. You can but try.

You know, the whole thing is: delay, deny, and then death. But I have my boys coming along behind me.'

Donna told her mother to hold on for another year so that she would have her day in court, just as the survivors and relatives of the Miami Showband victims did in 2021.

Not everyone was as determined to pursue justice through the courts and any other avenue. 'I know some think: let it go; he's gone now; it'll not bring him back. But they don't understand that we need justice. That we know nobody will ever do time.'

It's almost like grief, I suggest. There is an expectation that at a certain point, people grieving should … 'get over it', Donna finishes my sentence. '"But sure what good will it do now?" they say. Someone actually said an inquiry was a waste of taxpayers' money. I just said, well, it's a good job it wasn't up to them.'

In November 2022, months after our interview, Donna's mother received a 'significant' undisclosed payout as part of the resolution in her civil claim against the PSNI, alleging collusion between the killers and State agencies. Margaret described the outcome as vindication in her fight to secure justice for her late husband. 'I can rest easy knowing that I sued the British government over the failed investigation into Pat's murder and received a settlement.' Margaret died just over a year later, on 8 December 2023, having been forced to spend over fifty years of widowhood fighting for justice.

Donna said outside court that the State had failed in its duty to prosecute Jackson. 'They not only failed our family, but they failed the many families of his subsequent victims, and they failed this society,' she said. 'My mum can now rest easy knowing that she has done all she can to honour Dad's memory and to hold the State to account.'

The family's solicitor, Kevin Winters of KRW Law, described it as the end to a difficult and fraught eight-year legal journey.

I asked Kevin Winters how we should interpret the State's financial settlement in Pat Campbell's case.

'The State did not make any formal admission of liability or apology, but there was a payment of an undisclosed figure. For the man or woman in the street, it marks State recognition of wrongdoing – when they pay out damages even though they are not admitting liability. That's a concession.'

He explains that Margaret's age and recent history of serious illness were factors in agreeing to settle.

'The thrust of the case was that at some point immediately after the Campbell killing he [Robin Jackson] became an agent. It created the environment for that to happen. When he was picked out there was sufficient evidence to proceed to trial but they dropped the charges. There was a serious claim for investigative failure.'

Of the fact that Jackson had been named by a man in custody as having forced him to store arms, days before Pat's murder, Kevin says, 'Had Jackson's house been hit then Pat Campbell might still be alive.'

Jon Boutcher told me he intends to publish his Denton report – a court-ordered independent review into the activities of the Glenanne gang by a team of British detectives as part of the Barnard Review – by 17 May 2024, the fiftieth anniversary of the Dublin and Monaghan bombings.

If the British government does not shut it down, the Barnard Review could reveal a lot more about several of the murders covered in this book. It will flesh out a lot of details about collusion, Winters says, on top of the huge tranche of HET reports and investigative journalism, not least *Lethal Allies*.

Winters – whose first job was as assistant to solicitor Pat Finucane, later murdered by loyalists working as British agents – believes that the more we learn about the extent of British security forces' penetration of both republican and loyalist paramilitary groups, the more complex the apportioning of responsibility becomes. It will become clear that a share of the guilt in many more murders will ultimately be laid at Britain's door, if you strip away the idea of culpability only vesting in the person who pulls the trigger or plants the bomb. This 'brings into sharp focus why we are having a legacy bill'.

Roughly 60 per cent of Troubles deaths are attributed to republicans, 30 per cent to loyalists and 10 per cent to the British State. A deluge of judicial reviews, inquests and civil cases 'will serve to overturn that cosy statistic. It's a bit like a Venn diagram, the paramilitaries at one end, the State at the other, and the grey, shaded bit in the middle which starts out as a minor sliver starts moving out.' There are hundreds of cases like Pat Campbell's coming down the tracks, Winters says.

A key case for him was the overturning of the convictions of Danny Morrison and others, which exposed the existence of an alleged republican informant. The Court of Appeal's judgment was withering and called for an investigation, which led to Jon Boutcher's Operation Kenova, so it is 'the creature of litigation', he emphasises, not something delivered by politicians.

'It's a bizarre, backhanded compliment that we forced the British government to bring in legislation to shut everything down. We must be doing something right. If it was Putin's Russia you might understand the notion that a citizen can no longer take a case against the State over the killing of a loved one. I don't see politicians shouting loud enough.'

Eight

'Dad missed out on so much'

The living room in Eddie Rooney's Craigavon home is a shrine to Liverpool Football Club. A framed Steven Gerrard football shirt hangs alongside a metal replica of the club's crest, symbols of his son's devotion to the cause.

However, like many Irish homes, it is also dotted with memorials to loved ones who have died. These take the form of Mass cards slotted into the frame of the large family photograph above the dining table.

These cards typically include a photograph of the deceased – similar to the kind you might find in a passport – along with their dates of birth and death, and a prayer or hymn, the recital of which is believed to help speed the loved one on their journey from Purgatory to Heaven.

Their display in the home is an act of solidarity, a defiance of death, a statement that loved ones who have died are not truly lost but are still in the forefront of the minds and the lives of those left behind; part of the furniture, not forgotten in some drawer.

In a little alcove off the living room, however, is a much more unusual memorial. It takes the form of pages from the 1 May 1975 edition of the local newspaper, the *Lurgan Mail*, cut up so that they fit into five small A5 frames.

This is why I have come here to meet Eddie, accompanied by a family friend, Gerard McAvoy. Eddie and Gerard were both in Bleary Darts

Club on the night of Sunday, 27 April 1975, when loyalist gunmen burst in and shot dead three of their friends – Joe Toman, Brendan O'Hara (Gerard's brother-in-law) and John Michael Feeney – and seriously wounded a fourth. Eddie was 28 years old back then, Gerard 35.

Even at the remove of almost fifty years, the reports make bleak reading.

'Eighteen children have been left fatherless following what was described as the bloodiest terrorist attack on civilians in the Lurgan area since the Troubles began six years ago ...

'The scene of the shooting is only a stone's throw from where three soldiers were murdered in a booby-trapped cottage several years ago. Sunday's deaths bring the total number of persons killed in the Lurgan area during the past six years of terrorism to 28.'

The images stick in the mind. The blood up the walls and on the floor; the overturned beer bottles; the circled bullet casings on the ground and bullet holes in the walls – thirty-one in total – none more grimly memorable than the one that has penetrated the dartboard, marked and numbered as if in some obscene keeping of the score.

Bleary Darts Club after the murders. © Victor Patterson

'That's Brendan's car,' says Gerard, spotting in one of the clippings his brother-in-law's Mini parked outside the darts club. 'Jesus, it's good to have them, boy, them photos there. That brings back memories. This is powerful, right enough.'

***

Bleary Darts Club was formed in 1973 by Joe Toman and a group of his friends. Situated down an unlit, unsignposted laneway off Sugar Island Road, about three miles from Lurgan, it was based in an old weaver's cottage with whitewashed walls and a tarred roof that had originally belonged to Eddie Rooney's grandfather. There is a historical echo here. Almost two centuries earlier, approximately ten thousand Catholic weavers from Down and Armagh had fled persecution by Protestant gangs to settle mostly in Leitrim and Mayo, leaving behind cottages such as the one that would become the darts club.

Eddie's uncle had inherited the cottage but had moved out when he got married. He was happy to hand it over to Eddie and Joe so that they could start a club and keep the young ones off the streets. 'There was nothing in the Bleary at the time,' says Eddie. 'The club was about bringing the people together. And trying to get people off the street, instead of young fellas standing on the corners.' Although Joe himself was a teetotaller, the prospect of a local drinking establishment was an attractive one for his friends and neighbours.

The big room that housed the club was called the shop – meaning a workshop, not a retail space, Eddie explains, where a handloom would originally have stood. The members took down an old wooden partition to make the space bigger. The windows were blocked up to make the premises more secure. No cash was kept on site, but there was plenty of alcohol, spirits as well as crates of beer, which might have tempted a thirsty burglar.

The club was only open three nights a week: Thursdays for a

members' meeting; Fridays for matches in the Banbridge and District League or, if they were playing away from home, for a late drink after the match; and Sundays just for the craic, a friendly game, cards or a pint.

The Thursday before the shooting, the committee members made a practical decision that probably saved several lives. The back wall of the club was stacked tall with wooden crates full of empty beer bottles, which Eddie used to load into his van to return to the Village Inn in Waringstown, his supplier. 'We were just sitting talking about different things,' said Eddie, 'and I think Danny Toman just happened to say, "Boys, what about before we go, lift them crates and bring them up here behind that door, because there's nobody sits behind that door, it's too cold. And that's room wasted. We'll put another couple of tables in there for anybody wants to drink and play cards." So, if the crates hadn't been there and them boys walked in ...'

If you imagine the clubhouse as a dartboard, the way that the crates were stacked meant numbers 19 through to 3 were safe.

The gunmen didn't enter the room, just stood on the oche of the threshold and sprayed what they could see. There were twenty-seven people in the club that night, and over fifty shots were fired, yet only three people were killed, and a fourth injured. It was a miracle that it wasn't a massacre.

'If they had have walked in ...,' said Gerard, '... they'd have riddled all round them,' said Eddie, finishing his friend's sentence.

***

That Sunday evening – four weeks after Easter in 1975 – Brendan O'Hara, a 38-year-old barman, married to Gerard's sister Mina and father to four children, and his friend Patsy Cairns, a brother of Eamon Cairns, were enjoying a pint in the Ashburn Hotel in Lurgan when they witnessed the distressing sight of a young man being taken out to be kneecapped, a brutal form of paramilitary punishment for those considered to have stepped out of line. Two masked and armed youths entered the hotel, singled out their victim – a 25-year-old Catholic from Portadown – brought him to the car park and shot him in both kneecaps.

Brendan and Patsy understandably wanted to leave after that, but the night was still young – it was just after 10 p.m. – so they decided to head for Bleary Darts Club for a quiet drink.

'See the chair where Brendan O'Hara was shot, I was sitting in it before that,' says Gerard. It was five or six weeks since Gerard had been in the club. He didn't play darts or cards, but his friend Brendan Finnegan liked a game of poker, so he went along with Brendan for the craic and a few pints.

John Michael Feeney, a 45-year-old married father of eight, was visiting the club for the first time that night. He had brought his 18-year-old son Jimmy with him to show off the gold medal Jimmy had won at the All-Ireland senior boxing championships in Dublin just two nights before. He also wanted to talk to Joe Toman about a gun dog, a springer spaniel that a contact of his would train for Joe.

Joe Toman, a 47-year-old-joiner, was married to Betty and they had two boys and four girls, aged between 13 and 21: Geraldine, Joan, Micky, Christine, Gary and Eileen. As founder of the club, Joe opened the premises himself or often accompanied whichever committee member was rostered to do so, helping light the fire, set up the bar and generally get the place ready for the members. He was a character, a bit of a devil for the craic at times. A few nights before, he had thrown onto the fire some jumping jacks – small fireworks that hopped about in an erratic way as they burned, throwing off sparks and crackles – for a laugh, to give his mates a fright.

So, when the shooting started that night at about 11 p.m., Gerard initially thought it was another prank.

'Noel Toland, God rest him, pulled me to the ground,' said Gerard. 'And he says, "Get down, that's shooting." You would have thought they were never going to quit, to be honest. I was lying on the ground, afraid to get up. I was trembling, boy. Nerves was shattered.'

Joe Toman was sitting at a table by the fire with John Michael Feeney. Brendan O'Hara was sitting at the next table. Two others sitting with them, Mickey Green and Gerard's father, Hugh McAvoy, escaped unscathed.

Another club member, Michael Maguire, saw a gunman hold the door open with his foot. He was wearing black Beatle or Chelsea boots. When the shooting stopped, Michael ran across to Joe and pulled him away from the fire. Joe had been hit by eight to ten bullets. One small mercy is that his death would have been very rapid.

Joe's cousin Bernard Toman had been playing darts with Freddie Thompson. In the havoc caused by the shooting someone knocked him to the floor. Freddie had had his back to the door and heard someone say, 'Duck, boys!' and was diving to the floor when he was hit in the arm by a shotgun blast. When the shooting stopped, Bernard saw Freddie lying on the floor with blood coming from his left arm. He kicked the door closed and lifted Brendan O'Hara onto a chair, then realised he was seriously wounded. He tried to lift John Michael, but it was apparent he was dead. He took Joe's father, Daniel, home, then went to Lurgan Police Station to report the shooting. He returned to the club with police officers and took Freddie to hospital.

A man who survived the shooting spoke to the *Lurgan Mail* the morning after the murders. 'I just cannot believe that there are persons alive who would do such a thing,' the eyewitness, who declined to give his name for fear of reprisals, said. 'It was all over in two minutes, but three of our members were dead. Two were shot while sitting up to the fire, another was shot while playing darts and the fourth at a table. I have no idea why anyone would want to attack the club.'

The club's clientele was predominantly Catholic but a good few Protestants went too. But of course they weren't there as Catholics, Protestants or dissenters, just cards players, darts players and pint-drinking observers.

Freddie Thompson, the only person to be shot who survived, was a Protestant. Troubles narratives are rife with stories of attacks by extremists from one side or other in which a supposedly Catholic bar or Protestant pub is targeted, only for people of both persuasions to be killed. The killers almost certainly took the view that the mistake was not theirs – that their co-religionists should not have been consorting with the other side, fraternising with the enemy. Perhaps they considered them rotten Prods, what loyalist shipyard workers called socialists and communists in the 1920s, or – further back – the United Irishmen of 1798.

In fact, these victims were the mortar that held the North together, the best of us, the ones who crossed the aisle without even giving it a thought. This social fabric, the friendships that bind individuals and communities together, is purer and more precious than linen.

When the RUC and ambulances arrived, Eddie decided to go home. He lived just round the corner on Cranny Terrace. A neighbour who was in the club that night was saying to him, 'Get me home, you have to get me home here.'

The next day, a detective called to see Eddie. 'I tell you now, he asked me everything bar what he should have been asking me. He was more interested in what was the club for, who went to it, would it have been cross-community, was there ever any bother in it? Never, who do you think done this? Who did you see? Do you think there was one or two, do you think it was a car, what made them come? None of them questions.'

The day before the shooting, Eddie says, the UDR had been seen patrolling the field behind the darts club. 'The same as the O'Dowds [a triple murder nearby in January 1976]. That Sunday the Dowdses got it, that Saturday they [soldiers] were all round Barney's house. You can draw your own conclusions.'

And that's not all. 'Weeks before, the army broke into the club. Well, they said they were the British Army, you don't know. I can't mind if it was me went round to leave drink in it one Sunday, but the door was open. They had it wedged open, you could see they had it pushed open with a bar or something. They left a note saying the British Army had authorised this blah, blah, blah. We're sorry for any disruption and we took a couple of lemonades, we left the money for it. That's only an auld whitewash. A scrap of paper.'

Eddie says the killers had done their reconnaissance. 'They knew there was only one door into it. They knew all the windows were blocked up to stop anybody breaking in taking drink or anything.' They parked their getaway car on the main road, by a gate set back about six or seven feet from the road, like a lay-by.

Did they ever feel that the club was a possible target? Were they conscious that it was at all risky or isolated?

'It was in the back of your head because of the way the Troubles were going,' says Eddie. 'Yeah, Brendan and me would have talked about it,' says Gerard. 'You know, it was sort of dodgy now. Because there was a whole lot of shooting at the time. Every night, Brendan Finnegan and me would have been going out to it, you know in the dark nights, you came off the main road and all, you're into the dark ... you turned the lights of the car out, you got out and you couldn't see nothing.'

That night was the end of the club. It never opened again.

'No, it just knocked the heart out of us,' says Eddie. 'Just everybody was scared,' says Gerard. Another member who witnessed the killings told the local paper, 'Nobody has the heart to go back there after Sunday night. We couldn't risk another incident like that.'

In retrospect, you might say trouble had been brewing that weekend. But then again, trouble had been on the boil for six years by that stage. A Protestant, Samuel Johnston, had been shot dead in neighbouring Portadown two nights previously, on 25 April. The next day, Saturday 26 April, a train carrying 400 Orangemen to a rally in Belfast was stoned as it passed through Lurgan's Kilwilkie estate. One man was hospitalised with a fractured jaw and lacerations.

Also on that Saturday, Peter Campbell, a Catholic publican in Banbridge, had been seriously injured by a booby-trap explosion in his car outside his pub, the Bus Bar on Newry Street. He sustained serious throat and facial injuries, lost three fingers and the sight in one eye, and also suffered a broken arm and leg. He was giving two customers, a Protestant and a Catholic, a lift home, and they were also hurt. They had a narrow escape as when they came out to the car, Mr Campbell's pet Labrador jumped into the front passenger seat. Mr Campbell offered to move it so that one of them could sit there but both said they were happy to sit in the back. The dog was killed instantly in the blast.

Eddie Rooney felt that the soldiers' killings three years before at Cranny Terrace was linked to what had happened at the club. 'I mind that as well, because Jesus you'd hear the bang, boy. I was down home, because nobody went out of a Sunday around that time of the day. You just heard the people saying that's the army up there, because you seen all the Land Rovers and soldiers.'

When the explosion happened, the residents of Cranny Terrace ran to help, bringing blankets and coats, and doing what they could to comfort the injured. Nevertheless, they in turn would become the targets for a revenge attack; a drive-by shooting a few months later when the days turned dark early. Three houses in the stretch of houses pejoratively called Pope's Row by some locals were hit by gunfire, but no one was injured. Eddie says, 'The gunmen called out, "That's retaliation for the soldiers and there's more to come. We'll be back. We'll get yous." That's the way they put it. But that sort of died away then. When we opened the Bleary Club we didn't think of that because well, if you count '72, the soldiers getting blew up, and '75, the Bleary Darts Club getting it, that's three years.

'Do you see if the bingo minibus and the O'Dowds shootings [in 1975 and 1976 respectively] had been before the Bleary club, we never would have opened. We'd have said no, there's no point, it's too dangerous. But these two things happened after the Bleary club.'

Immediately after the shooting in 1972, the men of Cranny Terrace had set up a night-time vigilante patrol. Eddie, Joe Toman and others would take turns to keep watch overnight, carrying an old foghorn to raise the alarm if they needed to. A road loops round the back of the terrace so they put two barrels filled with stones at either end, with a steel post between them, so that a car couldn't complete a circuit.

Cranny Terrace was on a slope, which meant you had to go up four steps to Eddie's house whereas Joe Toman's was level with the road. 'The way Joe looked at it, if Joe was sitting at his window at night watching TV, you could have seen the top of his head. So, he had this row of concrete blocks along the windowsill inside the house in case somebody did shoot.

'But everyone then started taking precautions. I remember getting a plank and cutting it and putting the plank at the bottom of the stair, two rungs up and then I got another plank and put it across the door and got another plank and jammed it in between the two. You couldn't get that open. I wasn't the only one. You didn't know. You said to yourself they are liable to come back and throw a bomb through that window or leave a bomb at your door. You didn't know. But it never did happen.'

***

Gerard, already traumatised by what he had witnessed, had another ordeal to face. He had to break the news to his sister Mina that her husband, Brendan, had been shot dead.

'We were left, me and Brendan Finnegan, to go and break the news to Mina that Brendan had been shot. That's not a nice thing to have to do, like. Jesus, it wasn't an easy job. I hear that wee woman squealing yet, boy, whenever I said. Ah Jesus, it makes me cry nearly myself, like. Because it's an awful … it was an awful time, boy. Jesus, it was.'

Mina had multiple sclerosis, as did Gerard's two other sisters, May and Sheila, and was in a wheelchair, which made the prospect of raising four small children by herself so much harder. Catherine McEvoy remembers Barney O'Dowd carrying one of the sisters into the church. A few months later he would be shot.

Gerard doesn't mind admitting he was traumatised by the shooting. 'Oh God, see that time, boy. I got that at night if a rap come to the door I would hardly have answered it. Just my nerves was shattered,' he said. 'I didn't go to work for two or three weeks after it. I was working away up with the cement mixers away up at the top of the field and there was cows on the other side of the hedge, and they were rattling and I was jumping, the shite was scared out of me. I was not myself for a long, long time.'

To add insult to injury, a Sunday newspaper claimed that the darts club had been frequented by IRA members. Eddie and the rest of the committee members 'nipped that in the bud right away. And the following week they put an apology in for this misinformation.'

How does the memory of the horror of that night stay with them? Is it something they think about every day? No, is the answer.

'I think because I've them photos,' says Eddie, 'I don't think of it because if I just look at it, I say ach, there's the Bleary club. But if I hadn't got them and somebody says to me were you in the Bleary club, oh, I'd say you start thinking of that night and the door banging and … I tell you what the gunfire sounded like. It's like you throwing water on hot ashes. Just popping. That's what you heard. And then the bang bang.'

In 2012, Eddie wrote a poem about the murders, 'A Night To Remember (Bleary Darts Club)'. It begins, 'One Sunday night in April / Ruthless men lay in wait / Their minds warped with bitterness / Their hearts full of hate,' and it ends, 'But one day those cowards / Like their guns will lie rotten / But that night in the Darts Club / Won't ever be forgotten.'

***

The three victims were buried the following Wednesday: John Michael Feeney after a Requiem Mass in St Colman's Church in Laurencetown at 11 a.m.; Brendan O'Hara in St Colman's Cemetery in Lurgan after noon

Mass at St Colman's in Clare; and Joe Toman in Clare after 11 a.m. Mass there.

'I can still remember the smell of him – wood and putty – his work smell,' Joe Toman's daughter Eileen McCann told Anne Cadwallader, author of *Lethal Allies*. 'He was always spick and span. You could have seen your face in his polished shoes. He was great with his hands. He once built a boat. Dad missed out on so much. Life was never the same again.' Every Sunday evening, at the precise time of the attack, she meticulously went around her home, closing curtains and locking doors, her husband, Eugene, told Cadwallader.

Micky Toman is a joiner like his father. His father taught him to fish at Kernan Lough in the boat he made in the workshop they shared behind their home. On the night of the shooting he had just started the night shift at Goodyear in Craigavon when he was told by a supervisor he should go home. He had just turned 19 the month before.

He was a regular in the darts club too but would hang out with his friends playing table tennis at the far end of the room from where what he thought of as the ould boys sat or played darts. 'I included my daddy in that. I know now he wasn't an ould boy. He was young, only 48.'

As if it was not cruel enough for Joe to be murdered, the fact that he fell face first into the fire meant that his coffin had to be closed for the wake, depriving his family of the emotional closure of spending time with the body, acclimatising to their loss.

'The hardest part is that bloody fire,' says Micky, becoming emotional. 'That gets me every time. I know in my heart Daddy was dead. My daddy had that wee blue driving licence in his inside breast pocket and a bullet went right through it so he had to be shot in the heart. But why did it have to happen? We didn't need the fire on top of it.

'That affected us more, the fact that I didn't see my daddy dead. I went out of the house that night, he was living. I still dream to this day that he's not dead, because I physically never seen him dead. Even to this day it hurts. The hardest part was not seeing him. Still is. Mentally

I still find it hard. The fact that I'm dreaming them dreams, that's hard to believe after fifty years but I still do.' What does he dream of? 'The funeral and the wake house, the box is there but you're mentally saying it's only the [empty] box. The dreams change but they're all the same thing.'

As we speak, Micky is looking at framed photos of his father and Jimmy Feeney, who became his closest friend after the murders. 'Jimmy and me used to beat the crap out of each other at the club in Gilford, but then with our two fathers getting shot ended up best mates. The craythur never got over it. He would never even have talked to me about it.'

His father didn't want Micky to be a joiner, he says, because in those days tradesmen were not well treated. 'The week before Daddy was shot, he was off a half day to go to the dentist. His boss came out to Mammy with Daddy's wages after he was shot and he'd docked him a half day's pay and that was after twenty-five years' service. You weren't talking big money; a joiner's wages back then was probably £25 a week.'

The Troubles are over more than twenty-five years, but does he feel they are over for him? 'No, definitely not. Because there never was any justice. There was no justice because there was no investigation. Two weeks it lasted. I never would tell a policeman anything to this day because I don't trust them. I have no doubt the security forces were involved in the killings. Noel Toland and another man two weeks before the shooting went over to pee in a drain outside the club and a UDR man was lying in the drain looking up at him.' A neighbour told him he believed the gunmen had walked across the fields from Sugar Island Road because the magpies in the hedges had been disturbed.

'It was always going to happen,' Micky says. 'It was an easy target. Daddy was talking of packing it in. Protestants went to the club too but all but one quit coming a few weeks before the shooting.' They were told not to come, he surmises. Freddie Thompson, the sole Protestant in the club that night, was taken to hospital in Joe's car. 'I had to clean all that up, there was a lot of blood.'

The IRA tried to recruit Micky 'not long after Daddy was shot, that's when you are at your most vulnerable. Gary was only 14, he would have joined because he'd have been that scared to say no. He wouldn't have gone out for a bucket of coal after dark, that's how it affects you. They said, "We know who shot your Daddy, join up and you can get him." I said, "You tell me who did it and I'll shoot him myself; I don't need to be in the IRA to do it." I would honestly have done it at the time if I'd had the opportunity. Nothing to do with religion, just the fact that he killed my father. I blame the person, not the religion.'

Fishing is another thing that unites Catholics and Protestants.

'I fished a lifetime with Wilfie Tatton from Banbridge. We fished down Mayo all the time as well as in Corbet [lough]. Wilfie was always a bit wary about being a Protestant down south. One time in July one of the bailiffs winding him up said, "Did you come down with your sash on?" These two boys from Belfast were going to bate him. I said, "You go to hit him, you're coming through me first," and every man jack in the pub was standing up behind me. They turned and walked out.'

The clubhouse is long gone, but Micky intends to mark the day of the fiftieth anniversary by going to the field where it once stood.

Does he often visit Joe's grave? 'I've looked after Daddy's grave from the day and hour he died. It's something he would have done for me,' he says, his voice breaking. 'My daddy would never have let me lie without looking after me.'

***

The local RUC Chief Superintendent, A.V.L. Hodgett, issued an appeal for the public's help in tracking down the killers: 'No stone will be left unturned until we catch them.' In fact, according to the HET's 2011 report into Joe Toman's murder, the RUC investigation, while initially thorough, was of extremely short duration, effectively wound up after a matter of weeks.

The police checked out cars stolen in the days leading up to the murders, in particular one stolen from a Protestant part of Lurgan on the evening of the murder and found at Clare Hill, a mile and a half from the murder scene, the next morning. However, they did not release the exact information about where the cars were stolen from for fear of reprisals against the owners.

'We don't want another bomb horror on our hands, like that in Portadown following the Breen killing in Lurgan several months ago,' the chief investigator said. This was a reference to the murder of James Breen, a 45-year-old Catholic married father of two, the brother-in-law of a nationalist politician, shot dead in front of his eight-year-old son at his home in Lurgan's Kilwilkie area in February 1975. The stolen Ford Cortina used by the gunman was recovered and returned to its owner after being examined. Just over a fortnight later, the car's owner, Edward Clayton, a 27-year-old Protestant breadman and part-time community worker from Portadown, was killed by a bomb that had been placed under the vehicle.

Harold McCusker, the local unionist MP 'totally and unreservedly' condemned the killings. 'Whoever is responsible for any murder cannot be accommodated in a civilised society. No cause can be furthered by cold-blooded and calculated murder. Whatever a person's religious or political convictions, he is at least entitled to life itself.'

Malachy McGurran of Republican Clubs, a forerunner of the Workers Party, also condemned the killings: 'Three working people lost their lives, another was seriously injured and many left in a terrible nervous state, while the sophisticated purveyors of sectarianism continue untouched to stomp the land encouraging more such bloodshed. These people are as guilty as the people who pulled the triggers at Bleary on Sunday night.'

The inquest held in Banbridge returned open verdicts. A club member, Mickey Green, told the inquest he had been sitting by the fire when he saw the perforated black muzzle of what looked like a machine gun appear at the door. As the door was kicked open, he then saw flashes as shots rang out in quick succession and he dived to the floor. There was a lull during which some club member had the presence of mind and the courage to turn off the lights. Mickey had just raised his head again when the shooting resumed, a second burst of gunfire followed by several single shots. Then another club member managed to kick the door shut.

The inquest heard that about sixty shots were fired. An RUC constable said that he found fifty rounds of spent ammunition inside the clubhouse. The floor was littered with bullets of three different types, suggesting there had been the same number of gunmen. An RUC detective inspector told the inquest he had no reason to believe anyone in the club had any paramilitary connection and he believed the murderers' motive was sectarian. The coroner, Arthur D. Orr, described the deaths as tragic, noting that no one had yet been made 'amenable [*sic*]' for the crimes, which he described as 'a random shooting as no particular person had been sought out'.

Joe Toman's son-in-law Eugene McCann arrived at the club five minutes after the shootings. He recalled seeing what he believed to be a sub-machine gun on some kind of tripod outside the club and a box of shotgun cartridges, neither of which show up in any police report. McCann's house was raided the next day and he was served with a summons accusing him of transporting illegal alcohol. He was never interviewed by the police about the darts-club murders. However, in 2011 he told the HET that he had seen Robin Jackson, the leading local UVF gunman, scouting the area in a car with another man the week before. He recognised the driver as a local UDR man, who was later shot dead by the IRA. The RUC received intelligence in 1984 naming Jackson as one of two leading UVF men responsible for the darts-club shooting.

Forensic tests established that the weapons used had been a 9mm Sterling sub-machine gun, a Webley .455 calibre revolver and a 12-bore shotgun. The Webley was later found by a member of the public on farmland near Jackson's home in Donaghcloney, a few miles away.

It had also been used to shoot a Catholic shopkeeper, Paul McNeice, in Ardress, County Armagh, in October 1974. Mr McNeice's shop had been blown up ten days before, so his business was operating out of a hut when two men shot him. He survived.

The Sterling was found three months later at the scene of the Miami Showband massacre, ten miles away, on the main Belfast to Dublin road between Banbridge and Newry. It had been reported stolen from the Ulster Special Constabulary barracks in Donaghcloney in 1970. There is no evidence that the men convicted of these related crimes were ever interrogated about the Bleary shootings. 'The HET is aware of the family's belief that there was collusion involved in Joe's murder,' its report concludes. 'The family's fears cannot be satisfactorily allayed.'

On 30 April, the Banbridge unit of the Protestant Action Force, a cover name that the UVF used for its more outrageous murders, admitted responsibility for the Bleary Darts Club killings as well as five other deaths that month.

The first was the murder of Owen Boyle. He was a 40-year-old welder who had recently moved into a new home near Aughnacloy, County Tyrone with his wife, Winnie, and their eight children, built on a plot of land bought from a Protestant neighbour. On 11 April 1975, he was standing talking to his wife in the kitchen, facing the window that was so new it didn't yet have curtains, when he was shot six times through it. Owen, who was involved in no organisation other than the GAA, was still conscious when the police arrived, saying to the sergeant, 'Ah sergeant, why should they do this to me? I never did anything to no man.' He died eleven days later. One of the weapons used was linked to five other sectarian murders in the area.

On Monday 21 April, Marion Bowen, a 21-year-old hairdresser, who was expecting her first child a fortnight later, was visiting the family home she and her husband were renovating in Killyliss, County Tyrone, to check up on a new boiler with her brothers Michael and Seamus McKenna, when a booby-trap bomb exploded, killing all three instantly. Their bodies were taken to a morgue in Dungannon, where the pathologist conducting the post-mortems noted that Marion had been heavily pregnant, but the baby was missing. The hospital contacted the police at the scene and asked them to look for another body. An infant girl was found lying under heavy rubble in a bedroom, having been blown clear of her mother's body. She would have died instantly.

The HET report quotes the local undertaker, Massie McAleer, who said that when he was loading the baby's coffin into a hearse to be taken to the morgue, British soldiers stood around laughing and kicked the wheels of the hearse.

No one was ever convicted of the Derryliss murders. However, three men, including a UDR soldier, confessed to a remarkably similar bombing which occurred nearby a month later.

In *The Irish News* on 26 April 1975, Father Denis Faul accused the security forces of 'wilful neglect' and a '100 per cent failure rate' to protect Catholic lives. Former soldiers and those expelled from the UDR should be investigated. He found it extraordinary that 'people whose names were raised time and time again were not given a brisk interrogation without any of the twenty-eight methods of brutality that had made the RUC infamous throughout Europe'.

***

Four days after the Bleary murders, on 1 May 1975, an election was held for the Northern Ireland Constitutional Convention, a consultative body set up by British Prime Minister Harold Wilson's Labour government to seek agreement on a political settlement. A coalition of unionists opposed to sharing power with nationalists won 46 out of 78 seats, producing a report that November advocating a return to majority rule, which nationalists rejected. However, the terms of a future settlement were becoming clearer. The British government also rejected a return to unionist domination. William Craig, the hard-line unionist leader of

Vanguard, did accept the possibility of power-sharing with the SDLP, a move that split the United Ulster Unionist Council, a coalition of unionists opposed to the Sunningdale Agreement, and precipitated the eventual collapse of his party. David Trimble, one of Craig's lieutenants, would go on to become leader of the Ulster Unionist Party and sign the Belfast Agreement, winning the Nobel Peace Prize along with the SDLP's John Hume.

A month after the attack, a front-page headline of the 29 May edition of the *Lurgan Mail* read, 'Razor blade victim left unconscious'. A 13-year-old Catholic schoolboy had been abducted on his way to Lismore Comprehensive School that Tuesday morning by two men in a car, who slashed him with a razor blade and dumped him by the roadside. He was found semi-conscious with lacerations to the face and hands by a passing milkman, who brought him to Craigavon Police Station.

The following week, on 5 June 1975, a referendum was held on whether the UK should leave the Common Market, forerunner of the European Union. The Democratic Unionist Party declared to the *Lurgan Mail*, 'It is the open desire of the nations of Western Europe to achieve a Roman Catholic United States of Europe. Proof of this is the fact that the Vatican representative in Brussels has been given pride of place in the diplomatic corps.

'The loyalist cause has always been the maintaining of civil and religious liberty. These precious freedoms would be greatly undermined in a Roman Catholic dominated Europe. The real philosophy behind the EEC is not economic betterment for Europe but political union.

'Continued membership of the EEC will put in jeopardy our link with the United Kingdom. This will come about through relaxation of work permits for labourers from other European countries leading to an influx of foreigners.

'It is also possible that pro-Republican sympathisers within the EEC dictatorship will try to push us Southwards by threat of economic blackmail.'

The DUP predicted that the North's poultry industry would be wiped out within a few short years. (In fact, Moy Park, a company founded in Moygashel, County Tyrone, in 1943, now supplies 25 per cent of the western European market for chickens.) The DUP lost the European referendum in 1975 but played a controversial role in helping secure the UK's exit from the European Union in 2016, against the wishes of the majority of voters in Northern Ireland, destabilising both devolution and the peace process.

That same week in 1975, David Calvert, a Craigavon DUP councillor, complained that pupils at a local school had been forced to visit a Catholic chapel and 'versed on the Roman Catholic system of worship'. He said, 'I think it is a disgrace that this type of thing should be going on. It seems it is just a furtherance of the accursed ecumenical movement and another downward trend in the morals of our land.' Hugh News, an SDLP councillor, left the council chamber in protest and said, 'Craigavon Borough Council will now be recognised as the most bigoted of the twenty-six district councils in the province.'

On Saturday 7 June – in the parish of Aghaderg, which borders Tullylish – Josephine McGrath, the 61-year-old widowed caretaker of St Mary's Catholic Church in Lisnagade, received serious injuries to her face, hand and legs. She had picked up a wreath that had blown off a recently dug grave and triggered a 5lb pressure mine that only partially exploded, which probably saved her life. She managed to crawl 300 yards to a cottage to seek help. An RUC officer called it 'a diabolical and macabre sectarian attack'. Scarva's Presbyterian and Church of Ireland ministers offered prayers for Mrs McGrath during their Sunday services. Parish priest Father Hugh Connolly said, 'It's shocking to think that so little respect could be shown for both the living and the dead.'

Nine

'They kill us for their sport'

It says something for the ubiquity of Troubles atrocities that Declan Feeney's local, the Heights Bar, where we are meeting to talk about his father's murder in Bleary Darts Club, was the scene of the Loughinisland massacre in 1994, when six Catholics were shot dead while they watched a live broadcast of Ireland beating Italy in the World Cup finals.

I was at that game with my dad in the Giants' Stadium in New Jersey and remember reading about the Loughinisland atrocity after we'd travelled to Orlando the next day, ahead of Ireland's game against Mexico. Five men were wounded in the attack and as Declan and I talk below a framed Ireland jersey and a framed Down GAA top, one of them limps past, leaning on his walking stick. Declan introduces me to the barman, Aidan, a cousin of Matthew O'Toole, the SDLP politician who is a regular reviewer for me at *The Irish Times*. The North is a big village.

Declan and I arrange a follow-up meeting a few weeks later, this time in the Bus Bar in Banbridge, whose owner, Peter Campbell, had been blown up in his car by loyalists the night before the darts-club attack. When we get to the door, there's a note saying 'Back at 4', so we end up in Higgins's, where I attended more committee meetings of the Manchester City Supporters Club (Gilford branch) than were good for my mental health. Declan is immediately identified as a Feeney by some regulars, who reminisce about how his brother Jimmy was one of the greatest boxers they had ever seen. In the corner is the father of George Bailey, who gave Declan his first job with horses.

A shared love of horses and hounds has often made for strange bedfellows. Declan's father, John Michael, a working-class Catholic from Laurencetown, had just been appointed Brian Faulkner's second-in-command in the Iveagh Harriers when he was murdered. Faulkner had ruled Northern Ireland for just over a year as unionist prime minister until Westminster imposed direct rule in 1972, before serving an even shorter, five-month reign as chief executive of the North's first power-sharing government in 1974. Declan is now huntsman with the East Down Foxhounds, having served his apprenticeship in England, where he hunted alongside King Charles.

'I've done all right,' says Declan. 'I get up every morning to go out and do a job that I love.'

Declan was ten years old, the golden boy, when his father was killed. His sister Michelle was just three. Also left fatherless were Arlene, Jimmy, Alan, Peter, Cindy and Maria.

Declan doesn't know if his father will ever get justice but one thing he is determined to do is make sure people get his name right. In the documentary *Unquiet Graves* he is listed as John Feeney. Similarly in correspondence from the latest official investigation into collusion.

'I says to them, "Get it right, because my da was John Michael Feeney and everybody knew him as John Michael Feeney. It's just a name on a list. But he was more than that. You know? I missed him so much and I suppose a lot of things I done was things that would have pleased him. But I didn't do it purposely. It was me.'

***

Declan shows me a photograph of his grandfather in British Army uniform. John Michael's father, James, was born in 1896 and fought at

Gallipoli in the First World War with the Royal Inniskilling Fusiliers. If the welcome home was warm, it soon ran cold. 'My granny Feeney was put out of Hazelbank factory along with all the other Catholics in '21 or '22,' says Declan. Lloyd George's pledge 'to make Britain a fit country for heroes to live in' did not extend to the North, not to Northern Catholics anyway. Granny Feeney didn't take it lying down, though. A friend's mother told Declan that his granny had climbed up the factory flagpole and taken down the Union Jack.

The Feeneys lived in the gate lodge to Lawrencetown House, called the Point Cottage, which my uncle Joe later bought.

When John Michael left school at 14, he joined the Iveagh Harriers kennels in Seapatrick as groom and second whipper-in. By the time he was 21, he was married to Doreen Diamond, whose aunt Violet was married to the kennel huntsman, Johnny Flynn, a Tipperary man. Doreen was the oldest of sixteen and had to leave school at 14 to look after her siblings. Her dream had been to become a teacher.

The Master of the Hunt was Albert Uprichard, one of the last of the linen lords. He had been brought up in Elmfield, a castle near Gilford, and lived in another mansion, Millpark, in Hall's Mill, where he ran the boxing club. Although his wealthy Quaker family was staunchly unionist – two Orange lodges were named after relatives – he was a socialist and a nationalist. According to a tribute written on his death in 2012 by a friend, Jason Diamond, a cousin of Declan's, 'Boolavogue' was one of his favourite songs.

After John Michael got married, he needed a better wage. Albert got him a job in Down Shoes but factory work wasn't for him so he became groundsman for the factory and gardener for the managing director, Karel Kucek.

John Michael taught Kucek's wife how to ride, schooling her horse over boxes at the shoe factory. 'And, lo and behold, didn't she start hunting with the Iveaghs? And she took my da with her. So, he was back hunting again, through the side door.'

When Exquisite Fabrics opened in Craigavon in 1973, they were paying top dollar, so John Michael got a job there and left Down Shoes with a gold watch as a farewell gift.

John Michael loved his sport, had boxed professionally and beaten the Irish champion, Jimmy Brown. But if one thing defined him, it was his love for animals. 'My daddy, anything to do with animals he loved,' Declan says. 'He had an affinity with them.'

In many ways he lived the life of a country gentleman, hunting, shooting and fishing. Even at the height of the Troubles, locals in Laurencetown went hunting for rabbits and walked home with their shotguns broken over their arms. There is a sign nailed to a tree near my parents', which still makes me smile. 'Coose Gun Club. No shooting.' Whatever your view on blood sports, at least these hunters were not hounding fellow humans to their deaths.

An authority on gun dogs, John Michael won prizes with dogs he had trained at field trials all over Ireland. He tied his own flies for fishing in the River Bann, a skill that he passed on to his sons. Three became huntsmen: Peter in Kildare, Declan with the East Down, and Jimmy took over John Michael's position with the Iveagh Harriers.

The family home in Hall's Mill had a room full of birdcages with aviaries out the back. John Michael caught goldfinches and bullfinches and bred them with canaries. He broke horses for people and was one of the first in Ireland to have a Weimaraner. 'You name it, we had it,' says Declan. 'Mummy reared geese for Christmas. We had goats, a pet fox and a pet badger. There are photographs of Mummy with the fox round her neck and it looking at the camera.'

Two years after John Michael joined Exquisite, he landed his dream job. 'One day,' says Declan, 'our front door rapped and I opened the door and here standing looking at me was Brian Faulkner in a sheepskin coat, the grey hair swept back. He was never off the television then and he says to me, "Could I speak to your father?" He had a big Rover 3500 car, navy blue with a black roof. If you had a car like that, you were doing well.'

Johnny Flynn was retiring and Faulkner wanted John Michael to take over as kennel huntsman. It was just days before Doreen's fortieth birthday on 22 April. 'I remember Daddy saying to Mummy – because that's all the job he ever wanted to do in his life but he couldn't because he had eight children – "Doreen," he says, "life begins at 40."'

They moved on 18 April 1975. 'I'll never forget it. A lovely sunny summer's day. We come out of school and Daddy picked us up in the kennel van to lift the last bit of furniture from Hall's Mill. He lifted the ferret box, the dog, two cats and something else. I was in the back of the lorry and I remember my da going round the corner and the ferret box tipping over and the ferret got out and the fucking terrier was trying to kill the fucking ferret.'

A week later, on 25 April, Declan's brother Jimmy was fighting in the National Stadium in Dublin for the All-Ireland senior title, having won schoolboy and junior titles the previous year. His opponent, Damien McDermott from Derry, had beaten him weeks before in the Ulster final. John Michael was in the corner as Jimmy's trainer, with Albert Uprichard. A whole gang of Diamonds and Feeneys were in the crowd and this time Jimmy won. 'There's a cutting in Jimmy's scrapbook from the *Belfast Telegraph* and it says, "Feeney beat him and Feeney beat him well." They never came home to five in the morning. Sure they were all partying the bit out.' Jimmy was the All-Ireland senior champion at

Jimmy and John Michael Feeney with their boxing trophies.

only 18 years of age and was in line to compete in the 1976 Olympics in Montreal.

'So, there we were, the highest of the high. My da had got the job he always wanted. Jimmy had won the All-Ireland. Everything was going great.'

That Sunday morning, Declan helped his dad wash the yards down and then fix a puncture in a car tyre. 'I'll never forget, he had a grey, three-piece suit on him as he had been to Mass.' John Michael was leaving Doreen's sister home to Lurgan on his way to Bleary Darts Club and wanted Jimmy to come with him to prove a point. Declan heard him say, 'Jimmy, you come with me, because there's a man I know said I'll never rear an All-Ireland senior champion.'

Twenty-five years later, wanting to get closer to the moment when his family's life had changed forever, Declan had asked Jimmy to relive the experience. Jimmy had left the club to go to the toilet outside.

'And Jimmy said the next thing he just hears the gunfire. All he could see was the machine gun going [he imitates the sound], lighting the bottom half of your man up and then when the machine gun stopped, a revolver started. And then when it stopped, a shotgun went off, and then the machine gun started again. And he said he panicked and he run down the field through the hedges.'

Then Declan asked him, 'What did you see when you went in?' 'And he could hardly tell me, Marty. He wouldn't tell me what he saw. Daddy was dead. Daddy had been shot in the throat. They said he was dead probably before he hit the ground. Joe Toman fell in the fire. Jimmy says all you could smell was flesh burning when they went back in. And the other boy, Brendan, he was dead too.'

The morning after the shooting, Declan woke up and he remembers thinking, 'Why am I not at school?' He went downstairs. His uncle, Jim Diamond, was by the fire in a grey suit. 'And he had his hair to one side, the way my da's hair was.' Declan closed the door, and thought, That's my uncle Jim, there's something wrong; what's wrong? He ran back upstairs, then his cousin Maureen came and told him what had happened.

When he came back down, Brian Faulkner was there with his wife. 'And he says to me, "Declan, evil, evil men killed your father. If I could get them, I would tear them apart with my own two hands."' Declan went into the living room and saw Jimmy, barely able to stay awake having been up all night.

'He was all scrabs all over his face, and he was wearing my da's watch. I've still got his gold Omega watch and it's engraved on the back: "from his fellow workers of Down Shoes, July '73". His hand fell in the fire and all the glass melted but I got it fixed.'

Granda Feeney was there too. 'He was a hard man too, you know. He wouldn't have shown much, there would have been no such thing as a hug nor nothing. But I'll never forget when they brought my da's body through the front door, my granda Feeney just bursting into tears. A man who was 80 years of age, who came through the First World War and seen things that nobody would want to see, just crying like a wee child.'

Among the pall-bearers at John Michael's funeral were Faulkner and Uprichard. The boxing club paid a floral tribute in the shape of a boxing ring. Father Lynch, the parish priest, asked the mourners to pray not only for the bereaved but also for those who had seen fit to take away human life. In a few short minutes, he said, the parish had lost three decent, respected, innocent men. 'We pray that God in His goodness will awaken a new sense of brotherliness in our people.'

Declan is brutally honest about the fallout from his father's murder.

'That was the beginning of the end of our family. Everything went wrong from that. It just was a catalogue of disasters.'

Declan's memories stir up one of my own, his sister Cindy coming to our house for a parish group my parents ran for teenagers. We had a record player with about three records, I think: *The Sound of Music* soundtrack, which had more jumps than grooves by the end of its life; a Dubliners LP that couldn't have had more scratches if a cat had danced on it; and one single, 'Brown Girl in the Ring' by Boney M, which must have been for the parish youth. Cindy was beautiful, tall and slim like all the Feeneys.

'Except me,' says Declan, who was born with curvature of the spine and had to wear a brace but did not let it stop him riding horses.

The year after his father was killed, Declan had a steel rod put into his spine in Musgrave Park Hospital. 'We're going to put a stick up his back like a tomato plant,' is how the surgeon explained it to his mother. Declan spent eight weeks lying flat on his stomach. One day, Faulkner brought him a load of books. 'I've still got them: *Around the World in 80 Days* and two books about horses. And I wrote on them, "given to me by Brian Faulkner".' Later, when I see them, I realise they are hand-me-downs that had belonged to Faulkner's children. Declan also shows me a photo of him after the operation. A plaster cast like the breastplate of a suit of armour covers his torso with a cannonball-sized hole in the middle from scratching. He looks vulnerable yet invincible.

Faulkner went out of his way to help the Feeneys. As the architect of internment he was deeply disliked by many Catholics but changed course and led a power-sharing government, which was opposed by the IRA and brought down by unionist hardliners in league with loyalist paramilitaries.

Faulkner got Doreen a solicitor to represent her in her claim for compensation. 'I remember him saying, "This is the best solicitor in Northern Ireland." And do you know how much compensation my mother got? £5,000.'

Faulkner and Uprichard were keen that Jimmy should take over his father's job. Declan says, 'My mummy told me that when they were trying to talk our Jimmy into doing the job, Albert said, "I know the man," and Faulkner says, "Who?" And he pointed at me. "Declan. He would be the man to do that job." And Faulkner says, "Well, that maybe's right, but we just can't wait on him that long."

'And I have a letter that Albert Uprichard wrote me about the day's hunting that he had with me and told me how proud my father would have been of me, and he says, "You just have an affinity with animals." Same as my daddy. You just can't go and jump on a horse, going tally-ho, you need to have an affinity.'

Faulkner did persuade Jimmy to take over. When Jimmy got married, Faulkner found Doreen a house in Lenaderg.

Faulkner was killed hunting with staghounds near Saintfield in March 1977, aged 56. Declan lives just 500 yards from his old home, Highlands, outside Seaforde. 'A decent man,' says Declan.

After John Michael's murder, the family was harassed by the UDR. 'I remember lying in the house in Iveagh and the UDR coming up at night and banging the butts of their guns on the floor of their vehicle and laughing, driving round the yard. I remember my mummy and all of us probably overreacting but crawling round the floor to keep under the windows.'

Like Eddie, Declan felt that the UDR were ever present until 'some tragedy was happening, [when] there was none of them to be fucking seen. Sure they were stopping here [at the Heights Bar] the night of the shooting, knew nothing about it. The night my da was killed, Father O'Hanlon was rung to go to the club to give the boys the last rites, and the UDR stopped him a mile down the road and he told them where he was going, and they said, "We've never heard tell of it."'

Declan's teenage years were hard. 'My poor mother was drugged up to the eyeballs. I remember me and Maria coming home from school and me saying, "We're going into this house now again, this is desperate." At a time when everything's changing in your body and you might want to talk to somebody. No matter what happened, you just had to cope with it yourself. Because no matter what was going on in your life, it was far worse at home.'

Years later, Doreen would publish a book of poems, *Dreams and Things*, several of which touched on her loss. 'The Land of Dreams' ends, 'Reluctantly I open my eyes and see the grey unfriendly skies, / Beyond the window of my room, no sun to brighten winter's gloom, / And where your dear head used to be, an empty pillow next to me, / And then the heartache starts anew, my darling, I'm still missing you'.

Declan feels his father's murder and its aftermath made him very hard. 'I'm not that good now with my own children. Luckily my wife is. When I first met Kathy, I could have talked to her till the cows come home. But she would say, "What's wrong with you?" And I'd say, "Nothing, just leave me alone." And I would sort it out in my own head and put myself through shite. I said to Kathy, "You saved me." Christ knows where I would have been now.'

***

If Kathy saved Declan, England was the making of him. He had left school at 16 and drove a lorry for Tayto crisps but also looked after the boss's son's polo ponies. On a trip to England, he was unhappy with the stables he was offered, so sourced better ones – where he met Kathy. A love for horses led him to the love of his life.

As whipper-in with the Meynell & South Staffordshire hunt in Derbyshire, he was paired with Prince Charles for a day's hunting. 'I remember looking up at the sky and thinking, my God, Daddy, if you could see me now.' He recalls being amazed to see sweat running down the prince's face. 'I mean, he's an ordinary human being just like me and you.'

'Riding home, Charles said, "Declan, your father was shot." I says, "That's right." And he says, "You're the second youngest of eight," and I said, "That's right." He knew everything about me. And he says, "Will you do me a favour? Would you ring your mother for me and tell her that I said that she is a wonderful woman to have reared a family like she did."

'He'd fallen off that day and landed in a hedge. He was very brave. He would have jumped a hedge the height of that [wall-mounted] television but if the horse deviated in any way, he wasn't a real horseman. And he was a spoilt git. If the horse didn't go right for him, he'd have took a fucking tantrum, pulled grass out in a temper.'

Two weeks later Charles was back. "Well, did you tell your mother what I said?" And I says, "I did." "What did she say?" I says, "She said thank you very much for thinking about her and she said she would say a prayer for you. But I told her you fell off, so she said she would say two prayers."' Charles laughed.

Declan met Charles dozens of times and he and Kathy had dinner in Highgrove twice. He sent his mother a photograph of himself and Kathy with Charles, left it a few days, then rang home, but she never mentioned it. Eventually, he could wait no longer. 'I says, "Did you get the photograph?" She says, "I did." I says, "What do you think?" Big pause. She said, "I think if you put a beggar on horseback, they would ride to hell." Like, who do you think you are? Mummy was a hard woman like that. I suppose because she had to be.'

But when he went home, the photograph was framed on the mantelpiece. His cousin Fergie used to call in for a cup of tea and would turn the frame down flat and shout 'Traitor!'

'I loved England and I was taken by the hand in it. If you can do the job, you're their man, they don't give two fucks who your da was.'

'These boys here [in the bar] keep me going when I talk about Prince Charles and the mainland. But if I had have stayed here, I still probably would be working like a lackey. I went to tailors to have clothes made for me. I have boots made for me. The very cap I wear on my head's made for me. I says, "Yous wouldn't know what bespoke meant." I keep these boys going.'

***

Declan's love of a wind-up reminds me of a lock-in at the Pot Belly in Tullylish when he nearly got us thrown out by singing 'The Sash', a loyalist song, out of mischief. We were with Liam Campbell, who died recently of a brain tumour. Declan says, 'It's a bad sign when someone is taken from the same pen as you.' It's a farming metaphor I don't immediately catch.

In return for farmers letting the hunt use their land, Declan takes their dead animals, which he calls fallen stock, skins them and feeds them to the hounds.

Fallen stock is an unfamiliar term but it resonates. It makes me think of how killers treated Troubles victims, the North one great charnel house. On 5 December 1993, the UDA murdered 15-year-old Brian Duffy and John Todd, a 31-year-old taxi driver, Belfast Catholics. They used a shotgun, firing ammunition normally used for big-game hunting. The coroner said that large balls of shot 'exacted terrible injuries to both victims'. In the words of Gloucester from *King Lear*, 'As flies to wanton boys are we to th' Gods, / They kill us for their sport.'

Ten

What Light Could Be Darker?

All the Feeney children were profoundly affected by their father's murder, but perhaps none more so than Jimmy, who had witnessed it and who, as the eldest, was burdened with the greatest responsibility.

When you know how his story ends, its innocent beginnings are imbued with a painful poignancy. In the earliest photograph of Jimmy Feeney that I come across, while leafing through the back pages of the bound volumes of the *Banbridge Chronicle* from the 1970s, the 13-year-old shines with pride. All skin and bones, his joints like knots in cotton, a broad, open smile below what appears to be a home-cut fringe, Jimmy looks as if he could hardly lift an iron, never mind pump it.

But the boxing gloves and the singlet tucked into his silk shorts don't lie. He was a champion in the making from the first time he slipped between the ropes into a ring. 'One of the fighting Feeney brothers from Laurencetown,' he had narrowly outpointed the Ulster 4st 7lb champion Francis McAnally from Ballymena to record his twentieth win in twenty contests.

Four years later, with the Troubles now in full swing, the front-page lead story of the *Banbridge Chronicle* on 25 January 1974 was the sentencing of a 19-year-old Official IRA man from Lurgan for the murder there of Banbridge-born Constable George Chambers and the wounding of two other officers. The killer's unit had been on their way to rob a factory when they spotted the RUC men. The detail that stops me dead, though, is the IRA man's solicitor saying that the killing had been against 'company policy' and consequently the unit 'had been deprived of carrying firearms and visiting public houses in Lurgan for a month'.

Jimmy Feeney aged 13.

The back-page lead story was Jimmy Feeney winning the Irish Junior title at the first attempt in the National Stadium in Dublin. Beneath a photograph of Jimmy with his father and trainer, John Michael, and eight of his trophies, the report ran, 'Headaches must now ensue for his mentors at Laurencetown over the advisability of entering him in the Ulster and Irish Senior Championships … a forbidding prospect and one which on the face of it could hardly be deemed prudent for one so young … At 17 Jim has plenty of time on his side and the Laurencetown club would be well advised "to make haste slowly"'.

Instead of *festina lente*, Jimmy and his father chose as their motto *carpe diem*, seizing not just the day but the Irish Senior Championship a year later in Dublin's National Stadium. Jimmy, however, did not have time on his side. For the edition of the *Chronicle* that reported his triumph on its back pages also reported his father's murder on the front page.

On Sunday, 27 April 1975, two days after Jimmy's victory in Dublin, his world lay in ashes. Running for his life in pitch darkness as gunmen opened fire in Bleary Darts Club, he had scratched his face on briars and branches. While those superficial wounds soon healed, witnessing his father's murder and narrowly escaping assassination himself scarred him for life.

'His father took him over to this wee huckster of a place to show him off basically,' says Brenda, Jimmy's widow. 'And Jimmy had stepped outside to go to the toilet, because there wasn't even a toilet in it, when the gunmen came up the lane. So, Jimmy, whenever he went back in, he witnessed all that and it was a terrible sight and that changed Jimmy forever, like. There's no doubt about that.'

Jimmy told detectives that he could see by the light of the muzzle flash that one of the gunmen was wearing blue jeans. What light could be darker than that from the gun that is killing your father and two of his friends? That was the light Jimmy saw by for the rest of his days.

'The very seat that Jimmy was sitting on was absolutely riddled,' says Brenda. He had been sitting at a table with Brendan O'Hara, who was shot dead, directly in the line of fire from the doorway. Jimmy accompanied his father's body to Craigavon Hospital, loyal to the last.

With his father dead, Jimmy at 18 was now the man of the house. He also was saddled with his father's job of huntsman to the Iveagh Harriers.

'Jimmy wasn't capable of doing it,' says Declan. 'He was only 18. Jimmy had done more boxing than riding horses. Our poor Jimmy then, he couldn't cope. He had no counselling, he'd no nothing.'

***

Brenda and Jimmy had been teenage sweethearts, off and on. They met at St Patrick's secondary school in Banbridge and she lived opposite Jimmy's grandparents, Winnie and Billy Diamond, in Edenderry Park in the town. Jimmy was a regular visitor as he and Stevie, his uncle who was the same age as him, were very close.

'We had had a courtship during school and right throughout them early years,' says Brenda. 'Then Jimmy's father was shot and things took a terrible turn for him. And at that stage there was awful sectarianism in the town, terrible trouble, people being picked upon. Jimmy defended himself and to be quite honest, the RUC hated Jimmy. They seemed to pick on him. He got the blame all the time. Jimmy was very, very well-known because of the boxing.'

Brenda and Jimmy and their friends would go drinking in John Campbell's, the First and Last or the Thoroughfare and then on to the Castle Ballroom, which wasn't licensed to sell alcohol and where the music started about 10 p.m., and then the band played from 11 p.m. to 1 a.m. For a provincial dance hall, it attracted big names – The Troggs and even Cat Stevens had played there in the late 1960s. In the mid-1970s, however, the showband scene was at its height and The Miami, The Indians and Joe Dolan were all regulars, playing cover versions of chart hits and country favourites. The audience was typically made up of teenagers, 17- and 18-year-olds. Brenda remembers it as a dangerous place.

'There was an awful anger in people back then, a lot of fighting going on, and the Castle Ballroom had four flights of stairs up to it. I saw horrific things. The bouncers didn't tolerate any sort of inappropriate behaviour. Lads coming in drunk would have been thrown down them stairs.'

There was one big draw, though.

'Jimmy used to wear yellow parallel trousers. Oh, my God, I can remember looking down, looking round to see could I see the yellow trousers. That was the style.'

She was at the Castle Ballroom on 30 July 1975, just over three months after Jimmy's father's murder, to see The Miami.

Brenda and Jimmy had planned to get married in 1977 but Jimmy's mother, Doreen, just wanted out of the Iveagh Hunt kennels, haunted by their association with John Michael. 'She was demented. We brought the wedding forward a year to September 1976 so that I could move in … so that Jimmy could keep this job. I was only 18 and Jimmy was only 19. But this gave him a new drive. He absolutely loved the horses, he loved the hunt.'

His father's shooting 'had an awful impact on Jimmy', says Brenda. One consequence was that he joined the Official IRA, which while officially on ceasefire was still active in former strongholds such as Newry. 'He just felt it was the right thing to do.'

'Jimmy wasn't an angry person in sobriety. He really wasn't. He was bitter more than angry, but he kept it restrained till again the sectarian element came out in the town with things said to him. He was a very talented boxer, that didn't help either because people challenged him. Catholics didn't speak up in Banbridge, they just didn't.'

With the help of a man on the inside, the Official IRA planned an armed raid on a Securicor van, ambushing it with a spiked chain across a remote stretch of mountain road between Coleraine and Limavady in County Derry on 26 April 1977. The three robbers got away with almost £230,000 and rendezvoused with Jimmy at a nearby quarry.

Jimmy's job involved collecting dead animals from farms across the North, so the armed robbers' cunning plan was to transfer the stolen money bags into carcasses in Jimmy's lorry. However, an alert RUC patrol spotted the suspicious activity and recovered the money, along with an Armalite rifle and a pistol, before the crime had even been reported.

Jimmy was held on remand in Crumlin Road Gaol for months before pleading guilty to armed robbery and Official IRA membership. He was sentenced to four years in prison.

'Our Jimmy ended up in jail at 19 years of age and he was just a wee waif,' says Declan. 'Mummy said to me, of all the bad things that happened in our life, the worst thing ever, worse even than my daddy being killed, was seeing our Jimmy standing up in a white boiler suit in Crumlin Road Court. Jimmy was her blue-eyed boy.'

When Jimmy was arrested, Brenda was three months pregnant with their first child, Gail. He had told her the night before the robbery what was going to happen. He didn't want her to know a lot … what she didn't know, she couldn't tell.

Jimmy hadn't contacted her and she knew something was wrong. 'I saw a convoy of about thirty police vans coming up the hill. And I knew. They came into that yard with guns and it was shocking. They ripped that house asunder. But there was nothing in the house. That was the beginning of a nightmare, because Jimmy never was the same and the stigma that was attached to that.'

Jimmy was held on remand for eight months and Brenda was allowed three visits a week to see him in Belfast, as she became more and more heavily pregnant. 'It was a really, really horrible time then.' Gail was born in October 1977, just before he was sentenced.

He came out in April 1979, having served two years, eight months of which was on remand. Jimmy's arrest had cost him his job and the tied house that came with it. Brenda moved in with Jimmy's family in Lenaderg.

'My father was very angry, because my family weren't politically minded. They had watched the news that night and were laughing about this van getting stopped full of dead animals, and Daddy said to Mummy, "C'mere, do you see this? What will they be at next?" And little did they know it was Jimmy.'

When Gail was born, Brenda moved back in with her parents, but it was a three-bedroomed house and she was the oldest of seven, and now with a baby. So her mother went to the Housing Executive and got her a house just round the corner.

'I loved that wee house. Edenderry Park was a bit like Laurencetown. It was very much a community up there. It was a bit mixed, but it was mostly a Catholic estate. But there was no Protestants gave me any grief up there. It was whenever Jimmy came out. Applying for jobs was a nightmare. He got it hard. And the police were up at our door regularly.

There were death threats, and we were asked to move. Police said he was in danger. I don't know how true that was. But back then that frightens a young person. At one stage we were going to move to Drogheda. And I was worried when Jimmy went out, you know.'

Michael, Jimmy's son, says his father had offers to become a professional boxer, but that it was never the same for him after his father was killed. He tried to make a comeback in 1981, got back training and fought Danny McAllister, who had sparred with world champion Barry McGuigan. 'There wasn't much between the two of them, but my da had him down in the first round, and then your man come back and won the fight. He went on to win the Irish Seniors that year, he was a top lad. But my da was a shadow of himself. That was it, after the McAllister fight, Jimmy never fought again.'

Michael's son James is a boxer and in 2023 he won a national Irish title in the same National Stadium where his grandfather Jimmy won his. 'The family has experienced so much tragedy and this was a good news story,' Michael told *The Irish News*. 'There's something at peace in me now. I know my da was looking down and he would have been so proud.'

Jimmy's trauma was turned inwards. 'He bottled it up,' says Brenda. 'He talked to me a bit about it but never went on about it, never made it an excuse for the way that he was drinking. Jimmy wasn't able to handle alcohol. Jimmy was a very quiet fella. He was a great worker. But he was very withdrawn sometimes. He couldn't talk to people easily, so I think drink became a crutch.'

Jimmy was always good with his hands. While in prison, he took up woodwork. For years we had a windmill Jimmy had made on our living-room wall attached to a varnished, heart-shaped backboard inscribed with an Irish prayer. Inside it was a music box that you activated by turning the sails.

My parents were not particularly political. They admired John Hume, had supported the civil rights campaign and were horrified by the outbreak of violence. My mother once ran unsuccessfully as a candidate for the cross-community Alliance Party in the local council elections (held just after my headmaster's brother was murdered in March 1989). So this was our way of supporting Jimmy as a neighbour, not the republican movement. Most Catholics throughout the Troubles did not support the IRA or its political wing, Sinn Féin. Only in 2001, three years after the Good Friday Agreement and seven years after the first IRA ceasefire, did Sinn Féin overtake the SDLP.

Michael shows me one of the blackthorn sticks his father used to make. He had learned from his own father, John Michael, to gather the sticks and dry them out over winter. The thorns, the handle and a metal ferrule would be glued on, the wood straightened in a vice under a heat lamp. 'He spent hours and hours out in the shed making them,' he says.

'What he went through in jail, it was tough,' says Michael. 'The Official IRA and the Provisional IRA were at each other's throats. It was hard going in there.'

'He was only 19,' says Brenda. 'He struggled, like.'

Gail was 18 months old by the time her father was released. 'Gail and I had this really strong bond because of what happened,' says Brenda. 'It was only her and me, this wee world of ours, and when Jimmy came out, he drank a lot and frightened Gail. People were always at the door looking him out for a drink. They thought they were doing right, but I was this young person who was just married and I needed him to myself. So, he was torn. But he drank heavily then and there was a lot of anger within him that came out. So, Gail and him never pulled that back and that is the truth.'

Gail got married at 40, had her first child in 2021 and lives in the same estate as Brenda.

As well as Michael, Brenda and Jimmy had another son, Paddy. 'Jimmy wasn't very good at the father–son relationship when they were small,' says Brenda. 'He didn't have the knack. And always felt inadequate, that he never was good enough. I don't know if it was something in his upbringing, but he just never had that bond till they were about 13, 14 and started to play Gaelic football.'

'I loved going over the fields, Smyths' territory over Brookfield, with my da and the dogs whenever I was young,' says Michael. 'I was about seven and that was just the best days of my life, you know? I just followed him. We had lurchers and terriers back then.'

'Jimmy loved the fields; he loved the open air,' says Brenda. 'He went over one day for a walk; he came back he was near crying. He says, "They're building houses on them fields."'

Brenda separated from Jimmy in 1997. 'Jimmy's drinking increased and I was married to him for twenty-one years and I just couldn't handle it any more. In anger, I just said, "Take all that [Jimmy's handiwork], get it away from me; that part of my life is all over." I'm sorry now that I don't have all that for the kids.'

'Now, those few years we were separated before Jimmy died, we were very, very good friends and we were always parents to the children and it broke my heart and I've never, ever, ever been with anybody else and nor would I want to be. But I couldn't handle the drink any more. He tried to get help. He did a spell off the drink when we were broke up and he was at every football match the boys were at. He'd come up here with drink on him and I made him a drop of tea and then I took him down home. Do you know what he said to me many times? That he was tired saying he was sorry.'

Jimmy lived in Roes Green in Laurencetown. His son Paddy's back door faces the house where Jimmy lived.

'If I had my life to live over again, I'd live it differently because I know more about alcohol now and I know more about what Jimmy went through,' says Brenda. 'In the turmoil of rearing three children, I always felt isolated that he couldn't contribute the way that he should have. I struggled coping with them getting older and with Jimmy. But I wish I had handled it differently because I think he was very, very unhappy. He needed professional help.'

Jimmy took his own life on 24 October 2007.

'It was an awful shock. Nightmare,' says Brenda. 'I think many times, if we had stayed together, Jimmy would probably have been living today.'

Just weeks before, says Michael, he had attended the wake of a 15-year-old boy from the parish who had died by suicide. 'The parents came up to my da's wake and said, "We were talking to your dad a month ago and he said to us, "I don't know how anybody could do that [take their own life]."

'My da would have been the last person you'd have thought would have done that,' says Michael.

Another friend took their own life on the Isle of Man. Jimmy wondered aloud to Brenda how he could have done such a thing. 'And like, within weeks, he did it,' says Brenda.

'Our Jimmy put a bravado on, I suppose, but underneath he was a very vulnerable fella,' says Declan.

Back in 2007, Declan was building a house on land Albert Uprichard had sold him. His brother Alan was plastering it and Jimmy was to labour for him but hadn't turned up that 24 October and wasn't answering the phone.

His mother, Doreen, said to Declan, 'I haven't seen him from Saturday night and usually he comes here on a Sunday and brings me the papers. It's not like him, because he would have come over here. He could be lying over there dead or anything. And I'm not fit to go over.' The brothers concluded, though, that he was probably on the beer. 'He'll come back when he wants to.'

Declan drove home and had barely sat down when the phone rang. It was his brother Peter. '"Dec, we found our Jimmy." It near killed Mummy. That was the beginning of the end for her.' Then Arlene, their eldest sister, got cancer and died. Declan ran into an old neighbour, Paul, who had gone out with Arlene once. 'Paul says to me, "Declan Feeney, your family were dealt a fucking bad hand, boy."'

Brenda's brother Stephen was with Jimmy that Saturday. They were very close. He named his café Jimmy's after his brother-in-law's death.

'If only he'd come here that day,' says Brenda. 'But his wake was here. I went down to Doreen that night and she said, "Take him where he wants to be." We brought him home here where the children were, and I will never forget it. The people, the people. But he was a really good person. He just went on that path of self-destruction after the way his life went.

'But, you know what, if he'd have just held on, there was so much in store for him, because he has six beautiful grandchildren who he would have just loved. He would have taken them horse-riding, fishing, boxing. And he was to start working in Stephen's chip shop. He was going to be involved again.'

'I think too much had happened in his life,' says Michael. 'And at 51 he just sort of gave up.'

Northern Ireland has the highest suicide rate in the UK and Ireland, with about eighteen suicides per 100,000 people compared with nine in England and eight in the South, a figure that puts it among the fifteen countries in the world with the highest rates, according to the Northern Ireland Statistics and Research Agency. The rate for men is almost thirty per 100,000. Shockingly, suicide rates in Northern Ireland have doubled since the Good Friday Agreement in 1998. Diazepam, medication often prescribed to treat depression or anxiety, is prescribed five times more frequently in Northern Ireland than in England. Despite this, only 6 per cent of the health budget in Northern Ireland is spent on mental health, compared to 12 per cent in England.

Michael was born in June 1980 and came of age the year of the Good Friday Agreement in 1998. As he became a teenager, the conflict was ending. 'There always would have been that bit of anger in me, like, about my granda, and Pat [Feeney his father's cousin, who was murdered by loyalists in 1989] and my da and everything – I'd have loved to have met my granda, like. But I didn't go down that road. I'd opportunities to. I'm very much a republican-minded person and I know that the ballot box is the way to go now. Sport's a big thing with me, Gaelic and that. Sort of kept me right. I was probably the same mould as my da, like. I couldn't handle drink. My da was a strong man and drink weakens you. I says, I need to just stop this or else I'll be the same.'

Michael stopped drinking after his father's death. He and his wife split up but now get on really well. His three children live with him and Brenda. 'I tell you, they live in his pocket,' says Brenda. Paddy has twin girls. Michael and Paddy now manage Banbridge's senior GAA team. That her three children have become such devoted parents gives Brenda great solace. Love is being passed on, not the burden of the past.

***

'Jimmy loved fishing,' says Brenda. 'He made his own flies.' He was quiet and he liked his own company. 'Kernan Lough was his favourite haunt for rainbow trout,' says Michael. 'He used to go out there for hours on a boat, the *Kernan Queen*,' says Brenda. 'Sit in the middle of the lough with a flask of tea.'

Given its tragic past, Kernan Lough was a poignant place for a troubled man to search for serenity, fishing for rainbow trout on a lake whose dark depths were ultimately matched by his own.

Eleven

The Showband and the Silencer

A minibus leaves Banbridge late one night, full of people buzzing after the evening's entertainment. It never makes it home. It is Thursday, 31 July 1975.

***

The Castle Ballroom in Banbridge on a Wednesday, a midweek gig in a midsized town, was bread and butter for The Miami, a showband that had had seven Number Ones in thirteen years, but a lifeline for locals who wanted to lose themselves in music and dancing and forget the Troubles.

It was still fresh, though, for bass player Stephen Travers, who had joined only two months earlier. When the band reached Banbridge, he and singer Fran O'Toole, who had a sweet tooth, went to buy sweets. Stephen was unnerved when he saw skinheads running towards them, but one just wanted Fran's autograph on his plaster cast.

The gig didn't start till after 11 p.m., so it was 2 a.m. by the time the band set off home. Stephen sat up front with his bandmate Brian McCoy, who was driving, while Fran, Des Lee and Tony Geraghty played cards in the back.

At around 2.30 a.m., halfway between Banbridge and Newry, the minibus was flagged down by an army patrol. The musicians were lined up

The Miami, with Stephen Travers far right.

outside and asked for their names and addresses. The roadblock was fake, however, although at least five of the soldiers there were serving or former UDR members. They were also loyalist paramilitaries. As two of them, Harris Boyle and Wesley Somerville, planted a bomb on the bus, it exploded prematurely, killing them instantly. The explosion blew the musicians into a field, where four were hunted down. Fran was shot twenty-two times, mostly in the face, Brian nine times and Tony four times. Stephen was hit; Des hid in the long grass, playing dead, and was not hurt.

Stephen counted his fingers. As a musician that was important. Next, he clicked his platform heels. He still had his legs. He was disorientated, however.

'I didn't know I was shot. I couldn't figure out why my stomach was so distended. There was this terrible silence. The ditch was still on fire. I was crawling among the bodies, talking to them. I wouldn't accept that they were dead.

'I'd get up and fall. I found it difficult to breathe. After the dumdum exploded inside my hip, part of it had gone through my left lung, which had collapsed.'

James Blundell, the surgeon at Newry's Daisy Hill Hospital who saved Stephen's life, told him the anaesthetist had to compress his aorta to keep him alive until he received a blood transfusion.

Reverend William McCrea, a Free Presbyterian minister and later a Democratic Unionist Party MP, conducted a UVF paramilitary funeral for Boyle and Somerville.

UDR Sergeant James Roderick Shane McDowell and Lance Corporal Thomas Raymond Crozier were convicted in 1976 of the murders. Imposing the longest life sentences in Northern Ireland history, the judge said he would have imposed the death penalty, had it not been recently abolished. Former UDR soldier John James Somerville, Wesley's brother, was also convicted of the murders, in 1981.

Stephen spent months recovering. The Miami reformed, having replaced Fran, Tony and Brian, but it felt macabre. 'We became photo ops.' He left the following summer.

As part of a criminal injuries case, Stephen had to see a psychiatrist. 'He said, "I don't like the way you're handling this." I said, "Here's the bottom line: I went to a gig, on the way home the lads were killed, I was shot, I survived, I'm fine." There was no such thing as counselling back then. Only sissies complained about their feelings.' The psychiatrist told him his response wasn't normal. 'He said, "I must warn you, in six months or ten years the wall might fall on you."'

Stephen reflects with the benefit of hindsight and education. 'I stepped back for thirty years, said I'm not going to talk or think about it, but that did awful damage.' He felt that as a musician in Ireland he could never escape his past, so he and his wife moved to London in 1983.

One night he was having a drink in an Irish pub when the owner asked everyone for a business idea. Stephen saw a copy of *The Irish Post* and said that it needed competition. Within months, the *Irish Advertiser* was launched, with him as editor. The paper became *The Irish in Britain News*. Stephen co-founded another newspaper, *The Irish World*, in 1987.

Three years later, I got my first job on *The Irish World*, moving to *The Irish in Britain News*, the two papers Stephen had helped to found, before spending nine years with *The Irish Post*, where Stephen wrote for me about music.

I was in Harry's Bar in Banbridge in the mid-1990s when a former Academy classmate said loudly, 'I hear you're working for a Provo paper.' There is a certain type of unionist for whom anything Irish – be it the language, traditional music, the GAA or even a newspaper – is a republican front and a personal affront.

Stephen and his family moved home in 1998. In 2000, he testified at Justice Henry Barron's official inquiry into the Dublin and Monaghan bombings. Margaret Urwin, secretary of Justice for the Forgotten, a campaign group for its victims and survivors, told him that the Miami Showband massacre was not an isolated attack but one of many perpetrated by the Glenanne gang.

In December 2011, the HET report on the Miami killings raised 'disturbing questions about collusive and corrupt behaviour'. It confirmed Mid-Ulster UVF leader Robin Jackson's involvement and linked him to RUC Special Branch.

The report also revealed that on 11 June 1975, more than a month prior to the killings, Jackson, his brother-in-law Samuel Fulton Neill, and Thomas Crozier had been arrested for possessing four shotguns near Banbridge, but no charges were brought. Neill's car was reportedly used in the Miami ambush. He was shot dead in Portadown on 25 January 1976, allegedly by Jackson for informing.

Stephen said at the time, 'We believe the only conclusion possible arising from the HET report is that one of the most prolific loyalist murderers of the conflict was an RUC Special Branch agent and was involved in the Miami Showband attack.' As he explained to me, 'People said you now have the smoking gun of the culpability of the British State.'

An independent international inquiry, chaired by Douglass Cassel of the Law School of the University of Notre Dame, concluded that there was 'credible evidence that the principal perpetrator [of the Miami attack] was alleged RUC Special Branch agent Robin Jackson'.

On 19 May 1976, two of Jackson's fingerprints were discovered on a silencer home-made for a Luger pistol. The silencer and Luger were found in a police raid on former B Special Ted Sinclair's farm. The exhibit was mistakenly labelled, indicating that Jackson's prints had been found on insulating tape wrapped around the silencer.

Jackson, arrested on 31 May, denied having been at Sinclair's farm but admitted knowing him through the Portadown Loyalist Club. When shown the Luger, silencer and magazine (but not the tape), Jackson denied having handled them. Asked to explain why his fingerprints might be on either pistol or silencer, Jackson said he had given Sinclair adhesive tape in the club.

Although ballistic testing had linked the Luger (for which the silencer had been made) to the Miami attack, Jackson was never questioned about the killings, and the Miami inquiry team was never informed.

Jackson claimed that one week before his arrest, two high-ranking RUC officers had told him his fingerprints had been found on the tape and that 'I should clear as there was a wee job up the country that I would be done for and there was no way out of it for me.' Despite a detective inspector's recommendation, the officers faced no disciplinary action.

Jackson was only prosecuted for possession of the silencer. The trial judge, Mr Justice Murray, acquitted him, saying, 'I find that the accused somehow touched the silencer, but the Crown evidence has left me completely in the dark as to whether he did that wittingly or unwittingly, willingly or unwillingly.'

Former RUC officer and convicted loyalist paramilitary John Weir told the Barron Inquiry that Jackson coordinated the Dublin and Monaghan bombings. Justice Barron concluded that Weir's 'evidence overall is credible'.

Weir claimed Jackson had shot dead Catholic chemist William Strathearn in Ahoghill, County Antrim, in 1977. Weir and RUC colleague Billy McCaughey were convicted of the murder but both named Jackson and another loyalist, R.J. Kerr, as the killers. Jackson was never questioned for 'reasons of operational strategy', according to an RUC detective. Weir suggested that 'Jackson was untouchable because he was an RUC Special Branch agent'.

Weir had offered to testify against Jackson and Kerr if the murder charge against him was withdrawn. The prosecutor rejected this offer, saying that 'Kerr and Jackson have not been interviewed by the police because the police state [that] they are *virtually immune to interrogation* and the common police consensus is that to arrest and interview either man is a waste of time. Both men are known to police to be very active and notorious UVF murderers.'

Mr Justice Barron was highly critical of the RUC. In 2006, a Dáil committee concluded that some loyalists, notably Robin Jackson, 'were reliably said to have had relationships with British intelligence and/or RUC Special Branch and exchanges of information took place'.

The Irish News reported in January 2020 that British Ministry of Defence documents linked SAS-trained undercover officer Captain Robert Nairac to the atrocity. Nairac was abducted and killed by the IRA in 1977 and his body has never been found. The papers were disclosed to solicitor Michael Flanigan, who represented Fran O'Toole's widow, Valerie Andersen, in her legal action against the MoD and PSNI chief constable. It is understood the redacted documents contained suggestions that Nairac obtained equipment and uniforms for the killers. The file also claimed that he was responsible for planning and executing the attack.

A UVF handkerchief decorated with handstitched paramilitary figures and mottos was found among Robert Nairac's possessions. It is displayed in his regiment's museum in London.

The Miami victims' families and survivors took a civil action against the police and the British Ministry of Defence. A settlement was only reached in December 2021, exactly ten years after the HET report's damning findings. They received £1.5 million to settle claims of collusion without any admission of liability. Stephen received the largest settlement, £425,000. 'It's all very well to say they settled without admission of liability, but they don't pay you for annoying them. At the beginning they laughed at us, said we didn't have a case. The PSNI and MoD put up every barrier, the three Ds: delay, deny and, ultimately, death.'

That at least five UDR men were involved is only the tip of the iceberg for him. He dismisses the notion of rogue elements in the security forces and believes collusion was systemic.

'Far more sinister people were involved. So-called experts concentrate on individuals but that is just very clever deflection. It was policy from the very top. Some of the bravest men I met were in the RUC. There was a point in the chain of command at which good reports just disappeared.'

Almost fifty years have passed since the atrocity. How much of his life has he spent managing its repercussions? Should he prioritise his mental health over his feeling of responsibility to pursue justice?

In 2005, Stephen's friend Michael Gallagher, who lost his son Aiden in the 1998 Omagh bombing, asked him to take part in an anti-radicalisation project at Warrington Peace Centre, set up in memory of two children, Tim Parry and Johnathan Ball, murdered by the IRA. He was asked to bring an object that related to his trauma. He brought Tony Geraghty's guitar strings.

He listened to a British soldier who had been abused as a child and suffered from alcoholism. 'I felt I could help this man by telling him how I had coped, but I was in denial. When it came to my turn, I introduced myself, but when I went to take out the guitar strings, thirty years after the psychiatrist predicted it, the wall fell on me. I wasn't in Warrington, I was in the field, I could hear all the screaming, the obscenities, the gunfire, the terror all around.

'The soldier that I had been feeling sorry for had his arm around me and was telling me this is okay, it happens. This was the first time that I had shed a tear over the incident. I was ashamed that I had shown my feelings.'

Stephen describes his post-traumatic stress thus: 'It's like when a TV producer is telling people which monitor to look at. For me it's like there are two monitors. One is normality, which I'm focused on most of the time, but there is another big monitor and I'm drawn to that sometimes, and that is what happened on 31 July. When we went back on the road, sometimes I heard the fans screaming and thought it was something else.'

When Stephen's father served in the British Army, he contracted malaria. It resurfaced from time to time over the years, just like Stephen's trauma.

'No one back then ever mentioned PTSD. I'd never heard of enduring personality change. It was first used for people who had been in concentration camps. I have been in the incident for forty-seven years. It doesn't happen that they take out the bullets and sew you up, and it is gone. The trauma lasts for ever.'

Stephen helped set up a victims' support group, the Truth and Reconciliation Platform.

'I think the best way to speak up is to talk about your own experience. We wanted to get people from both communities to tell their stories. It has been a great education, but it came with a price.'

Is it good for him, though? I am conscious of the irony. I am interviewing him about his trauma.

'It's essential,' he replies. 'I certainly don't have peace of mind but I would have less if I didn't process the trauma by using it to help others. I think I'm stuck with that for the rest of my life and all I ever wanted to be was a bass player.'

What good does it do? 'An immense amount. I heard a woman on a radio show, coming back on the day after she spoke about her husband's murder: "Yesterday I was nobody and my husband was nobody but today I am somebody and my husband is somebody."'

***

In 2005, to mark the thirtieth anniversary, Dana and Dickie Rock sang at an interdenominational service in Dublin's Pro Cathedral. Brendan Bowyer headlined a memorial concert in Vicar Street. Another service was held in Portadown, with fifteen marching bands, to commemorate two of the killers.

In 2015, The Miami played their final gig at the Linenfields Festival in Lenaderg. The month before, 200 people had gathered at the ambush site to lay a wreath on the fortieth anniversary. In Dublin, Stephen attended a ceremony at the memorial in Parnell Square.

In 2019, Netflix released the Emmy-nominated documentary *ReMastered: The Miami Showband Massacre*. Yet in Banbridge, where Fran O'Toole, Brian McCoy and Tony Geraghty played just before they were murdered, there is nothing to acknowledge what happened. The Castle Ballroom is now a bingo hall.

I am struck by the parallels between two of the UK's most notorious serial killers in the 1970s. Peter Sutcliffe, the Yorkshire Ripper, born in 1948, murdered thirteen women and attempted to murder seven others between 1975 and 1980. Most of his victims were sex workers, whose low standing in the eyes of the public and particularly the police was believed to be a factor in the failure to apprehend the killer sooner. He was given twenty life sentences, converted in 2010 to a whole life order. He died in prison in 2020.

Robin Jackson, the Jackal, was born two years before Sutcliffe, and his first murder was two years before Sutcliffe's too. They were both HGV drivers, exploiting this to prey over a wide area. The low standing of Catholics in the North, perceived as pawns in the war against the IRA, is the likeliest reason why he was never convicted of any of the fifty or so murders attributed to him. He died at his home in Donaghcloney in 1998.

Twelve

Republican Roulette or Loyalist Lottery

A minibus leaves Banbridge late one night, full of people buzzing after the evening's entertainment. It never makes it home. It is Friday, 1 August 1975.

***

Jimmy Marks would never have left you standing at the side of the road, says Philip McConville. His Ford Custom minibus, cream-coloured with a distinctive red stripe, was a familiar sight on the roads around Bleary in the 1970s, as it ferried locals to bingo nights, pubs and relatives' houses. At a time when rural public transport was limited and far fewer people had cars, he provided a vital service. The minibus might have had only a dozen seats, but 'on a normal Friday night you wouldn't have got moving,' says Philip's aunt Julia. 'You sat on people's knees, or you stood. There was up to twenty on that minibus. There was no such thing as seatbelts in them days. Jimmy would have set you on the roof.'

Philip's great-grandfather Joe Toland, a 79-year-old retired textile worker, got the bus from Bleary every Friday night, but rather than taking him to the bingo, Jimmy dropped him off in Gilford to visit one of his daughters. 'Granda used to say, I hate going when it's all women in the back, I don't like sitting with the women,' Julia recalls. 'So Jimmy

From left to right, back row: Pat Toland, Danny Toland, Nora Reynolds (Toland), May Toland (Green), Joe Toland, Mary Agnes Toland and Rosie Toland (McConville). Front row: Marie Toland and Bernie Green, c.1960.

Marks bought a wee three-legged stool and he said, you can sit there, Joe.' Joe sat with his back to the front windscreen so he was facing Jimmy in the driver's seat as they talked.

Joe's granddaughter Rosie McConville, who was Philip's mother and Julia's sister, didn't like pubs so the bingo was her night out. A 31-year-old mother of five, she worked hard all week, hemming handkerchiefs by the dozen at home for Blane's factory while Philip, Stephen, Kieran, Leon and Conor were at school, and again after they went to bed. (I can't help thinking of the hundreds of thousands of hankies manufactured in this valley of blood, sweated labour and tears.) The work did not provide a living wage. It was pocket (handkerchief) money. It was exploitation.

'Rosie loved bingo,' says Julia. 'It wasn't big money. It was just to get out.' The bingo was in St Patrick's Hall in Banbridge that Friday, but she used to go to Mullavilly near Tandragee too. The other regulars on the bus that night were her friends and neighbours Eva Quinn, Eileen Sheehy, Mary McKeown and mother and daughter Pauline and Eileen Moore.

I can picture the scene at those evenings and understand the appeal as I used to love going to bingo with Granny Doyle and her next-door neighbour, Janey, while on holiday in Gorey. The atmosphere in the big hall was a cross between that of an exam hall and a bookie's during a big race. I lapped up the suspense and the high drama, the nicknames for numbers, the rumble of excitement when someone called out that they had got a line or a full house, the women doing two books at once like Wall Street traders. It was communal, theatrical and social. It was, above all, innocent.

Paramilitaries in the North, meanwhile, with their cavalier attitude to civilian casualties, more interested in their cause than its effects, made life itself a game of chance – republican roulette or loyalist lottery – with the odds of being caught in a no-warning explosion or in crossfire incalculable but not negligible. Cause of death: the Cause.

***

Julia Campbell, who was 15 back in 1975, was meant to be on the bus that evening as there was a dance in Gilford Catholic Club but she fell asleep and her younger sisters, Imelda, 14, and Mary, 13, went without her. When she woke up and realised they'd gone, she went to bed in a huff. As it turned out, the dance was cancelled, so the girls went to visit one of their aunts nearby. When it was time for the girls to go home, the minibus was late coming back from Banbridge, so they got a lift instead. This small act of rule-breaking may have saved their lives. Because they weren't supposed to take a lift from anyone, they went to their aunt May's in Bleary to wait for the minibus to arrive so they could pretend to their mother they had just got off it. Except it never came.

Sixteen-year-old Fergal Anderson from Waringstown was also on the bus to go to the dance but as his girlfriend lived in Gilford, he just went to her house instead.

Rosie almost missed bingo that night. She and her husband, Ricky, had been visiting their son Leon, Philip's brother, in Craigavon Hospital, where he was recovering after an operation to remove his appendix, and by the time they got home the minibus had already left. 'So she browbeat my da to bring her to Gilford to catch up with it,' says Philip. 'He crucified himself for years after that; if he hadn't have brought her, it wouldn't have happened.' Philip and his brothers spent the evening at their granny's a few doors down because their dad was going out for a drink.

Philip still lives in the old family home. He shows me out the back window the spot on the treeline where the darts club used to be, in a cottage that belonged to a relative, Sammy Toman. It was an easy target, says Philip. It lay derelict for a good while after the murders, then it was burned to the ground. From the front window, he points out the spot a couple of fields away where the three British soldiers were killed in Seán Moore's booby-trapped house back in 1972. These are our killing fields.

***

Jimmy Marks collected the women in Banbridge just before 11 p.m. for the journey home, then stopped in Gilford to pick up Joe Toland and young Fergal Anderson. Fergal headed down to the back of the bus, while Joe took his usual spot on the stool at the front.

On the Moyallan Road just outside Gilford, heading towards Portadown, there is a beautiful straight stretch lined by trees on either side, where the branches meet overhead in a leafy canopy. But the minibus didn't make it that far. Barely two minutes after Jimmy picked up Joe and Fergal, as he slowed for the bad bend near Bannvale Hospital, known as Bannvale Corner or Highwall Bend, gunmen opened fire from the grass bank on the right-hand side of the road. Joe was hit by several bullets in the back of the head and was killed instantly. Jimmy too was hit multiple times in the head and the bus came to a stop in the middle of the road. Rosie was hit by at least eight bullets and left paralysed. Eva

Quinn and Mary McKeown were shot and seriously injured. A bullet passed through Eileen Moore's coat but she escaped with just a few cuts from flying glass. Fergal Anderson was unhurt. He recalled seeing a flash across the front of the vehicle, someone shouting 'Get down!' and the sound of machine-gun fire.

A Mrs Whiteside from Castleview in Gilford was the first on the scene. She rushed home to ring the emergency services. At this stage she didn't know who was injured but she knew it was the Bleary bus. She lived near Joe's daughter Annie McInerney, so alerted her before returning to the scene. She helped Rosie out of the minibus and sat her on the ground, kneeling against her back to support her. Annie drove to Bleary to tell the family what had happened.

Jimmy's wife Florence, then 38, told the *Lurgan Mail*, 'The women have been going all over the place for sessions and my husband drives them to Portadown, Lurgan and Banbridge all the time. No one ever dreamed anything like this would happen. It's shocking.'

***

Joe Toland was one of the oldest victims of the Troubles, but just because he had had a long life does not mean that it was finished. 'People say "Oh, he was 79"', says Philip, 'but he was a sprightly wee man. He cycled every day to Lurgan and back. Joe was nowhere near done.'

His funeral was huge. He had twelve children, six boys and six girls, and his daughter Kathleen alone had ten of her own, including Julia and Rosie.

Kathleen was a remarkable woman. She had just lost her father but had to care for her now wheelchair-bound daughter and help rear her five grandchildren. If most of the victims lowered into the ground during the Troubles were men, most of the heavy lifting and the picking up of the pieces afterwards was done by women.

'It was a week of violent and evil deeds,' said Father Aidan Hammill in his homily at Sunday Mass at St Patrick's in Banbridge two days after the shootings, 'yet the victims of two of these terrible actions – the ambush of the Miami minibus and the minibus carrying pensioners from the bingo in St Patrick's Hall – are more to us in Banbridge than just more statistics in the roll call of death and injury.

'Both atrocities were the work of madmen, ruthless psychopaths who have not only rejected the Christian gospel but lost all belief in God. With belief in God, morality is based on His Law – without God, morality becomes relative, the individual deciding for himself what is right and wrong in a given situation.'

Rosie was one of ten children. She was the only girl in the first batch of four, then, after a ten-year break, there were five more girls and a boy in the second batch.

'Rosie was 16 when I was born,' says Julia. 'Do you know what she said? "I loved you, and other times I could have strangled you, because I was the only girl and then you come along."'

Before the shooting, Julia and Imelda would have helped Rosie when she was hemming handkerchiefs at home. 'We got the job of clipping the loose threads,' says Imelda. Did they get paid? 'No, we did not. You maybe got a cigarette. We were her little helpers.' They had fun, though.

As well as the five boys, Ricky and Rosie had had a baby girl, Kiera, who died of cot death. When Rosie was shot, Stephen, her eldest, was 12, while Conor, the youngest, was four and just about to start primary school. 'She had cycled him into nursery and back the year before,' says Julia.

I ask whether it was clear straight away that Rosie had been paralysed. The answer is even more sobering.

'At the start they didn't think she was going to [survive],' says Julia. 'At Granda's funeral someone came up to my daddy and said, "Dan, I'm awful sorry to hear your daughter died this morning."'

'Technically, they weren't telling lies,' says Philip. 'She died twice; her heart stopped.' At one stage, says Julia, 'they were actually wheeling her out of intensive care only the nurse felt her pulse and then they hooked her back up again. The doctors had said that if an accident came in she would have been taken off life support as everyone was entitled to a chance. Mummy said, we'll just pray nothing happens to anyone else.'

'I remember them two days,' says Philip. 'There was nothing but Rosaries said.'

'I remember the night after Rosie was shot going into the front bedroom and there was mattresses everywhere,' says Imelda. Rosie's family moved in with Kathleen for a few days. Then Philip went to stay with relatives in Andersonstown in west Belfast for a fortnight, until it was time to go back to school.

'We didn't see Mum for months,' says Philip, 'and even then it was only for a few minutes. She was in intensive care for a long time. Mum was in ridiculous pain. This was nerve damage, her spine wasn't damaged at all, but she was paralysed from the waist down. They tried nerve blocks, everything, loads of tablets, they killed her in the end, I think. When she got a bit of relief, which wasn't often, she'd have knit jumpers for the family.

'She lived on for twelve years, but she had no quality of life. She would have been as well dying that night, to be honest with you. When you look back on it, she was in constant pain. She didn't sleep well, then she would have dozed during the day.'

'She would have told you she was afraid to sleep at night because of the shooting of the houses,' says Julia. 'She said she would sleep at daybreak.'

The 'shooting of the houses' can be explained. Rosie was worried because she and her family, and her parents, lived on Cranny Terrace. As Eddie Rooney, who had survived the Bleary Darts Club shooting, had also told me, it had become a target for drive-by shootings, and residents had had to mount a night-time patrol after the soldiers were blown up nearby in 1972.

As if Rosie hadn't suffered enough, after she'd been in Craigavon Hospital for a nerve block, she came home with a terrible bedsore, 'as if someone had sliced up her spine bone'. When the local GP saw it, he immediately called for an ambulance and she was sent to Musgrave Park Hospital in Belfast, where the wound took months to heal.

'[Her husband] Ricky put in a complaint and all they said was she was a very uncooperative patient. Ricky said she was an uncooperative patient at home too "but if I had sent her to hospital like that, you would have had me before a court".'

Religion is often depicted as the accelerant that made the conflict in the North so combustible. While sectarian attitudes did exacerbate the division between many who identified as Irish or British, it should be acknowledged that people of faith on both sides actually acted as a brake on those within their families or communities intent on revenge.

Philip says, 'I told my mum when I was about 15 – I was rubbing her leg because that was the only way she could get a bit of relief – I says, "See the people who done this to you, Mum, if I ever find out who they are, I'm going to kill them." She said, "Son, I pray for them every night." I was just dumbfounded. You just have to say, she's a better woman than me. Her faith was unbelievable.'

'My mummy did as well, every night,' says Imelda. 'She always dedicated the last decade of the Rosary to the people who done it 'cause they were the ones who would have to face their Maker.'

These acts of great faith in both houses did mean Philip had to plan his visiting carefully when he was young. 'My granny used to say the Rosary every night at six,' says Philip. 'If you were very unlucky you might get the Rosary in your own house and then in your granny's house. So you'd time your visit to half six, but if you ever forgot, the minute you opened the door you were snared, you couldn't back out.'

Parish worker Catherine McEvoy said of Rosie, 'She was never bitter, she just accepted her lot. There used to be a prayer that people carried, to pray that you wouldn't have a sudden death. She said, "I don't believe in that any more. My grandfather carried that every day of his life and he was killed in the shooting."'

Misfortune had not done with Philip's family. Ricky was diagnosed with cancer and died in 1982, two weeks before his fortieth birthday. Rosie died on 13 March 1987, aged just 43, leaving Philip and his four brothers orphans.

'Them two certainly didn't get any good luck,' says Philip of his parents.

Philip points out Jimmy Marks's house just a couple of fields away. While he was critically ill in hospital, Julia says, 'the police brought the minibus and parked it in front of Jimmy Marks's house. Mrs Marks came to Mummy in floods [of tears]. She said, "Kathleen, there's blood, there's bullet holes. I can't look at it out the window." Mum got our Jim to come and drive it away.'

The callousness, the cold-hearted contempt remains shocking.

Jimmy Marks lived for 159 days after being shot, but he never made it home. He died aged 44, leaving behind his wife, Florence, and their two young sons. The cause of death was bronchopneumonia and infection due to paralysis following brain and spinal injuries. The day that he died, the latest three victims of the Troubles in the parish – Barry, Declan and Joe O'Dowd, two brothers and an uncle – were being buried in Clare churchyard. He joined them two days later.

***

Almost five decades on, it is still not entirely clear who was responsible for the murders. The victims were all Catholics and the attack had striking parallels with the Miami Showband massacre carried out by the UVF less than forty-eight hours earlier. In both cases a minibus had been ambushed within minutes of leaving Banbridge late at night. Jimmy's bus had been followed and stopped by the RUC a few weeks before because some youths on board had taken a UDR man's flag down.

The RUC, however, immediately blamed the IRA for the attack. Philip McConville says Fergal Anderson said to him that almost immediately after the shooting he was put in the back of a police car and told it was an IRA attack. How did they come to such a swift conclusion? 'Your obvious conclusion to that is prior knowledge,' says Philip, who suspects an IRA informer alerted the RUC that an attack was planned.

One theory was that it was a revenge attack for the Miami killings. The minibus supposedly resembled police personnel carriers, which had been in Gilford for a loyalist parade earlier that evening. RUC vehicles, however, were usually grey or bottle green, not cream with a red stripe. More convincingly, the weapons used – an M1 carbine, an Armalite rifle and a Thompson sub-machine gun – were usually associated with republican rather than loyalist paramilitaries.

The *Republican News* of 9 August 1975 denied that the IRA was responsible. It said, 'It is common knowledge that there is a loyalist murder gang operating in this area.'

Another theory is that the intended target of the attack was Norman 'Mooch' Kerr, a 28-year-old disc jockey from Portadown, who was a close friend of Harris Boyle, one of the UVF men killed when the bomb he was planting on the Miami Showband's minibus exploded prematurely. Kerr was shot dead by the IRA in Armagh on 15 August 1975, a fortnight after the Bleary minibus shooting, as he was loading his disco equipment into his van. The IRA said it had killed Kerr because it claimed to have Boyle's diary, which implicated Kerr as an associate of SAS captain Robert Nairac.

An RUC officer arriving at the scene at Gilford saw two men running across fields towards the Bann, but a police dog and its handler lost their trail. There was, however, what appeared to be a solid lead. A green or grey Mini car or van had been seen parked down the laneway to Bannvale Hospital near the ambush site. Eva Moore, who was on the bingo bus, saw it drive off towards Portadown after the shooting. Two other witnesses confirmed this but saw the vehicle reverse into Sinton's Lane and then return past the ambush site towards Gilford. An alert was put out and about ninety minutes later, a 19-year-old Loughbrickland man driving a green Mini was stopped by the UDR outside Newry and handed over to the RUC, where he was held for questioning until 6 a.m. There is no record of the interview or of whether the vehicle was examined.

According to the HET report, the driver claimed he had bought the car that evening from the owner Declan O'Dowd's brother Noel at a pub in Banbridge at 10 p.m. and at the time of the shooting was in another pub in the town. Declan recalled the sale as having taken place there over an hour later. Noel O'Dowd recalls the transaction happening outside KD Cars in Gilford at about 7.30 or 8 that evening, but he was never interviewed by the police, nor were the friends who were with them, and there is no record of police investigating the discrepancies in the accounts.

The case papers are very incomplete, with very few records, briefing reports or witness statements. A hardback book, seemingly a record of enquiries in the case, starts on 1 August and only recommences on 15 August.

Six Catholics – Declan O'Dowd, the man he sold the car to and four Gilford men, none of them with any IRA connections – were arrested on 26 August for questioning but released the same day. A green hood found in an outhouse near the murder scene was linked forensically to one of the Gilford men arrested. Two more were arrested in June 1978. Finally, three Catholics from Portadown were arrested in January 1982 after a tip-off claimed they were members of the Provisional IRA and had been seen in a green Mini in Gilford on the night of the shooting. But no one was ever charged.

In 2011, a HET report revealed that a rifle used in the bingo bus attack was also linked to the IRA killing of two Greenfinches (female UDR soldiers). Gillian Liggett, 33, married with two children, was shot in the head in an IRA ambush on the Armagh to Middletown road on 6 April 1976. Only the second Greenfinch to be killed, she was from Leominster in England.

On 8 October 1977, the IRA shot dead Margaret Ann Hearst, 24, a part-time member of the UDR, in her mobile home in the garden of her parents' home in Tynan, near Middletown. Her three-year-old daughter was in the room next door and a bullet went through the toy frog she had been cuddling. A 16-year-old boy from Middletown admitted he fired the fatal shots. Margaret's father, Ross Hearst, was murdered on 4 September 1980. A civilian, he was abducted while visiting a friend after attending a religious service in Tullylush, County Monaghan. The IRA claimed he had admitted 'under interrogation' to supplying information to the security forces.

A second gun used in the Gilford attack was also found in the possession of two IRA members in St Paul's churchyard in Lurgan in 1979.

Former RUC officer John Weir told *The Irish News* in 2017 that the bingo bus attack was carried out by the Glenanne gang including Robin Jackson, UVF commander and suspected British agent. 'HET say it was a republican job and they have proof of it – it was not,' he said. 'It was a Robin Jackson job with Glenanne, the day after Miami was done.' *Lost Lives* states that 'according to reliable loyalist sources the attack was carried out by the UVF'.

The killings are being reviewed by former English police chief Jon Boutcher. Boutcher told Philip that his reach was greater than anyone else's. Philip replied, 'Jon, I don't mean to be disheartening but Sampson was here, Stevens was here and Stalker was here [three other former English police chiefs who headed inquiries] before you and they all got run out of Dodge.'

The victims' families want to know if the RUC chose not to act despite knowing that an attack was being planned by republicans. Martina Marks, Jimmy's niece, told the press in 2015, 'We're starting to think that an informer was involved and that the RUC knew what was happening.' She questioned why an RUC minibus had left Gilford early that evening and why it took weeks for the investigation to get off the ground.

'There was no investigation,' says Julia. 'I remember them coming the day after the funeral to question Granny. She said, "What are you asking me for? How would I know? I was standing on my own street waiting on my husband coming home and he never came."'

Julia says she would like to know the truth about who murdered her grandfather and destroyed her sister's life but, like her mother, she wouldn't pursue it. Her mother's philosophy was: 'It's happened, nothing I can do about it, it's not going to bring them back. I just hope nobody belonging to me ever goes out to shoot somebody. I could live with one of my own being shot, but I couldn't live with the fact that one that I reared would go out and shoot anybody.'

Julia was sceptical of the RUC's claim, however. 'I did ask, why would the IRA be hitting a minibus full of Catholics?'

Philip too had his doubts, but he now thinks it was the IRA. 'The HET report points in that direction but the investigation was shoddy at best. The RUC knew this was going to happen and did nothing about it.' It has been suggested that the investigation into the much more high-profile Miami killings detracted from the Bleary bingo bus investigation. Philip says that given the involvement of security forces in the Miami murders, they were more focused on covering their tracks.

'The Miami made huge headlines, ours really didn't,' says Philip. He is not wrong. Bizarrely, the front page of the first *Banbridge Chronicle* issue to be published after the Miami Showband murders and the fatal Bleary bingo bus attack relegated coverage of the atrocities to the bottom of its front page, choosing to lead with a threatened drought at Spelga Dam, a local reservoir.

Martina Marks's father, Michael, was the youngest of Jimmy Marks's four brothers and three sisters. 'Jimmy was like a father to him,' Martina says. 'He would have done labouring jobs and taken my dad along.' Michael worked as caretaker of Gilford Health Centre, one of whose staff, Dr Connolly – my own doctor – rushed to the scene to treat the wounded.

As is often the case with victims' families, there was never much discussion about the exact circumstances in which their loved one had been killed until the HET issued its report on the original investigation, exposing its flaws and often raising more questions than it answered. The end of the Troubles in 1998 also meant people felt free to start the conversation.

'We didn't talk about it a lot,' Martina says. 'That changed with the HET report. The family, including Jimmy's wife, Florence, who was still alive then, and their two sons, came together and had the first discussion since it happened. The HET report confirmed what we suspected. The Miami investigation took up a lot of resources, things weren't done that should have been done, there were a lot of holes.'

Before Michael died in April 2020, he asked Martina to continue pursuing the truth about his brother's murder. 'I don't think it has been properly investigated,' she says. There was a possible civil case against the police for its alleged failure to carry out a proper investigation. However, other relatives didn't want to go down that route. She wonders whether there was possibly an IRA informer. Otherwise, how were the RUC so sure on the night?

Like so many others, she is pinning her hopes on Jon Boutcher's team of investigators. While his remit is specifically crimes associated with the loyalist Glenanne gang, he may uncover information that was kept from the original RUC investigation.

Thirteen

'You blank it out, you know'

The year 1975 had been a terrible one for violence in the North, with more than 250 lives lost. The village of Gilford in County Down had not been spared, with the fatal attack on the Bleary bingo bus on its outskirts that August. So the people celebrating New Year's Eve in the Central Bar on Mill Street in the village on Wednesday 31 December, if they were not simply living in the moment, were most likely looking forward, not back.

Of the hundred or so people there that night, about eighty were in the lounge bar, with a few upstairs playing or watching pool and the rest in the public bar facing the street. Sylvia McCullough, a 30-year-old factory worker, was there with her husband Sandy, while 44-year-old father of five Richard Beattie, a joiner by trade, had just popped in for a couple of pints with his friend William Scott, a 30-year-old civil servant. Richard had entered one of his racing pigeons in a competition at the clubhouse next door and he was waiting to hear the judges' verdict.

At about 9 p.m. Richard – who was in a generous mood – had just offered to buy pints for 22-year-old Denis Fulton and his friend, who was upstairs playing pool, when a customer came rushing in, shouting that someone had left a bomb in a duffel bag in the pub's front porch. Before the place could be evacuated, the device – containing 7lb of commercial explosives – went off.

Richard Beattie, left, with a friend on a construction job in the Falkland Islands, c.1968.

Although they were not killed instantly, Richard Beattie, William Scott and Sylvia McCullough bore the brunt of the explosion, while more than twenty others were injured, several of them seriously.

Sandy McCullough was standing right beside Sylvia when the bomb went off, yet miraculously he was unscathed. 'The building just caved in around us,' he told the *Belfast Telegraph*. 'One minute my wife was standing beside me, the next she wasn't there. I never saw her again.'

Denis Fulton told the newspaper, 'I went upstairs to tell my friend that a drink was being put up for him. If I hadn't accepted the offer and then gone upstairs I would almost certainly have been killed.'

Richard and William were still alive when the emergency services arrived, but they died soon afterwards. Sylvia hung on but died the next morning in Craigavon Hospital, becoming the first fatality of the Troubles in 1976 – the death toll of that year would be the second highest of the entire conflict.

Reverend Edwin Armstrong, the Church of Ireland vicar of St Paul's in Gilford, told the *Banbridge Chronicle* that he had been at home

The aftermath of the Central Bar bombing in Gilford. © Victor Patterson

watching television when there was such a blast that they thought the windows were coming in. He, his son and a neighbour went to the scene to see what help they could offer. His next task was to break the news to the widowed mothers of William Scott and Richard Beattie that their sons had been killed, and to console Richard's wife and children.

Mr Armstrong described relations in the village and locality as extremely good. At the funerals of Richard and William, Mr Armstrong referred to having seen many people weep openly after the bombing. There was nothing unmanly in this, he said. Jesus had shown his compassion by weeping at the grave of his friend Lazarus.

Assistant Chief Constable Charles Rodgers described the killings as 'a terrible blow to the small community of Gilford, which has been completely free of sectarianism and which is totally integrated … This community has always lived and worked together very closely and this is the first incident of this nature in the area.'

Both the South Armagh Republican Action Force and the People's Liberation Army, cover names for mainstream republican paramilitary groups, claimed responsibility for the triple murder. It was supposedly carried out in retaliation for a loyalist bomb attack on Kay's Tavern in Dundalk on 19 December, which killed two Catholics, Jack Rooney and Hugh Waters, and a gun and bomb attack hours later on the Catholic-owned Donnelly's Bar in Silverbridge, south Armagh, which killed 14-year-old Michael Donnelly, the owners' son, Patrick Donnelly (no relation to the owners) and Trevor Bracknell.

Cecil Harvey, a local unionist politician, said after visiting the homes of those bereaved in the Central Bar bombing, 'If the person or persons responsible could have made the same visit to see the misery and heartbreak and sadness they have caused by their foul and evil deed maybe they would not be so proud to claim responsibility for their action.'

William Scott, 31, a health inspector in Lisburn, was the only son of Elizabeth and the late Edward Scott. 'He was a most devoted and dutiful son to his widowed mother and his tragic death is an irreparable loss to her,' the *Chronicle* wrote. He was chaplain of the local Orange lodge and a member of the Royal Black Preceptory, as well as a keen supporter of Gilford United FC.

Sylvia McCullough, 30, a native of Banbridge, lived in Tullylish and worked in Wades factory in Portadown. She was honorary secretary of the local branch of the Vanguard Unionist Party, a hard-line faction led by William Craig. She was survived by her husband, Sandy, her mother and three sisters.

Reverend David Coe, speaking at Sylvia's funeral, expressed the hope that the good community relations in the village would not be destroyed and that there would be no retaliation. His hope would be dashed the very next day when loyalist gunmen would shoot dead Joe, Declan and Barry O'Dowd, three local Catholics.

Just over a year later, Reverend Coe and Reverend Armstrong would offer prayers when a plaque was unveiled and dedicated in the Uprichard Memorial Orange Hall in Tullylish to Gilford's three murder victims. If you google Gilford pub bombing, however, the algorithm redirects you to the 1974 IRA Guildford pub bombing in Surrey, adding the insult of erasure to the fatal injuries sustained by its three victims. How faint a trace our commonplace atrocities leave on the historical record and national consciousness, yet how indelibly they mark the lives of loved ones left behind.

***

Richard Beattie, who shares his father's name, was 17 when his dad was murdered. He lives a few miles away from Gilford, between Portadown and Lough Neagh, in a fine, modern house with huge windows overlooking the River Bann, which on the October day we meet is swollen with rainwater and looks like it might burst its banks. Nearby fields are waterlogged and where they slope down to the road the water running off them is a muddy brown. God knows this land must be well used to the rain but there is only so much even it can take.

Until today, Richard has never talked about his father's murder. He speaks at all times very calmly, and laughs a lot as he tells stories, finding the humour in small things, but occasionally the emotions he is tapping into threaten, like a saturated water table, to spill over onto the surface.

'It was only after you rang that I started thinking about it,' he tells me straight away. 'It was a horrific night that it happened. I sort of blamed myself a wee bit for it. I was 17 going on 18 and I had long hair and used to spend ages in the bathroom. That night I remember saying: "Do you want to go to the bathroom first, Dad, before I wash my hair?" because I knew he wanted to go down to the pigeons.

'It seemed like only seconds from when he left the door till the bang went off. Something went in my head: I knew exactly what it was. I knew where it happened. I was there like that,' he says, snapping his fingers. The Beatties lived in Castleview, a housing estate about 200 yards away from the pub. I know it well. Our doctor's surgery stands at the entrance to the estate. A footpath brings you directly onto Mill Street, which means you can run there faster than you can get there by car.

'I run down the town and I run into the place and it was falling down round with people,' says Richard. 'I went up the stairs and a couple of guys I knew were there but they were traumatised. I came back down the stairs and I remember shouting for my dad and he answered me. I went into the bar and I seen things that you never want to see. I remember putting my hands under his shoulders and him saying, "Don't lift me, I've no legs." His friend Billy Scott was lying beside him. It was horrific. I went outside, I couldn't take it another second. Crowds were gathered up, then it got a bit muddled for me. I remember just standing. It seemed like ages and ages before they brought the bodies out. You blank it out, you know, altogether. I went from there to the hospital.'

On New Year's Eve 2021, I posted on social media about the atrocity. I had written a full-page article about the O'Dowd murders, which was published in *The Irish Times* on 1 January 2022 to mark the anniversary, and I wanted to make it clear that I was not ignoring or indifferent to the atrocity that preceded it. A friend, Noelene, replied to my post to say that Richard Beattie was her uncle. I had no idea that she had lost a close relative in this way. Some people might think Northerners do nothing but talk about the Troubles, but the truth is we are all far too silent and circumspect about those thirty years of trauma.

Noelene later told me that her father, who was a firefighter based in Portadown, was one of the first emergency services personnel on the scene and had discovered Richard, his wife's brother, amid the wreckage and the carnage of the Central Bar that night, even lighting him a cigarette while they waited for an ambulance. The trauma experienced by the emergency services during the Troubles is worthy of a book in itself.

Richard talks about his dad and his pigeons. The pigeons and the pub went together, he says. 'The pigeon thing was maybe an excuse.' The clubhouse – basically a big room with birdcages lining the walls –

is still there. Gilford United used it for changing rooms.

'My dad used to keep pigeons for years and years in the back garden,' he says. 'We used to live in Hill Street and there was a massive stone in the backyard. He used to sit on it and every time birds went overhead he used to whistle, to call his down.' He laughs at the memory.

I ask him how you proved your pigeon had won a race. 'For races you had a clock, and a rubber ring clipped on to the pigeon's foot. When the pigeon came home you took the ring off, put it in an aluminium capsule and put it into the side of the clock and pulled the handle, which punctured it with the time.' The innocent ingenuity amazes me. Then I think of the evil ingenuity of bomb-makers and the use to which they put timers.

Richard's father worked as a joiner with a local builder, Jim Stevenson, and Richard in turn served his time as a joiner with him. I ask Richard what sort of things he and his dad used to do together.

'We used to go swimming in the River Bann, out the Portadown road. There are big stones in the river there, and deep parts.' They also used to swim at a place they called the falls, between the mill race and the Bann and the lock gates, which were used to fill the mill pond. 'He also taught me to clean out the pigeons. I was lucky that way,' Richard adds, laughing.

Some people like to exaggerate the difference between Northern Catholics and Protestants. Catholics, they say, tend to have much larger families. But Richard's father had six brothers and sisters, his wife Maureen is from a family of ten and he himself has four brothers and sisters.

'Gilford was a good place to grow up,' he says. 'There was never any trouble. Some of my mates that I run about with was Roman Catholic, nobody thought anything of it 'cause we were all living on top of one another.' Their two-up two-down in Hill Street had a toilet in the backyard. 'Everybody's door was open or if they weren't you knew rightly the key was hanging on a bit of string. You just put your hand through the letterbox. People would come in the front door, out the back, just looking a shortcut. We had the best of craic.'

The family moved to Castleview in 1972. 'I remember me and my dad carrying stuff down under the darkness of night – bed ends, all your belongings.' The pigeon shed came too. It filled the backyard. 'There wasn't a lot of light came into the kitchen.' Did they get rid of it after he died, I wonder? What odds? The shadow cast by the murder blocked more light than any pigeon shed ever could. In Castleview, Richard could watch Gilford United matches from his bedroom window.

Another memory surfaces, from the night of the bombing, after Richard got home from the hospital. 'I can remember going back to the house to my mum, going round to my grandmother's as well. I can remember sitting on the floor and her holding me, my grandmother. I think he was her pet really. She took it very bad too. He was a bit of a rebel, my dad, he ran away and joined the army. He wasn't allowed to go but he went anyway.' He served three years with the Royal Inniskilling Fusiliers along with his brother Sammy just after the Second World War, some of it in Cyprus.

'It took my mum an awful length of time to get over it,' Richard says. 'Because my dad was self-employed she got very little money off the government. Five kids to rear so she done well. She worked in the mill.' Richard was the eldest; the youngest only four or five. Did he and his mother or his siblings ever discuss what had happened?

'It was something we blocked out,' he says. 'I don't think I've ever had a conversation with one of my siblings about it.'

Did they mark the anniversary?

'You can't forget it, it's New Year's Eve, it happens every year. No, we never ever marked it. It's just something that hurts every year. You can't have a new year's celebration without thinking about it. It's not something that I want to commemorate or dwell on; I think we were all so young when it happened we just try to blank it out. I don't mind talking to you about it. It's not something I've ever done before, even thought about it, to be honest. It's weird.'

I wonder if his mother had spoken to her children about becoming bitter or getting involved in anything, but Richard says there was no need for that conversation. They weren't a political or sectarian family.

'Even though that tragedy happened, it didn't change us in any way. One thing it never did, it never made me or any of my siblings bitter. You would have thought maybe one of us would but none of us; we all have Catholic friends. You'd almost think we'd gone out of our way. None of us were involved in anything.'

In December 1979, a 29-year-old INLA member from Portadown was given four life sentences for the murders of Sylvia McCullough, William Scott and Richard Beattie, and also that of a 14-year-old Catholic schoolboy from Portadown, Thomas Gerard Rafferty. Thomas had been blown up less than six weeks after the Central Bar bombing by a booby-trap bomb in a shed near his home, which was intended for the security forces. An anonymous caller to the police confidential phone line had tried to lure security personnel to the area by saying that guns were concealed there.

It seems likely that the Central Bar bombing was a revenge attack for the murder a fortnight earlier on 15 December 1975 of 17-year-old Ronald Trainor by the UVF in a bomb attack on his home in Portadown. He was a member of the IRSP, the political wing of the INLA. His mother, Dorothy, a Protestant, had been shot dead that April and his father seriously injured in a UVF gun attack. His brother Thomas, an INLA member, was killed by the UVF in 1978.

Did the trial and conviction of the man responsible for his father's murder affect Richard? 'Do you know, I only read that yesterday?' says Richard. 'I didn't want nothing to do with it. I remember the police coming to say there had been developments and my sister talked to them. I didn't want to know.'

At the time of the bombing, Richard was serving his time as an electrician at Goodyear, where my father worked, and got a lift once a week to a training centre in Lisburn with his father's friend Billy Scott. What was he like?

'I was probably a bit too young to take much notice, but by all accounts he was a nice guy. He didn't have pigeons; he was just there with my da that night. I don't know how that friendship started. All I can remember about the guy is he was a bit like yourself, a bit portly' – I am in fact just very big-boned – 'and he had a gold tooth.'

One of the odd things about Gilford is that it has no graveyard. Dunbar McMaster, the mill owner, donated the ground and 50 per cent of the money to build the village's Catholic, Church of Ireland and Presbyterian churches, but stipulated that they could not have graveyards. So Richard's father was buried in Tullylish.

'I go to the grave regular. It does, I think, give you a wee bit of comfort, but I think mainly I go because I know they would want me to go.'

Richard and his wife Maureen are both saved, in other words, practising Christians who have accepted Jesus as their Saviour. Does his faith help him reconcile himself to what happened to his father? He interprets this, I think, as asking whether he saw his father's murder as to do with religion.

'It doesn't. I've seen and I've read and I'm not stupid; definitely the Catholic people in this country were put upon, some of the things that was done were terrible, a fool would know it wasn't right. But I never really associated what happened to my dad with that. I was too young. I just know my dad was taken from me too early.'

The Central Bar was rebuilt and renamed the Pheasant Lodge. Richard can now pass it without thinking about what happened there.

'It was hard for a long, long time, but when they got it rebuilt it wasn't as bad, it didn't look the same. I worked in it, as a waiter, years later, when Jim Dawson [the owner] got it going again.'

Richard's mother Phyllis never remarried but did have a long-term relationship with Joe McCart, 'maybe one of the very few Protestants in Laurencetown! He died of throat cancer. My mother nursed him the whole time, then she died of cancer two years after in 2015. She had it when she was nursing him but she held it back. Some people get an awful easy way out of this life and some people suffer, it's just a raffle.'

How did his mother's death affect him?

'When my mum died it was far worse. She had been everything to us,' Richard says, becoming upset. 'Now I wish I wasn't talking about this.' I feel guilty that I have disturbed this man's equilibrium and share the story of my own loss to try to bridge the gap.

'Grief is a funny thing. It affects everyone differently,' Richard says. 'I think the way we did it was the easiest way. You blank it out. Ninety-nine per cent of the time it doesn't affect you as you don't even dwell on it, but when it does, it hurts, probably hurts for longer, because you don't deal with it when you don't talk about it.'

Richard's dad was 44 when he died. When he reached that age himself, it hit home hard.

'When I was 44 I felt so young,' he replies. 'I realised my dad was only a young man. I was 17 when he died. When you're that age, anyone over 40 is a right age, but it's very young, and then – you would know – life's just snatched away from you, too young. That's what makes it hurt so much. He never really got the chance to live, and I never really got the chance to know him as an adult – whenever you're a child you look for childish things – to have proper conversations with him.'

Did his father's absence make itself felt particularly at life's landmarks, such as his wedding day or the birth of his children?

'It was disappointing he was never there, that he never got to see his grandchildren. I'm getting very emotional now, Martin.' Richard stands up and looks out the window at the swollen Bann.

Did he feel the pressure, when his father died, to become the man of the house?

'Do you know? I never shed a tear,' he replies, 'that night or the next night. But I remember the following night, sitting on the stairs and my auntie Peggy said that to me [about becoming the man of the house].' The memory upsets him. 'That was bad, her saying that, I can remember that.' It's an awful burden to put on a grieving boy.

I wonder whether belief in God helps. 'I think your faith helps you with all aspects of life, if you walk with the Lord, but everyone is different, I wouldn't preach to anyone. Because I didn't have any faith at that time [when his dad was killed], it wasn't there to help me, it was very hard, especially with all your siblings and your mother having to go out to work. It would have been better if she had been able to stay at home and look after the kids but yet they all turned out well.'

Richard shows me two ornaments, wire birds painted white, which once belonged to his mother. 'My mum was an awful one for oul' footery stuff in the house. She was always footering, always painting. Them's the only two things of hers I took out of the house, because she was always happy doing it. Whenever you went down to visit her, she was always either sitting in the kitchen on the high stool reading the paper or painting something. She was the only woman I ever seen who polished the copper pipes to her radiators, and in the hot press. They were gleaming,' he says, laughing. 'I don't know what it was.'

I remember my mum scrubbing our house's front step in Millar Park. The step was cement but it was treated like marble.

'What did they have, them wee tiny houses?' asks Richard. 'There was nothing in them, but they used to scrub the front doorstep or else they put that cardinal red stuff on the threshold. My mother used to bleach the front doorstep, the front path down the entry and the whole backyard, every week. She never used the bins, they were like brand new, she put rubbish in plastic bags and her sister Lily would put it in bins down the town.'

There could hardly be a greater contrast between the image I have of Richard's mum's immaculate home and the way once-proud Gilford is today, with its general air of dilapidation. 'Since the mill closed there's no employment in the town. It's a shame to see,' says Richard. 'I think the heart has been knocked out of the people in Gilford – it's dying on its feet.'

Fourteen

A Ghost Estate

Even within a single parish, the burden of the Troubles is ill-divided. Bleary and Ballydougan suffered far more than anywhere else in Tullylish. This may not have been inevitable but it was predictable. In Ireland, when history repeats itself, it is usually as tragedy again.

Two centuries before, even as egalitarianism was gaining ground with the formation in Belfast in 1791 of the Society of United Irishmen, consisting largely of radical Presbyterians inspired by the ideals of the French Revolution, the rival spectre of sectarianism was resurging. In 1795, in Loughgall, County Armagh, twelve miles from Tullylish's western boundary, nine Catholics were killed in the Battle of the Diamond between rival agrarian gangs, Catholic Defenders and Protestant Peep o' Day Boys. Following this victory, the Orange Order was established on 21 September 1795.

The Peep o' Day Boys, now known as Orange Boys, burned down the Clare townland's Mass house. In the neighbouring parish of Aghaderg, Loughgall yeomanry torched Lisnagade Mass house.

Threatening letters were sent to Catholics in Tullylish and Protestant sympathisers. 'John Hollan, you are desired to abandon your house and if you don't we will reck you … you pretend to be a Protestant, and is not, moreover you have a Papish wife … Given under our hand this day of March, being the second year of the destruction of the Pope, the great scarlet whore of Babylon, and his infirnal imps the Priests.'

Even if their motivation was enlightened or economic self-interest, Protestant landlords had their Catholic tenants' backs. What is a landlord, after all, without tenants?

Seapatrick, Tullylish and Donaghcloney parishes were fined for Orange outrages in 1795. Lord Downshire's agent Thomas Lane briefed him the following March: 'Lord Moira's estates of Bleary, Clare etc. are in a most distracted desolate state, and on Thursday and Friday nights 14 houses were demolished in Tullylish … The depredators, Orange Boys.'

Two months later, he wrote, 'Clare is nearly depopulated and many of our own [Catholic] tenants are applying for leave to dispose of their situations acknowledging their intentions of going to the South … I cannot confide in the militia around us. They would in my opinion more rejoice to become parties in a bloody scene than be active to suppress it.'

The onslaught prompted an exodus of 10,000 Catholics from Down and Armagh to Mayo and Leitrim, which had their own weaving industries.

On 19 October 1796, Francis Rawdon-Hastings, 2nd Earl of Moira, landlord of Clare, Bleary, Ballydougan and Ballynagarrick, wrote to Thomas Pelham, Chief Secretary for Ireland, who had claimed that violence suffered by Catholics had been exaggerated, to tell him that if anything the violence was under-reported.

'The place where this has happened is in the heart of the linen manufactories, and is one of the most industrious parts of Ireland. It will not escape your observation, Sir, that Catholics of the lower class (such as these sufferers are) are not permitted by law to have arms for their own defence, and it must occur that they thence have a peculiar claim upon government for protections against lawless depredation.'

He listed 150 Catholic tenants and dependants who had been driven out in the previous year by Protestant gangs.

Among the names given for Bleary were Nicholas Doud (aka Dowd) and Hugh Dowd. The list for Ballydougan is headed by James and John Dowd. Some Dowds, however, stayed on in the heart of the Linen Triangle, in what would become the heartless land of the Murder Triangle.

***

Joe Dowd, a descendant of one who stayed, married a local farmer's daughter, Dinah Byrne, in 1911. Doubtless influenced by the Gaelic Revival, they decided to christen their children O'Dowd. They also decided to send them to the predominantly Protestant Ballydougan National School, as the nearest Catholic schools, in Laurencetown and Gilford, were too far to walk. It was a pragmatic decision, rather than an ecumenical one, but it suggests a family uninfected by sectarian prejudice that put their children first.

Noel O'Dowd, one of Dinah and Joe O'Dowd's grandsons, credits this education with teaching his father, Barney, and uncle Joe the value of money and land, and giving them a strong work ethic. However, listening to Barney, his mother was clearly a huge influence.

In Barney's telling: 'My mother was the best and hardest-working woman in the world. She worked at the school every morning and every evening. She milked the cows, she churned the milk, turned it into butter, carried it into Lurgan – which was two and a half miles – paid for her groceries with the butter.

'My father was a bit of a charmer but he had different values to what I would have had. He was a good enough worker yet he could sit there while my mother swung a big pot on a crane over the fire. Women were only a chattel. Very few men appreciated their wives.'

One day, Canon John Doyle, the parish priest, came with his curate to ask Barney's father, Joe, to transfer his two youngest children to school in Laurencetown. The pretext was that it was their duty as Catholic parents to provide their children with a Catholic education. The subtext was that a fall in pupil numbers meant the school risked losing a teacher.

When Joe O'Dowd pointed this out, Barney recalls, the priest asked whether he was interested in Catholic education but, free of the deference to clergy typical of the time, he gave as good as he got. 'My father said, "I'm very interested in Catholic education, Canon Doyle, but you got B Specials to paint the Clare chapel and some of your own parishioners walking about." For every defence he brought up, my father tore it asunder. My father said, "You weren't concerned about the souls of the other four children who went to the local school, so these two may as well go to hell along with them."'

The O'Dowds got on fine at school but the pupils could be casually cruel. One of Barney's classmates was known as BTB – BT were his father's initials; the second B an insulting reference to his parents being unmarried. Northern society, still relatively conservative today, was even more so ninety years ago. This was one way that people were taught to know their place, be they Catholic or, in the official language of the day, illegitimate.

When Barney left school, he had two options: work in Gilford Mill or as a labourer for Blane, a local farmer. The money wasn't great in either place, but the farm work was closer to home, outdoors and came with a hot meal. The Blanes treated him well. One day in 1942, however, an opportunity presented itself.

'There was a big dairy farmer beside us selling milk. He was stopping doing the country area because it was taking too much time. The milk wasn't bottled at the time so I got containers made by a tinsmith the shape of a milk keg. I delivered it off a bike.' In 1964, he was delivering twenty-two crates. A decade later it was eighty, each holding twenty pint bottles – that's 200 gallons a day. Deliveries were seven days a week as few people had fridges.

One of Barney's customers was Sinton, a linen lord in Tullylish, so he got to know the housekeeper, Kathleen Durnien from Lisnakea,

County Fermanagh, one of whose five siblings, Tommy, had captained the county's Gaelic football team. Kathleen and Barney married in 1950, renting in Gilford before stretching themselves to buy the farm in Ballydougan in 1953, with two toddlers in tow and a new baby on the way.

***

Long before the collapse of the property market south of the border, the North had its own ghost estate, a scattering of homes abandoned after paramilitary murderers had made it unbearable for the survivors to stay.

The O'Dowds' remote farmhouse is one such place. An L-shaped, single-storey cottage, its windows and doors are blinded by breeze blocks, the poor land surrounding it sold for rough pasture. It is only fit for cattle now.

But it was a full house on the evening of Sunday, 4 January 1976. To mark the end of the Christmas holidays, Barney, Kathleen and five of

The O'Dowds' abandoned farmhouse, Ballydougan. © Martin Doyle

their eight children – Barry, Declan, Mary, Eleanor and Cathal – were entertaining Barney's brother Joe, seven other members of Joe's family and a neighbour's child. UVF gunmen burst in and shot dead Barry, 24, Declan, 19, and Joe, 61. Barney was gravely injured but survived. It is striking how often these sectarian murders of Catholics happened on the Sabbath. Did the killers think of it as God's work?

Ten minutes earlier and twenty miles south, a coordinated UVF attack in Whitecross, County Armagh, claimed the lives of two brothers, John Martin and Brian Reavey, and gravely injured a third, Anthony. The next night, ten Protestant workmen were massacred by republicans in neighbouring Kingsmill. The North seemed to be teetering on the brink of all-out civil war. The news cycle churned, leaving the O'Dowds to bury their dead. For the first time.

Kathleen O'Dowd's grief-stricken face at the funerals captured the heartrending toll of the Troubles in a few etched lines. Barney, fighting for his life in Craigavon Hospital, mourned his dead alone.

***

Kathleen O'Dowd is comforted by her daughter Mary and sister Patsy McManus at the funeral of her sons Barry and Declan and brother-in-law Joe. © Keystone/ Getty Images

Everyone in our parish knew the O'Dowds. They delivered the milk that you put on your cereal or in your tea in the morning, and the coal that you burned in the fireplace to keep you warm at night. So when word of the atrocity broke, it sent a chill through the entire community. If such a harmless, hard-working, peace-loving family could be targeted, who was safe? My mother remembers putting us to bed in the dark that night for fear of what a light might attract.

After the publication of my article 'Dirty Linen' in *The Irish Times* – when I met Barney again, still sharp at 98, and some of his children – his son Noel shared with me his file of papers on the murders: the HET review of the original RUC investigation; his own recollections of that time; and the official witness statements of the adults who survived the attack. This reconstruction is based on those statements.

That Sunday evening, there were ten adults and six children in the farmhouse for a family gathering. Barney, 52, was in the living room with his children Barry, 24, and Cathal, 11. Barney's brother Joe, 60, was there too, with his daughters Deirdre, 21, a student, and Bernadette, 17, a trainee nurse, and his granddaughter Áine McCorry, 7.

Barney's wife, Kathleen, was in the kitchen preparing dinner with her daughters Mary, 23, and Eleanor, 13. Her son Declan, 19, was also there, along with Joe's daughter Una McCorry, 32, her husband, Joe, 36, their two other children, Michael, 5, and Philip, 3, and a neighbour's daughter, Áine Gaffney, 12.

At 6.30 p.m., there was a knock at the front door. When Kathleen opened the door, she was confronted by three masked men. Mary heard her mother shout in a strange voice, 'What do you want here?' Kathleen could describe only the one who spoke. He was about 5ft 11in, of thin build, wearing an odd mask, which 'was to his shoulders and was like white cheesecloth'. 'This is a hold-up,' he said, in a local accent. 'We're here for your money.' He was holding a gun in his two hands. It appeared short and thick, but it wasn't a pistol.

Kathleen tried to kick the door shut but they pushed on in. Mary looked up and saw her mother standing level with the kitchen door, and heard her screech, 'Three masked men with guns, I've let them in.' Kathleen recalled: 'I backed off and then went into the kitchen and closed the door and stood with my back to it.' Mary pulled out the settee and crouched behind it with her cousin Una and sister Eleanor.

Joe McCorry, Joe O'Dowd's son-in-law, had just finished carving a leg of lamb with the new electric carving knife, Kathleen's Christmas present. He and Declan were talking when they heard a scream from the front door. Declan immediately went to investigate. As Kathleen was closing the kitchen door, Joe saw his five-year-old son Michael's arm appear through it and pulled him into the kitchen. 'Just as I did this,' he recalled, 'there was a burst of automatic gunfire from the direction of the front door. I cradled my sons Michael and Philip in my arms and I hid down behind the kitchen door. I then heard further gunfire, which I presumed was in the living room. Then there was silence.'

Bernadette was in the living room sitting near the piano beside her sister Deirdre with her niece Áine on her knee. Her cousin Barry was by the piano and her father Joe was on the sofa talking to her uncle Barney. Bernadette heard a noise in the hall then the door burst open and she saw a man in the doorway with a gun. He was about 5ft 6in tall with short hair and a round face, obscured by a stocking with no apparent eye or nose holes.

'The gunman said, "This is for money, get over there" [but] he did not indicate where he wanted us to go, he just looked at Daddy and Uncle Barney. Uncle Barney got up and took a few steps towards this man. It was then I heard shooting. At this I held tight onto Áine and pulled her into the corner beside the piano. I saw Barry coming towards me and then he fell up against the wall beside the fireplace. After this there was still more shooting. I closed my eyes and put my hand over Áine's mouth. When the shooting had finished, I heard Uncle Barney talk. He said, "My God, my poor son." Deirdre and I decided to get up. We did not know if the man had left. Barry was lying on his back with his head to one side. Daddy was lying on his stomach at the sitting room door. I went out into the hall and I saw Declan lying on his stomach beside the kitchen door. Uncle Barney was lying over Declan's legs. Aunt Kathleen was in the kitchen in a very distressed state.'

Deirdre's recollections are very similar to Bernadette's, but she remembers the stocking mask was dark grey, that the gunman was stocky, wore a black or dark brown leather jacket and had very short hair 'as there was no sign of bulges inside the mask'. When the gunman told them to 'get over there', she thought he was going to line them up. The shooting started in the hall, she believes. She then saw Barry fall and thinks the shooting continued after that but wasn't sure when her father was shot. 'After this there was a silence and then I heard my uncle Barney crying.'

The two sisters agreed that the man who killed their father and cousins and seriously injured their uncle had a local accent.

The way Barney remembers it, he and his brother were having a drink and he had just got up to set Joe's glass back on the drinks table when he turned to see an armed man facing him. He was wearing a khaki-coloured combat jacket and a fishnet-type mask, 'similar to a ladies' hairnet only closer knitted'.

Back in the kitchen, Joe McCorry had watched bullets come through the door. One was later found lodged in the door frame. When the shooting stopped, he went to open the door but Kathleen screamed that the gunmen were still there. But when he saw the door handle move very slightly, he pulled the door open to find Barney slumped over Declan, moaning. Deirdre, Bernadette and Áine came out of the living room and Joe took them into the kitchen. He then went into the living room and saw Barry and his father-in-law, Joe, lying dead on the floor. His wife, Una, said an Act of Contrition into the ears of her father, Barry and Declan: 'O my God, I am heartily sorry for all my sins because they offend thee, who are so good and with thy help I will not sin again'. Joe rang 999 for the police.

'As I was ringing,' Joe McCorry told the police, 'my wife was in the hall and I heard her shout that Barney was hit. Up unto this time I had thought that he was uninjured and crying over Declan. I was going to take him to hospital but owing to the state of the womenfolk and children I decided to wait for the ambulance. At this time everyone was in a panic and were terror-stricken, not knowing if the gunmen were still outside.'

Kathleen left the kitchen and saw Barney lying across their son Declan's body. She then saw Joe lying in the doorway. 'I asked where was Barry. Someone said he had gone to Mass with Noel but I knew he had been in the morning. I came on into the sitting room and Barry was lying in the corner by the piano.'

Una asked Barney if he knew the gunmen and he mentioned a particular family. Mary remembers her sister Eleanor shouting, 'They've shot Declan', and her father saying, 'Declan's dead.' She got whiskey for her mother and father, but as she tried to give him the glass she noticed he was bleeding.

Amidst the darkness of the witness statements, the little acts of love shine like candles: Joe McCorry pulling Michael to safety, then cradling him and his other son Philip; Bernadette holding Áine tight and covering the child's mouth, perhaps lest a scream might draw the gunman's fire; Barney's lament: 'My God, my poor son'; Una's Acts of Contrition; Mary's offering of whiskey.

No one heard a vehicle enter or leave the yard and the family's Alsatian dog had not barked at any point, which was most unusual, Kathleen said.

***

No one has ever been convicted of the murders and now it is most unlikely, although they are being reinvestigated by Jon Boutcher's team. The murders' case file was re-examined in 1978 as part of an investigation into terrorist crimes committed by RUC officers, and in 2006 by the HET.

The HET report criticised the original investigation. The officer put in charge of the triple murder investigation was George Christy, a temporary detective sergeant. Today a more senior officer would have headed it. Also, the crime scene was not preserved, and furniture had been moved before forensic examination and photography commenced.

Nineteen bullet casings were found at the scene but only seventeen bullet heads, so two were clearly missing. How confident can one be in the thoroughness of an investigation if the police do not even find two pieces of evidence they know are present? The mystery was solved when Ronan O'Dowd told HET investigators that a month after the shootings he had found two bullet heads when moving the settee.

There is no information in the original case papers, the HET says, that indicates whether searches were conducted in the vicinity of the property, or if fingerprint examinations were carried out.

The getaway car, an Austin Morris 1300, had been stolen that Sunday afternoon in Lurgan and found burned out in Laurencetown at 11.45 a.m. the next day. The HET report notes some confusion as to whether it had been destroyed by the killers or by a controlled explosion. There is no record in the case file to indicate if any evidence was recovered from the vehicle or from where it was found. House-to-house enquiries along the route from the O'Dowds' home to the dump site were not conducted for fourteen days.

The day before the murders, Barney's son Ronan had seen a car very similar to the getaway vehicle parked down a laneway giving access to a field adjoining the family farm. He had spotted two masked men whom he assumed to be soldiers, holding bulky radios with long aerials, looking towards his home as they entered the field. Detective Sergeant Christy walked the route with Ronan a couple of days after the murders, but there is no record of this line of enquiry being pursued. The HET also found no record of investigators linking the vehicle Ronan saw and the getaway vehicle, 'although it seems likely'.

That same day, Noel and Declan noticed a UDR patrol in one of their fields, the only time Noel ever remembers seeing them on their property. 'It's suspicious now but wasn't then,' says Noel.

Liam Moore, who had been with Declan the afternoon before the murders, told police he felt they were being followed all that day.

Weeks after the killing, Barney and Kathleen found a local UDR man's wages slip near their house, but the RUC presumed that a patrol member protecting their investigation had dropped it, or that the wind might have blown it onto the property. The family felt it much more likely that it had been dropped by one of the UDR men their sons had seen on the day before the murder, and that its owner should have been questioned.

When police interviewed Barney sixteen days after the murder, he identified the gunman as a local man he had known for twenty years, claiming to have recognised both his voice and his face behind its amateurish mask. 'Before any shooting started I remember this man say, "This is a hold-up." I feel that this was [—'s] voice who lives in [—]. As this man was about to leave, after shooting Barry, Declan and Joe, he turned to me and fired more shots. That was when I got my stomach wounds. The first shot hit me on the wrist ... I would not do an injustice to any man and I realise there is always an element of mistake, but to the best of my knowledge I know this man is [—].'

This man was arrested the next day and questioned over three days. He denied involvement and provided four alibi witnesses who, though accepted at the time, were adjudged by the HET to be unreliable as three had been drinking heavily – they had attended a wake and visited people who had been injured in the Central Bar bombing in Gilford – and all were vague on timings.

An anorak seized from this suspect was tested by a forensic scientist who found traces of lead and antimony (firearms residue) on the left cuff, right front shoulder and inside both lower pockets. When questioned, the suspect said that he had last owned a firearm in 1964, and that was the last time he had fired a gun. He had not recently been near firearms.

There is no record of either an explanation by the suspect or any follow-up investigation.

Interviewed by the HET in 2006, Mr Christy couldn't remember what effect this discovery had on his view of the man as a suspect. He did remember Barney naming the man as a suspect 'but felt that Mr O'Dowd had in fact only been saying that the person he named looked very similar to the gunman'.

The same man was also named in an anonymous phone call to the confidential Robophone telephone recording service on 14 January. The Friday after the shooting, when Noel was delivering coal in Gilford, he saw the man drive up past the coal lorry and circle back. Noel felt someone had alerted the man that the O'Dowds were back in business and he wanted to see for himself.

Mr Christy was adamant that Barney had been mistaken; the gunman, he insisted, bore a strong resemblance to notorious loyalist Robin Jackson. It is possible both suspects were present. Anne Cadwallader in *Lethal Allies* also blames Jackson.

In 2006, Barney told an Oireachtas sub-committee on the Barron report that a detective had told him they had a suspect but could not charge him, explaining, 'This is a hard man … He is head of the UVF and we have tried to break him but we cannot. Even if we did, we could not charge him because the UVF had said that if ever this man was charged with murder, they were going to start shooting policemen the same as the IRA were doing. Therefore our hands are tied; we cannot charge him with the murder of your children.'

Similarly, Barney told the HET in 2006 that Mr Christy had told him that Jackson was head of the UVF and 'couldn't be touched'. The detective told the HET that he did not recall specifically discussing Jackson with the family but conceded he may have done in the course of resolving the issue of the suspect named by Barney. If he did use the expression 'could not be touched', it would only have been in the context that there was no evidence against him and therefore he could not be arrested (touched).

The RUC arrested three men from the Lurgan area the day after the murders and held them for three days. Their interrogation produced the first piece of intelligence about the murders: the RUC's interviewing of Declan after the bingo bus attack in August had brought him and his family to the attention of the UVF. A man related to a Mid-Ulster UVF member had requested a 'person' to gather 'details' about the O'Dowds. There was no intelligence that pre-dated the attack or anything to suggest it could have been prevented, the HET report says.

The HET commented that it had 'not found anything ... [to] explain: why (within hours of the murders) the three Lurgan men were identified as suspects; who provided the information about the information gathering on the O'Dowds; who carried [it] out ...; who arrested the three Lurgan men; what the men said during their interviews.'

John Weir, a former RUC man and member of the Glenanne gang, named Jackson as the murderer of the O'Dowds and the coordinator of the Reavey murders that same night.

In 1977, intelligence indicated that the Mid-Ulster UVF had murdered the O'Dowds and the Reaveys. Jackson was named, for the first time, as having been 'involved' in the O'Dowd murders. The HET said, 'This is the first time that there is any documented record of the RUC linking the murders of the O'Dowds and the Reaveys.'

Again, in July 1984, Jackson was named as the 'headman/shooter'. It was also recorded that the suspects had made their escape 'across the fields', 'hid the weapons behind a telegraph pole in Waringstown' (the weapons were collected the following day).

As well as the Robophone tip-off naming the man Barney had identified as his attacker, there was another, received between 9 a.m. the day after the murders and 9 a.m. the following day, that said, '[—] will know something about the murders at Ballydougan on Sunday night.' The HET noted that there was no record of any RUC action following this tip-off.

A few years later Eugene Reavey told Noel and Cathal that he had been given the name of the man who shot the O'Dowds. It was the man Barney had identified.

The O'Dowds wanted another local man investigated. He had called to their home days before the murders with a car full of strangers looking for coal. They had thought it odd as he had had a recent delivery; after the killings, they thought it suspicious. The HET report said this was part of an ongoing investigation.

On the first day Noel returned to work, six weeks after the killings, a friend told him that a mutual colleague had told her the day after the murders, 'I knew it was going to happen.' Noel questioned the mutual colleague and she said that she had been in Harry's Bar, Banbridge, on Friday 2 January, when people in her company were discussing the Central Bar bombing on New Year's Eve. Declan's name was mentioned. The colleague claims to have said, 'I work with his brother Noel and he is OK.' Noel informed the police but heard nothing more. According to the Barron report, Robin Jackson and his accomplices were seen celebrating in the same bar after the Silverbridge and Dundalk bombings on 19 December 1975.

Justice Barron concluded: 'The suspicion that there was collusion between the paramilitaries and the security/intelligence services is neither fanciful or absurd.'

On 29 February 1980, there was a breakthrough. Three UVF men were arrested shortly after the murder of Brendan McLaughlin in Belfast. Ballistics examination showed that the murder weapon, a Sterling sub-machine gun, found in their possession had also been used to kill the O'Dowds and eight other victims: Daniel Hughes in Boyle's Bar, Cappagh, County Tyrone, on 17 January 1974; James and Gertrude Devlin, at Congo, Dungannon, on 7 May 1974; Eugene Doyle and Arthur Mulholland, at Hayden's Bar, Dungannon, on 10 February 1975; and Fran O'Toole, Tony Geraghty and Brian McCoy of The Miami at Buskhill, Newry, on 31 July 1975. Between the attack on the O'Dowds in January 1976 and the murder of Brendan McLoughlin over four years later, the weapon's whereabouts is unknown. It may have been in storage as it was heavily greased and there are no ballistic records of it having been discharged in that time.

Of the four men convicted of these crimes, three were serving members of the UDR.

The weapon itself was standard British Army issue – very likely one of those stolen from a UDR base in Portadown on 23 October 1973, less than three months before the weapon was first used to commit murder.

The murder weapon might alternatively have come from a much larger raid on a joint UDR/Territorial Army base in Lurgan exactly one year before, on 23 October 1972. As the armed men left – with their haul that included 85 rifles, 21 sub-machine guns and 1,300 rounds of ammunition – one raider told the guard, 'Don't worry, we won't harm you. All we want are the weapons which we'll put to better use than you before December.' (An internal British Army briefing paper concluded: 'It is quite apparent that the offenders knew exactly what time to carry out the raid. The possibility of collusion is highly probable.')

An August 1973 British government report, 'Subversion in the UDR', found that 5–15 per cent of UDR soldiers 'have paramilitary links with widespread joint membership of the UDA.' Indeed, joint membership was 'positively encouraged', Anne Cadwallader writes in *Lethal Allies*.

Despite this briefing being sent to the then prime minister, Harold Wilson, and Margaret Thatcher, leader of the opposition, the UDR was given an enhanced role.

Of all the crimes committed with the same weapon that killed the three O'Dowds and wounded Barney, the Miami Showband massacre the previous July was geographically closest and the links to Robin Jackson most obvious. (Another weapon used in the Miami murders was also used in the Bleary Darts Club attack.)

In 2015, the O'Dowd and Reavey families jointly accused the British government of covering up collusion. 'It beggars belief that the British government is still hiding behind "national security"', said Barney. 'What are they afraid of? Is it because of the probable involvement of RUC agent Robin Jackson in the attack on our home? The HET report on the Miami Showband massacre established beyond any reasonable doubt that Jackson was an agent linked to the RUC.'

Barney's point was reinforced in 2021 when the Miami victims were awarded nearly £1.5 million (€1.75 million) in damages to settle claims against the British Ministry of Defence and the PSNI over suspected collusion with the loyalist murderers.

A month later, in January 2022, Northern Ireland's Police Ombudsman Marie Anderson found that police had demonstrated 'collusive behaviours' in relation to nineteen loyalist murders in the northwest between 1989 and 1993. In February 2022, relatives of some of those killed and wounded in a mass shooting at a Belfast bookmakers in 1992 settled High Court actions over alleged State collusion. Confidential resolutions were reached in claims brought against the chief constable of the PSNI, the British government and the Ministry of Defence. One of the weapons used had been given to a police agent within the UDA by the RUC's Special Branch.

***

The HET report concluded that the O'Dowds' religion, their relatively high profile, their involvement with the SDLP and Declan's arrest over the Bleary bingo bus shooting, even though he had been exonerated, might have been made them targets of the Glenanne UVF gang that included security force members.

In 2021, Boris Johnson's British government announced plans to stop further enquiries into allegations of wrongdoing during the Troubles. That same year, the North's Police Ombudsman asked the Public Prosecution Service to consider charging a former RUC officer over the loyalist murders of the three Reavey brothers.

In the words of William Faulkner, from *Requiem for a Nun*, 'The past is never dead. It's not even past.'

Fifteen

An Empty Grave

Noel O'Dowd and I arrange to visit the place where he grew up, and other parts of the parish touched by the Troubles, to converse in the tense that those who have lost someone dear to them know all too well as the ever-present past.

As we drive towards the O'Dowds' former home, we discuss the Bleary bingo bus attack on 1 August 1975 – the driver, Jimmy Marks, also drove the O'Dowds' school bus. That shooting would lead indirectly to the murder of the O'Dowds. Declan had satisfied the police of his innocence, but loyalist paramilitaries now had him and his family in their sights. 'Even though we were totally innocent, we felt we were marked men,' says Noel. 'A family discussion followed and it was felt that maybe it would be better if we left the North altogether.'

The milk round was sold. Barney, Barry and Plunkett Campbell, a family friend and the boys' former teacher, travelled to Ballina, County Mayo, to look at a pub for sale. A friend of Noel's had moved to London, so Noel applied to the civil service for a transfer. He told his department head that he thought he and his family were in danger. 'He told me if I thought my life was at risk I would have to get a letter from the police or a priest and I would be in London the following day.' Without any proof, Noel stayed put.

A few days before the shooting, Barry, Noel, Mary and Declan, the four oldest siblings, had sat up late over a few beers discussing the future. It was one of those days between Christmas and New Year's Eve, when daylight is fleeting and the wider world seems to be on hold. 'We all talked about the possibility of getting killed as it [the violence] was very close to us,' Noel recalls. 'I remember Barry saying that he wouldn't be afraid of dying, just for the people left behind.'

Noel and I visit the O'Dowds' family plot in Clare chapel's graveyard. Barney, echoing his father's standing up to the parish priest, had stubbornly refused a request by the clergy to permit his parents' plot to be moved to facilitate an extension to the vestry. Eight O'Dowds are buried there, dating back to Eleanor in 1858.

My neighbours are house-proud people. Grave-proud, too. They tend their plots with such a practical tenderness. It's not that the dead will know; it's that the living know what those now dead would want, that the gravel on their grave be as clean as the doorstep they scrubbed when they were alive, that their pride in their appearance lives on in the spruceness of their final resting place.

A woman we meet cleaning her family's grave remembers Barry helping her escape the Fairways nightclub in Dundalk via the fire exit during a bomb scare. It could have been New Year's Eve in 1975. Noel remembers he, Barry and a friend, Jim Thompson, had been at the Fairways that evening, 'not a great night as there was a bomb scare and the place was emptied and we all had to go home'.

When Noel and Barry got home, they learned that three people had been murdered in the Central Bar bombing. They were shocked but also scared that Gaffneys, the Gilford pub where they sometimes drank, might be next.

With the milk round gone, Noel had got himself a Saturday job in a clothes shop in Lurgan. On Saturday 3 January, Declan gave him a lift and as they were going up the lane they saw a large group of UDR soldiers in the field to their right. They thought nothing of it. Despite bomb scares and bombings, Saturday night was still Saturday night, so after work Noel rang his friend Jim and begged him to go to another dance in the Fairways. It was a good night and they didn't get home till after 2 a.m. Barney, Joe, Barry and Declan had spent the evening in McCartan's pub in nearby Donaghcloney, a rare night out for Barney.

Having established the context in which his family became victims, Noel drives us to his old home, 47 The Slopes, off Plantation Road in Bleary. The farmhouse is invisible from the road, 150 yards down a grassy laneway. You would have to know it was there. This suggests the killers had local knowledge. Noel regularly visits family nearby but rarely comes back here. 'There's nothing left. It only makes your heart heavy, you know.'

There is a modern house by the laneway leading to the O'Dowds, with a trampoline and toys in the garden, and I give thanks for a generation growing up in peace. The O'Dowds had a harder childhood, delivering milk and gathering ice-cold glass bottles at the crack of dawn before primary school. In winter, the frozen cream would turn the foil cap into a cone. The only day off they had was Sunday – but they had fun too, says Noel, playing football in the meadow behind the house. He was Pelé during the 1970 World Cup but mostly he was Martin Chivers, the Spurs striker.

Tucking the ends of my trouser legs into my socks to protect them from the mud, then clambering over a padlocked five-bar gate triggers memories of an innocent country childhood, but I chide myself that this was where innocence died. Where the lane turns to skirt a hedge as it enters a field, a stone gatepost lies in the grass, a stricken sentinel, like a milestone in the fall of civilisation.

'This is the scene of the crime as they say,' says Noel, as a rabbit darts across the lane. 'This was a hive of activity, with the coal lorry, the milk van, people coming and going, but no one heard a car that night.'

That no one heard a car that night is something all the O'Dowds remark upon, as if in that mystery an explanation is hiding in plain sight.

Listening to the sound of our feet reminds me of the BBC archive footage of the funerals, the only sound the scrape of hundreds of mourners' shoes following the all-too-traditional route to a country chapel. I think, too, how almost silent the killers' feet would have been, creeping down a green boreen and over fields.

The sinister sound of cars prowling in low gear on city streets is a feature of *Resurrection Man* by Eoin McNamee, his brilliant fictionalisation of the barbaric Shankill Butchers in Belfast. The implication of its absence in this case – the suggestion instead of the stealth of feet creeping across fields, of native scouts and trackers – hints at neighbourly treachery, local knowledge of back roads, shortcuts and weak points.

'There used to be a nice lawn there and a lovely apple orchard,' says Noel. Armagh nearby is the Orchard County. I think of the ground clotted by a glut of rotten apples, the rot that spread throughout the Murder Triangle and the lives destroyed as a result.

On the morning of the shootings, Sunday, 4 January 1976, Noel woke up alone in the house. Everyone else had gone to 9.30 a.m. Mass, which was also the funeral of a local man, Dan Murphy. Declan spent the afternoon working on his latest car, a Triumph 2000, with his friend Liam Moore. Noel, Barry and their friends – Seamus Cairns, Jim Thompson and Tony Rafferty – played poker for pennies. Noel's luck was out and Barry's was in. He had no luck either in his efforts to avoid church – he gave in to his mother and, at the third time of asking, set off for evening Mass in Craigavon, the Sabbath's last-chance saloon. He told Barry he would see him later and Barry replied, 'God willing.' He also spoke to Declan, who was planning to go to Belfast to see his girlfriend, Patricia. (Noel had the sense that both Barry and Declan were saying goodbye.)

Noel drove off just as his uncle Joe arrived. 'He took my place really. I drove out, he drove in.' If Noel had a narrow escape, so did his brothers Ronan and Loughlin, only 16 and 17, but old enough, in the Troubles' callous calculus, to have been shot. They were at their uncle Frank's.

Noel would normally have left Mass at Communion time but perhaps because he had arrived late, he stayed to the end. On the way home he stopped at a shop for cigarettes. He got back minutes after the shooting. Everything seemed normal. His uncle Joe's yellow Lada was parked at the front door. He parked beside Declan's Triumph in the backyard but had barely got out of the van when he heard his mother shouting, 'Is that you, Noel? Go and get your uncle Frank, your father and them have all been shot dead.'

Noel didn't ask any questions, just got straight back in the van and set off for his uncle's, a two-minute drive away. He knocked Frank's back door. His aunt Jean answered and he cried, 'Is Frank in?' Jean grabbed him by the shoulders and said, 'What's wrong?' Noel blurted out what his mother had told him. Jean said she would look after Loughlin and Ronan, who were in the yard. When Noel and his cousin Gregory got to the lane, they were stopped by a policeman who asked who they were. Noel told him and just asked, 'How many?' and the RUC man replied, 'Three.'

Inside the front door, Noel found Barney lying on blankets, his head on a pillow, being comforted by Mary. Declan was behind him but there was no sign of life. Mary was frantic and kept insisting her brother was still alive. Joe was in the doorway of the sitting room, face down and obviously dead. Barry was lying against the wall of the sitting room having been shot in the head. Kathleen was running around the yard with her head in her hands and could not be consoled. Noel remembers thinking, how are we going to recover from this?

Patricia rang from Belfast and had to be told that Declan, who was still lying beside the phone, had been shot dead.

Just before the ambulances arrived, Barney asked for Noel, who knelt down beside him and took his hand. 'I won't be back,' he said. 'Of course, you will,' Noel replied. 'Anyway, when this is all over,' Barney said, 'sell up and bring your mammy and the rest of the family to the Free State.' Noel told him, '*You* can do it.'

The first ambulance took Barney away, the next took Declan and Joe, then the first returned for Barry. A doctor arrived and gave Kathleen a sedative. Noel declined one for himself. No one asked him for a statement. 'There was no crime scene, no forensics were done but the bullet holes were all pinpointed.'

BBC Radio Ulster wanted Noel to do an interview. 'I was mad [keen] to do it but Mary wouldn't let me,' said Noel. 'Very wise. God knows what I would have said.' They did, however, issue a statement appealing for no retaliation.

Noel and Mary drove to Craigavon Hospital to see Barney, who was just out of the operating theatre. 'I sat down on the bed beside him and he scolded me,' Noel recalls. 'At that point I knew he was going to make it.'

It was a miracle that Barney survived the attack. Years later, he had an operation for a hernia carried out by the same consultant who treated him after being shot. His son Loughlin recalled, 'The consultant said, "Barney, I don't know if you remember me. I worked on you after you were shot. I always remembered you. Your case was so unique. We deal with car accidents and bomb injuries and all sorts of trauma, but you are the one we all remember. The bullet was going straight for your heart and for no reason the bullet turned 90 degrees. We never saw anything like that before."'

Seamus Cairns told Noel, 'Don't be ashamed to cry. If you can't do it here, go down to the fields by yourself. You will feel better for it.' But he couldn't cry. He was too numb. Later, he and Seamus went to the churchyard to pick graves. Loughlin and Ronan went to the hospital to accompany their brothers' bodies home. The house was full of people. News of the Kingsmill shooting broke. The family's plea for no retaliation had been ignored. They were horrified. The next day, they attended their uncle Joe's wake. Tuesday 6 January was a holy day of obligation, the Feast of the Epiphany, and Noel was astounded to see his mother go to Mass with her sister and friends. Her faith was what would get her through. Noel listened to his cousin Vivian and two friends tell hilarious stories about Barry. He felt guilty about laughing. Memories were all they had left, the connective tissue that would in time help bind the wounds.

The day of the funerals, Wednesday 7 January, dawned cold but clear. Noel was shocked to see TV cameras and so many mourners. Lots of Protestant neighbours were there. The funeral cortège did not follow the most direct route to Clare chapel but detoured past Blane's factory – Noel measured his height against its wall as a boy – to join Joe O'Dowd's funeral procession. Noel walked the three miles alongside Declan's girlfriend, Patricia. The chapel is only small so loudspeakers were set up outside so all the mourners could follow the service. 'I remember Father Lynch's eulogy,' says Noel. 'He said they were cut down like dogs.' 'Afterwards I felt so empty,' he recalls. His last memory of that day was ringing to tell Barney he was going to cancel the coal lorry that Friday, only for Barney to say, 'You will do no such thing – you have that lorry in Gilford for Friday morning.'

The Reaveys, despite their own grief, visited the O'Dowds the next day to comfort a family they did not know but who had suffered the same loss. Heart-mending humanity in the face of such evil. The North's saving grace. (Alan Black, the sole Protestant survivor of the Kingsmill massacre, met Barney and his family a few years ago. There is a photograph of the two together and they could be brothers.)

One week after the shooting, family friends, the Brewsters, had their newborn son christened. They asked Ronan to be the godfather and the baby was named Declan after his brother. That evening, Ronan and Loughlin flew to Manchester to stay with their uncle Frank Durnien in Sheffield, out of harm's way. Mary went back to college, so now there were only four around the table for dinner, when the week before there had been ten.

Kathleen became anxious about staying in the house at night, so for a few days they stayed overnight with Uncle Vincey and Aunt Bridie.

Ronan and Loughlin returned home after a fortnight and Barney was discharged from hospital around the same time.

Noel and his cousin Seamus visited the Reaveys on 18 January. Anthony, 17, had been seriously injured in the attack that had killed two of his brothers but was home from hospital. It struck Noel how much he resembled Declan, with his long red hair and easy charm. Twelve days later he collapsed and died of a brain haemorrhage. Noel and three uncles represented the O'Dowds at the funeral. 'My God,' says Noel. 'I have never seen such grief. For the Reavey family to have to go through it all again must have been too much to bear.'

The Month's Mind, to mark the passing of one month since the O'Dowds' deaths, was awful. 'I remember standing at the graves at the end of Mass with everyone bawling their eyes out.'

Terrified that the terrorists might return and fearful that their remaining sons might be lured into the IRA to seek revenge, Kathleen and Barney decided to move south. Navan, County Meath, was mentioned, as there were jobs at Tara Mines. A house was found. The coal round was given away. But weeks before they were due to leave, Noel and Kathleen were stopped at an illegal loyalist checkpoint and Noel was forced out of the car. Kathleen was traumatised and told Barney that they had to leave urgently. Noel left home for the last time on 2 August 1976. 'I was very emotional to be leaving my home where I was born and where my brothers and uncle died.'

Almost unbelievably, some people questioned the family's decision to go.

'We've been criticised for leaving, running away,' says Noel. 'People would say, you shouldn't have left your home, but they don't understand the deep trauma of what happened.'

***

Noel and I walk around the outside of his old home. (It strikes me later that it would not be out of place in the Ulster Folk Museum in Cultra, which tells the history of the North through vernacular buildings. A bleach green watch-house from the parish and a weaver's cottage from Ballydougan itself were moved there brick by brick to tell the story of the linen industry.)

The O'Dowds' abandoned farmhouse sums up the horror of the 1970s. The windows and doors are sealed, the house a silenced witness to the needless damage done. The steps to the back door are gone but the corrugated sheet blocking it has come away so we climb in. It feels like entering a mausoleum. There is some light from a hole in the roof and from our phones. Pigeons are roosting high up in the kitchen, where Kathleen retreated to after being confronted by the gunmen at the front door, Declan passing her to see what the commotion was.

'He was shot dead here,' says Noel as we stand in the hallway. 'He just fell there. That was one of the bullet holes.' He indicates a strike mark on door frame of the kitchen. We move into the sitting room, where Barney, Joe and Barry were shot. Noel describes the scene, the couch where Joe was sitting, the piano near which Barry was sat. The room had just been renovated, with a new picture window and fireplace, its crazy paving the height of 1970s fashion. Joe's last words were to compliment Barney on the fine job.

'Joe got up and made a dive. Joe was lying here, Barry was in this corner. Dad crawled over Joe's body into the hall.'

We move on to the bedrooms and I note the tiled floor and old lath and plaster. 'That's where the two of them were laid out. Do you see this room here? I was born in this room, myself and Loughie. Could have died here. Probably should have. I don't know why I escaped.' Cathal (11) was standing here when he saw the gunman.

There is a sleeping bag recently abandoned in one of the rooms. Who would sleep here?

Outside again, in the light, there are green fields and rosehips and hedgerows as far as the eye can see. It is so peaceful now. 'You'd wonder what it's all about, wouldn't you?' says Noel. 'Think of my poor mother.'

When the ambulance men lifted Barry's body that night, Noel says, the coins he'd won at cards fell from his pockets. Noel wanted to fetch a pail of water to clean up the blood and gore but neighbours insisted they would do it. Instead, he lifted the cards that were scattered on the floor. 'There was one spot of blood on a card. You know which one? The ace of spades, no word of a lie.'

***

When we remember loved ones we have lost, we reanimate them, put flesh on their bones, make them come alive even for those who never knew them.

Barry was christened Joseph Bernard but was always called Barry. He suffered when he was young with osteomalacia, a soft bone in his leg, missing out on schooling when he spent six months in hospital. Noel and Mary remember a teacher at primary school – a disgrace to the profession – calling Barry a useless lump of lard, but it didn't bother him.

He had weights put on his leg to build up his muscles and had to wear a calliper. 'But he broke it so many times,' Mary told me in a phone interview from her home in England, 'that they said it was too expensive to repair, yet he ended up with no limp. He rode our Connemara pony bareback and went flying through fields and rode it right into Cairnses' kitchen. He swung from the rafters in the barn, he was fearless. When the gunmen came, he tried to get away. Dad said Uncle Joe died mid-air as he leapt at the gunman. It was poignant that there was nothing Barry could do but try to hide like a child, there was no escape.'

The O'Dowds normally kept their licensed shotgun by the piano. That day – because there would be children at the family gathering – it had been moved to a bedroom. Part of me wants to think Barry was instinctively diving for it, and not for cover, as if seeking shelter needs any ornamentation.

'Barry was naturally very musical and had charm by the bucketful,' says Mary. 'He was a hard-working guy; a big, strong, physical lad, on a different trajectory to Declan, who was the repository of all Dad's hopes and dreams.'

'Barry's life was very short,' says Noel. 'Did he enjoy it? He certainly did. The best way to describe him is devil-may-care, he had no fear. He was extremely popular. He would do mad things. He was very, very strong but never abused his strength.'

Barry had been working as a dumper driver, constructing oil rigs on Shetland, but came home early for Christmas as he had broken his arm. He had remarked on the increased tension locally. His return trip had been booked for two days after the shooting.

Noel's cousin Niall recently met a man in Castlebar who had worked with Barry on Shetland. 'He was 19 and Barry looked after him like a child, he said.'

Barry had been going out with Imelda, a nurse from Camlough, but they had broken up as he had wanted to get married and she thought she was too young. For years after the murders, she came to visit the O'Dowds. 'Would he have had a great future ahead of him? I think he would. I think he would have been a good husband and a good provider. He would have loved children. One of my biggest regrets is that the boys both died young and there were no children.

'Barry had a good attitude to life. Nothing ever worried him. We were never in trouble with the police. We were respectful if boisterous. We had a work ethic. Our social life started when we were 17 and able to drive; before that there was football in the meadow. Barry preferred cars.'

'Declan was the most like Dad,' says Mary. 'Dad was clearly very ambitious in terms of being seen to be a Catholic who'd against the odds built his business. Declan was very friendly with customers. He was meticulously clean and tidy. I remember we were looking after someone's baby and it dirtied its nappy. The rest of us reacted in total disgust, whereas Declan changed the child's nappy. He just did things and did them well; he was highly domesticated.

'We only learned afterwards what a blow it was for Dad losing Declan because he was the one he intended would take over the business – he had the aptitude. Obviously, he never lived past 19, but he was emerging into the young man my father felt gave him the confidence to do almost anything.'

Noel says, 'When our house was raided and Declan carted off to Castlereagh [RUC interrogation centre], our mum made Declan give up the milk round. That was done to keep him safe, but it would have been a huge personal blow to Dad's idea of his business.'

Joe was Barney's oldest brother, 'a great man, very resolute, a great businessman,' says Noel. He worked in England during the Second World War, saving enough to buy a farm although his mother had to ask a Protestant friend to bid for him. He was always expanding, buying land, dealing in cattle and pigs at marts in Keady and Castleblayney.

'He was small and stocky but had a big voice. He knew how to enjoy himself, would have brought his daughters and his wife, Winnie, who he absolutely adored, to the seaside. He loved watching the wrestling. He was a very generous man, gave a lot of money to charity. That only came out after he died, people commented on how good he was.'

'When Joe died there was huge upheaval. Their eldest son, Seamus, moved to the home house; Gabriel, another son, moved to Seamus's house and Aunt Winnie moved to Gabriel's house in Craigavon. Winnie was a beautiful, elegant lady. Not only had she to cope with the loss of her husband, she also buried her daughter Una in 1988 when she died of cancer, aged only 44. I have no doubt that was brought on by the trauma of witnessing the shootings. Winnie bore her grief with great dignity on both occasions.'

Noel has lived in the South for almost fifty years but feels he never really settled.

'I hated it down here, even though I was married and had a family, I never felt at home. I felt like a refugee at first. But Navan has been very good to us. We have all done well. Some days you feel better than others. It took me about five years to cry.'

Mary, by contrast, had already got used to life away. She had graduated from Trinity College Dublin in 1975 and was training to be a teacher in Newcastle when the murders happened. 'I had got to hate it [Northern Ireland], I still hate it, I have to say, absolutely hate it. The day after the boys died, I woke up and for a split second forgot what had happened, then you realise the life that you thought you had had completely vanished. That was horrendous.

'Every night instead of setting the table for ten people, suddenly there were so few knives and forks, cups and saucers round the table. Even though the damage had been done we were terrified at night. When Dad came home, we thought, what if they feel the need to come back and finish him off? I insisted on pulling wardrobes across windows, which was ridiculous. My mum was terrified. I couldn't face coming back until they'd moved; the absolute terror and fear of being back in that place never left me. I was convinced we were all going to die.'

Mary recalls with gratitude the community's support but singles out Eamon Cairns. 'A quiet, intuitive man, he made no fuss, just sat, chatted and soothed us with his steady presence.'

Noel agrees. 'Eamon was a great neighbour. From Barry down, there was pretty much a Cairns for every one of us. We were very linked as families. The kindness they showed us. After we left, we used to go back twice a year, in January for the anniversary Mass and in June for the blessing of the graves. The Cairnses had us back for breakfast every year. We always dreaded the possibility of something happening to them.'

Barney, speaking to WAVE, a victims' support group, said, 'I wasn't half myself really. I'd wait till Kathleen went to sleep and I slipped out and I walked the roads, some nights all night until daylight, I used to go and look at people's cattle in fields, one thing or another, anything at all. You outlived it by the fact you couldn't hate and got away from any reason to hate. While you were there, hate was being driven at you and there was the chance of you adopting it yourself. We were so fortunate that Kathleen forced us to go south, because neighbours went through the same thing but they stayed and they went through hell. It's not away from us, do you know what I mean? Oh, by no means, it can't go away, it just can't go away.'

***

Violence can provoke radicalisation as well as revulsion. A cousin of Noel's was 22 when he was convicted of murdering 34-year-old off-duty UDR man David Chambers in Lurgan in 1984. A 200lb bomb exploded in a nearby derelict building injuring two policemen as they arrived at the scene. He served fourteen years in prison before he was freed in 1998 under the early release scheme of the Belfast Agreement.

What strikes Noel is how his father's generation all went to school together and so Barney and the Blanes, McCombs, Sergeants, Chambers, Wilsons, Larmours and Joyces were all very friendly because they knew each other. 'We never had that with people [Protestants] of our own age group. We'd bump into them at the shop, some would be customers, we knew them to say hello to but we never knew them properly.'

These Protestant neighbours 'would have been very, very sorry about what happened to us, very supportive. An old Protestant farmer, Norman Chambers, in his innocence, a couple of days after my father was shot, went to visit him in hospital with a bag of sweets. My father was under police guard! There was such goodness in that parish. The local shopkeeper sent down food and cigarettes. There was a lot of kindness destroyed by the Troubles.'

The memory stirs another recollection.

'Mary and myself went on the milk round every Saturday and Mrs Watson always came out with sweets for us without fail. There were also three McComb sisters, Jenny, Rita and Lily, and every Saturday they gave us two bars of Cadbury's chocolate, which were sixpence each. Your da wouldn't even buy you that!'

In 2010, Barney and Noel were home visiting family when they heard that Lily, then 95, was in hospital. 'I bought the biggest box of chocolates I could find,' says Noel. 'In the hospital they didn't know her as Lily, they knew her as Bertha. They told her these two men want to talk to you. She said, "Who have we?" My father said, "Who delivered your coal and your milk?" And she said, "Bernard O'Dowd. Is that you, Bernard?" He said, "It is," and she burst into tears. And she said, "Is that you, Noel? You were a lovely young boy." I handed her the chocolates as a payback for all she had given me. That was special.'

***

When Kathleen died in December 1999, she was buried not in her native North but near Navan, her adopted home in County Meath.

The family then made a decision that would not be out of place in a Greek tragedy; a decision that speaks to the unresolved trauma of the Troubles, and the fathomless depth of familial love. Kathleen's four surviving sons would exhume their brothers' bodies and rebury them beside their mother. A family torn apart would be reunited.

'An awful lot of people would disagree with it,' says Noel, but his father 'didn't want the grave in the North to go to rack and ruin. There'd be no one there to look after them.'

Ronan applied for permission on behalf of the family. The health service supplied protective clothing, disinfectant and a tent to screen them. The RUC stood guard. Watched over by Barney, on 31 August 2000, Noel, Ronan, Cathal and Loughlin took turns shifting six feet of soil. They were helped once more by Eamon Cairns, whose two murdered sons lay buried just a few yards away. Kathleen's sister Patsy came from Fermanagh to represent her family.

'My sisters were against us doing it ourselves,' recalls Noel. 'They thought it would be tough on us, but why would you involve anyone else? It was very rewarding in a funny sort of way. It sounds horrific but it wasn't, believe it or not. It was a good experience.'

As it had rained heavily the night before, the digging only took a few hours. They transferred their brothers' remains into body bags and then into new coffins.

They travelled south together, passing the Fairways Hotel, once a regular Saturday night haunt for Noel and his brothers. 'I thought that was quite poignant,' says Noel. 'I lost not just two brothers but my two closest friends. You don't realise your best friends are your family at that age.' Barry and Declan were reburied that evening after a short prayer service. 'My son got the chance to carry the coffins,' recalls Noel. 'He knew it was the closest he would ever get to them. It wasn't a bad experience at all, it was quite a rewarding one, just an emotional day. They were our own flesh and blood.'

'It gave dad the chance to bury his children,' Loughlin said. 'It gave him the chance to carry their coffins, which is a big thing up North.'

The writer John Berger once captured exquisitely how one's final resting place can draw the sting from death if it means being reunited with a loved one.

'What reconciles me to my own death more than anything else is the image of a place: a place where your bones and mine are buried, thrown, uncovered, together. They are strewn there pell-mell. One of your ribs leans against my skull. A metacarpal of my left hand lies inside your pelvis. (Against my broken ribs your breast like a flower.) The hundred bones of our feet are scattered like gravel. It is strange that this image of our proximity, concerning as it does mere phosphate of calcium, should bestow a sense of peace. Yet it does. With you I can imagine a place where to be phosphate of calcium is enough.'

***

It is a cold and crisp February afternoon in 2022, the day after Ireland's first Six Nations match of the season, for me the unofficial start of spring. Eleanor O'Dowd has invited me to dinner to meet Mary – the eldest of the surviving O'Dowd siblings, who is home to visit her family – in person. I'll also be meeting Cathal and Loughlin for the first time. But first, there is something I want to see and Noel again has agreed to be my guide. We drive once more along country roads then pull up at a laneway barred by a locked gate. This time, there is a side gate on a latch so I am spared the acrobatics. The laneway, like the one leading to the O'Dowds' old home, has a grassy fringe up the middle.

As we round the bend, an old church in ruins comes into view, surrounded by a scattering of gravestones, old and new. The O'Dowd family plot is large, but mostly unoccupied. The kerbing can't be that old but it already looks weathered, venerable with age. Purple heather adds a dash of colour to the grass-covered grave. Up until very recently, Barney took sole responsibility for its maintenance. The gravestone records the family story one last time: 'In loving memory of Kathleen O'Dowd (née Durnien), Kilcarne, Navan, Died 15th December 1999. Her beloved sons Barry, aged 24 years, Declan, aged 19 years, who died tragically because of their faith in an attack on their home, 4 January 1976, reinterred from The Clare, Tullylish, County Down, 31 August 2000. May they rest in peace.'

This is, of course, no happy ever after. But there is serenity in the simplicity of the scene. I tell Noel how Nikki and I visited the monastic settlement of Glendalough when my youngest was very young. As we ambled past the gravestones that surrounded the old round tower that looks like a Stone-Age space rocket, Martha studied one gravestone with a particularly long list of interred relatives for a while, then said, 'Aw, all family dead together.' To a child's eye then, there was something sweet about siblings and parents together for eternity. To an adult's eye now, taking in this grave and its surroundings, the boys' reburial beside their mother, far from the site of trauma, makes complete sense for the first time. I can truly believe that there is peace in this place in which to rest.

Barney died on 10 April 2024, a few weeks shy of his 101st birthday, his impressive longevity only emphasising how cruelly abbreviated were the lives of Declan, Barry and Joe.

Micky Toman made the journey south to pay his respects. He grew tearful as he spoke of his father's looming anniversary. 'The loss is still there,' he said. In the words of Emily Dickinson: 'They say that "time assuages,"– / Time never did assuage; / An actual suffering strengthens, / As sinews do, with age.'

At the wake and the funeral, Northern and Southern accents mingled. Southern society, in turning its back on violence, often turned its back on victims too, but the wound of partition has been cicatrised by this Northern family forming new bonds down South. All but one of Barney's children live within a few miles of each other, recreating the tightly-woven extended family they had left behind them.

Fr Martin McErlean, who celebrated the funeral Mass, had worked with Barry on Shetland and they had been due to fly back together the day after the party at which he was murdered.

'Barney achieved his own justice,' he told mourners, 'by outliving the forces that had sought to destroy him and his family. One of Barney's grandchildren remarked that a life lesson he learnt from him was not to hold hatred in his heart. Barney had every reason to be consumed by bitterness. He chose a different route … the belief that understanding must win out over hatred.'

Barney refused to let tragedy loosen his grip on life or to define him as a person. He was laid to rest with Kathleen and his two murdered sons, whose plot he had lovingly tended well into his tenth decade.

One of Barney's eighteen grandchildren, Katie, is a cardiac surgeon in a Belfast hospital, so the O'Dowd bloodline and tradition of serving the community lives on in the North. A reminder too that broken hearts can with time and care be mended.

Sixteen

A Soldier, a Musician, a Policeman, a Nurse

The night before our conversation at his home in Richhill, a pleasant village halfway between Gilford and Armagh city, Robert Harrison got out the scrapbook that tells the story of his father Bobbie's life and untimely death and went through it with his wife, Lorna. We go through it together too. There's Robert on a donkey in Omeath with his dad. Here's Bobbie in his nurse's uniform. But I wince when Robert turns a page and I see the bullet-riddled police car that illustrates the newspaper report of his father's murder.

Bobbie Harrison with his son Robert in Omeath, Co. Louth.

I can well imagine why, when he set it down the night before, he then said to his wife, 'We've looked at all these letters and photos. We'll have a look now at some of the happy ones, nice places we've been as a family, the boys growing up.'

***

Serving the Crown has long been a tradition for Gilford's Harrison family, whose eldest sons for generations have been christened Robert.

Bob Harrison fought in both world wars, serving in the Second World War in a British Army regiment made up of First World War veterans. Family lore has it that when his troop's train stopped at a station in Belgium, he bumped into his brother who was serving in another regiment and whom he had not seen in over a year.

When a telegram arrived at Bob's home in Gilford some months after he had been reported missing, his wife, fearing the worst, told her eldest son, Bobbie, to open it. The news, however, was good. Bob was recovering in a field hospital.

There was a rain barrel in the backyard of his old mill house on Gilford's High Street and when he got home, he washed himself bare-chested at it every day of the year, his braces hanging down. He had been gassed in the war, however, and all Robert Harrison can remember of his grandfather is an old man sitting coughing in the corner with a spit bottle.

Bob's son Bobbie Harrison was born in 1927 so he was spared or missed out on the war, but in 1947 he joined the Ulster Special Constabulary, better known as the B Specials. If you were a Protestant and a unionist, like Bobbie, the force was a bulwark against the republicans who threatened to overthrow or undermine the State. If you were a Catholic and a nationalist, the Specials were a constant source of sectarian harassment. Bobbie was no bigot, though, and had Catholic friends and colleagues all his life.

About the same time as he joined the B Specials, Bobbie was serving his apprenticeship with a local farmer called Kidd, who had a butcher's shop by the railway bridge in Laurencetown.

The parish priest used to joke that if anyone told him in confession that they had eaten Kidd's sausages on a Friday, back then a day when Catholics were supposed to abstain from eating meat, he would dismiss the idea of it being a sin as the sausages consisted mostly of breadcrumbs. My mother, however, says they were delicious. 'I remember thinking when I'm a big girl and earn any money I'll buy a pound of Kidd's sausages and eat them all myself.'

She also remembers walking with her friend Katherine Duffy one snowy winter's morning in about 1950 to the village pump on the other side of the River Bann to fetch a pail of water. 'Bobbie had a striped apron on and had a white pail in each hand and he ran in front of us, and filled the two pails, and called out, "Ah girls, I got in front of you" – but he only went a few steps when the feet went from under him and the water went flying. We laughed and laughed and so did he. He was a perfect gentleman, a lovely man.'

So Bobbie was a well-known figure in my village, popular and good-natured.

Bobbie's wife, Gladys (née Browne), grew up in Tullylish. Her father and mother had met in Castle Coole in Fermanagh, where she was a cook and he was a farm labourer. They moved first to another big estate in Loughgall and then to Gilford Castle, where the job came with a tied cottage in Tullylish. One of Gladys's best friends growing up was Eileen McInerney (née Byrne) and even after Gladys married and moved to Gilford, they still met up religiously every Sunday. Eileen, a Catholic, would go to early Mass in Laurencetown, at 8.30 a.m., to be back for 10 a.m., when Gladys would call for a cup of tea and a chat, until the second bell rang at 11.20 a.m., calling Gladys to her service in All Saints', the Church of Ireland church in Tullylish. Bobbie would often go too, and if Barney O'Dowd called to deliver the milk, the two men would enjoy a good argument about politics. Noel O'Dowd remembers, 'Barney would have been friendly with Bobbie and his wife, Gladys. They were his customers and they were lovely people.'

'Obviously they were complete opposites but each gave as good as he got,' says Robert.

There is more to life than politics, though. 'Eileen's husband, Jimmy McInerney, developed cancer,' says Robert, 'and my father would have sat with him when he was dying because my father was a nurse, you see, and he knew him. That's the sort of thing he did, like. I'm near sure he was with him when he died. People were different then.'

Robert and Micky McInerney, Eileen and Jimmy's son, were also close friends. When Micky got married a few years after Bobbie's murder, his bride, Catherine, wore Robert's wife Lorna's wedding dress.

***

Bobbie Harrison spent most of his adult life in uniform but the one he wore the longest, for twenty-six years, was that of a nurse at Bannvale Hospital in Gilford, a residential facility based in a former linen mansion that cared for more than a hundred people with intellectual disabilities.

'He was the longest-serving nurse when he was killed,' says Robert. 'My father would have gone down on his days off and played the accordion for them. All the boys loved him.'

One Sunday, the head nurse, Billy Bogues, had a problem. He had no Catholic nurse available to accompany the Catholic patients to Mass. Bobbie volunteered. One of the boys, Victor, used to shout things at people. 'Everything was going grand,' says Robert, 'till whatever the priest said, Victor shouted out, "You're a bloody liar." My father says, "I was doing a good deed and I know rightly they'll think I put him up to it."'

'My father was a prankster,' says Robert. Another colleague, Sid Deans, had an allotment in the grounds and Bobbie planted plastic daffodils in it in the middle of the night one winter. 'Another man said, "My God,

Bobbie Harrison, right, with the Gilford Memorial Amateur Flute Band.

Deans, I never seen daffodils at this time of year." They all went up and Deans effed and blinded, but my father could keep such a straight face. It was all innocent fun, though, not making fun.'

Music was Bobbie's big passion. He was the leading drummer in the Gilford Memorial Amateur Flute Band. Robert in turn became a musician. 'All the kids ran down Keady Row to see the band,' says Robert. 'The Catholic children were saying, I wish we could play in the band. But all that changed. Our band played music; we had armrests with cards. The so-called bands of today wouldn't be able to read music. I would only listen to a good flute band, or silver band – that's what I call a band.'

Bobbie could play any instrument, says Robert. He made a xylophone out of hardwood in the Bannvale workshop and painted it different colours to help teach the boys how to play it. He played accordion in a showband in the 1960s and even featured on local television on a show called *Teatime with Tommy*, performing with his brother Tommy and a friend, Billy Chambers. The same trio performed for the Marquess of Hamilton in Fermanagh every New Year's Eve.

He had a beautiful voice and was in great demand to sing and perform at fundraising concerts for everyone from the Salvation Army to the St Vincent de Paul in Banbridge. He used to say to Danny Hollywood [the St Vincent's organiser], 'Them people will be sick listening to me,' but Danny would reply, 'Aw no, they all want you back.'

'My father never took a drink or smoked in his life,' Robert says. 'He didn't like it if a man spent half their week's pay on drink on a Friday night in Molly Smith's and his wife had five children. But he didn't mind a man having a drink. My mother would have been more, 'Aw, that's terrible.' But if you went into a room and he was playing the accordion, he would have the neck open and his face would have been as red as a beetroot and you would have said, that man's half full, but it was just because he enjoyed it.'

But in 1966, after his daughter Diane, Robert's sister, died of cancer aged just three years and nine months, Bobbie was not able to sing in his church choir for over a year. 'He had a lot of tragedy,' says Robert, who has a letter from the local vicar saying what an absolute delight it was to hear that voice again. Sadly, however, he has lost the tapes he once had of his father singing.

'My father was always busy,' says Robert. 'If he wasn't working in the hospital, he was on duty wherever he was serving. If he wasn't doing that, he was entertaining. My father always worked for his family. He took a week off every year to pull apples at McNab's out at Moyallan, and he got a bounty each year for a week spent at a UDR camp. That extra money was always spent taking us on holiday. It might have been a tin hut in Newcastle with no running water, but we always had a holiday. When Granda wasn't fit to go on holiday, Dad stayed behind to look after him.'

Bobbie liked shooting, be it rabbits, pigeons or ducks, and the local gentry let him shoot on their estates, but Robert thinks the part he really enjoyed was being out in the fresh air. He taught Robert how to shoot and took him to band practice and taught him to swim in Gilford lido, an old mill facility that US troops had converted into an outdoor pool during the Second World War.

***

When the Troubles broke out, the report that the British government commissioned into policing in the North recommended the disbandment of the B Specials. In their place, the British government established the Ulster Defence Regiment, a locally recruited British Army regiment whose members would serve only in the North. Many of its first recruits, including Bobbie, were former B Specials. He joined on a five-year contract as a lance corporal, rising swiftly to sergeant and then staff sergeant. Bobbie was attached to a unit in Banbridge – where Robin Jackson also served for six months but Robert does not remember his father ever mentioning him. 'There is bad apples in every barrel,' he says. He does recall another of his father's UDR colleagues, Jim Elliott, who was 'tortured and murdered' by the IRA.

Three nights a week, after a twelve-hour shift at the hospital, Bobbie would be picked up at 9 p.m. and be on patrol till 4.30 a.m. He could have pulled rank and stayed at the base 'but he always said he wouldn't ask men to do something he wouldn't do himself'. The UDR wanted him to stay on and apply for promotion to the rank of major, but when his contract was up, he was 48. 'He said, "I've done enough now, I want to spend more time with my family."'

However, the RUC in Gilford approached him as they were short of men and needed an experienced hand to man the station. 'He said, "No, I'm finished, I don't want to be out to three in the morning any more, it's not fair on my wife and daughter,"' says Robert, who had joined the RUC Reserve himself the year before. 'They knew all that had gone on with my sister dying. They said, "Look, Bobbie, you can come in on some of your days off and do 10 a.m. to 5 p.m." Of course, ironically, he was murdered at 20 past 8 on a Saturday night.'

Bobbie was on duty on New Year's Eve in 1975 when the Central Bar was blown up. Robert's father-in-law would have been in the pub that night except his wife had a terrible migraine. Robert and Lorna were at a police dance at Bannville House in Lenaderg. 'They stopped the music and announced that there had been a serious incident in Gilford and asked anyone who hadn't been drinking to get ready to go on duty. I was sure my father had been killed.'

Did he worry about his father all the time? 'God help the people who were murdered [in the Central Bar bombing], but I was never as glad to see anyone in my life when I saw him in the square,' Robert says. He spent the night protecting a damaged premises across the road from the pub from looters.

***

Robert vividly remembers the night that his father was murdered, 5 February 1977.

'I left my dad down at the police station at 20 past 6. He had a big heavy police coat for if he was going out doing road stops. I asked if he had his keys. He says, "They're in my pocket," and then he said, "I'll see you in the morning and we'll go to church." That was his last words to me.'

Later that evening, a woman rang from a phone box to say that incendiary bombs had been planted in Kane's drapery store in Gilford. Bobbie and a colleague, Jim Davidson, went to investigate.

Mr and Mrs Kane, an elderly couple, lived above the shop. Bobbie and Jim searched the shop but found nothing. 'The boys who done this are probably standing about laughing at us wasting our time,' Bobbie said to Mrs Kane. She told Robert that these were his father's last words to her. 'Bobbie phoned the station on the landline, as this was more secure than the police radio, to say that they would stay local so that if the Kanes were worried, they could ring and the officers could come back. The Kanes had every reason to be worried. The year before, Willie Herron, his wife, Beth, and their daughter Noeline had been murdered in an IRA firebomb attack on their drapery shop in Dromore, a nearby town, while they slept in their home above it.

The IRA gunmen struck just as Bobbie and Jim returned to their car. Jim was kneeling on the driver's seat to reach across to lift the button to unlock the front passenger door for Bobbie. Robert describes his father's murder. 'They came up behind him and fired forty shots from three feet in twenty seconds. He didn't even see them.' Jim miraculously survived as most of the bullets went under him. However, his injuries were so severe that surgeons had to amputate his whole forearm.

The gunmen drove off in the direction of Lurgan, but Robert believes there must have been another gang member who gave the signal to the gunmen as they lay in wait around a corner. 'They were as guilty as the ones who pulled the trigger.' So too the woman who made the hoax call.

He believes there had been a dummy run earlier that week to test police response times. On the night of the shooting, the IRA had also made hoax calls to Tandragee, Portadown and Lurgan so that by tying up a lot of police resources they could escape more easily. A burned-out car was found at Silverwood, Craigavon, the next day.

'Everybody thought it was me that had been killed because I was the greenhorn, the inexperienced one,' Robert says. 'It's sod's law. I was on duty the day before. There was actually a force order came out that two brothers or a father and son, blood relatives, weren't to go out in the vehicle together. That only came out a few months before my father was shot. We would often have been out together in the same car. It would have finished my mother off.'

A certificate from the RUC chief constable – dated the day before Bobbie was murdered, confirming that Bobbie had met the standards required of an RUC reservist – arrived in the post as he lay in his coffin. Robert points out his father's serial number. 'He was number 5523, I was 5408.'

He shows me a photograph of his father's funeral. He was one of the pall-bearers, but the photographer had been instructed not to take his photograph to protect him. He points out two of the other RUC men carrying his father's coffin. One, Jim Wright, who sang in the Salvation Army, would also be killed by the IRA, while another, Kenny Vennard, would be shot but survived.

A letter of thanks from the RUC benevolent fund to Mrs Harrison acknowledged receipt of £613.75 'in lieu of wreaths at your late husband's funeral. It is very gratifying for us to know that at a time of great personal tragedy you remembered others who have trod a similar path to yourself.' This was the largest amount ever received, it said, which showed the esteem in which Bobbie was held by the RUC and in the community.

Mrs Harrison received £3,500 in compensation for his murder and their daughter Jill got £500. 'As my mother said, it wouldn't matter if they'd offered her a million,' said Robert. 'I remember being in court with my mother and the judge saying, "You do realise when your husband put this uniform on it was like putting a target on his back."'

Robert was only 21 when his father was murdered. His mother was ill with pleurisy and his little sister was just nine years old 'so I was sort of left man of the house,' he says.

Robert remained in the RUC Reserve for a time without going on duty again. He had been informed that his name and his father's name and their personal details had been found during a search operation in Lurgan, so among other things he had to change his car. 'They wanted me to go out on duty and I could carry a firearm, but off duty I couldn't have one because they were afraid of what I might do. Basically they were saying, I couldn't trust you.'

Even after he resigned from the RUC Reserve 'for a lifetime after that I had to get under my car every morning [to check for explosive devices]. That threat was always there. As ex-police, you're just abandoned.'

Four years after Robert's father was murdered, four local youths were convicted for daubing IRA slogans on the Harrison home and that of Robert's in-laws a few doors down. Before he was sentenced, the ringleader had told Robert's mother he would burn her out the next time. Another of the culprits, though obviously unrelated, was also called Harrison. It is one of the tragedies of the North that many of those who intermarry, and their descendants, have not formed a middle ground but merely crossed from one camp to another.

***

There is no shortage of memorials to Bobbie Harrison. His name appears on a plaque to murdered officers in Lurgan PSNI station and on a memorial in Banbridge to security forces personnel killed in the Troubles. There are also personal plaques in the Orange hall in Gilford, where he was a member, and in All Saints' Tullylish, above the pew where his wife, Gladys, used to sit. Robert and Lorna visited the National Arboretum in England, where his name unusually appears in three different places, reflecting the three forces in which he served.

'Ironically,' says Robert, 'the only place his name is not on is where it should be, on Gilford war memorial, 200 yards from where he was murdered.'

Another very personal tribute was the decision in 1978 of the Gilford Amateur Flute Band, in which Bobbie had played for a lifetime, to rename itself the Robert Harrison Memorial Band. However, when a younger generation fell for bands with lots of big drums which made the most noise – 'Rumble come thump as I call them,' says Robert, 'no music, plenty of noise' – and did not require hours of practice to learn the tunes, the memorial band faded away.

'My father had no time for flag-waving people or throwing stones,' says Robert. 'He was a unionist. His father had fought in both world wars. He honoured that. If someone said, "Oh you're putting your flag out for the Twelfth," he said, "No, I'm putting it out for the Battle of the Somme." He was in the Orange and the Black and the band, but my father's motto in life was give no offence but take no offence. Everyone knew what he was, that he was in the B Specials, the UDR and the police reserve. He would say, "Wait till I tell you something, you see where I work, there's boys and young men and they're mentally handicapped and I never ask anyone what church they go to." He was uphold the law, honour the Queen, keep the laws of the land and that's what I am here to help do.'

Robert shows me an article about his father's murder by a local journalist, Stephen Preston, which he says summed him up the best.

It was the largest ever funeral in the parish, Preston wrote, adding, 'Perhaps the greatest if unremarked tribute to his memory was the great number of Catholics who were present.'

How did Robert's mother cope with her husband's murder? 'To the world she was all right,' he says. 'The RUC welfare were very good to her. She always said to me, after my sister was married and moved out, it's all right being out but when you turn the key and there's no one in the house, that's when it hit her.'

Her doctor, Dr Davin, who was also my doctor as a boy, knew Bobbie well from visiting sick patients at Bannvale. He thought it would be good for Gladys to get out of the house, so she got a job as receptionist in Gilford health centre from 1979 to 2000, which she loved.

Robert doesn't know why, but twenty-three years after Bobbie was killed, Gladys started losing weight. 'Something just triggered with her. She just gave up,' says Robert. She wrote to friends saying that she thought she had cancer. She went to see a consultant, who diagnosed depression. She began talking about her daughter who had died. 'She'd only ever talked about her on her anniversary or her birthday.' She died in Robert's arms in her bed on a Saturday night. The day after the funeral, Gladys's RUC liaison officer, Alison, received a letter from her thanking her for all she had done.

***

No one was ever charged with Bobbie's murder. Robert waited until his mother had died before he asked the HET to re-examine the case. 'I didn't want to do it while she was alive; it's raking up a fire that's almost out,' he said. 'I asked for the investigation to be reopened. It looked like nobody ever done anything about it.'

The HET team were 'nice enough people', Robert says, but the whole thing was 'a papering-over exercise'. It was, however, confirmed that the same weapon used to kill Bobbie was also used in the murder of RUC inspector Harry Cobb in Lurgan a few months later, on 24 July 1977. One of the two men jailed for that murder became a hunger striker. Inspector Cobb's widow, Florence, is quoted in David Beresford's *Ten Men Dead*: 'After they die, they will be forgotten, just as those policemen and soldiers who died are forgotten after a while, except by those who loved them.'

Robert would still like to see his father's killers convicted, even though the punishment will never fit the crime. 'You still would like to see justice, but justice now means they're out in a year so it's no justice.'

On anniversaries, at Christmas and Easter and on Mother's Day, or if they are passing, Robert and Lorna visit Bobbie's and Gladys's grave and tend to it. 'We have artificial flowers. I hate to see dead flowers.'

How does he feel now about his father's murder?

'I still would feel very bitter, not at Catholics but at republicans,' he replies. 'To me it's just pure poison, not just what they did to my father. Lorna's dad is 92, her mother was 84 when she died. They saw us married, they saw both our children being born, both those boys being married and every one of their children. I would feel very bitter on that count. My father never even seen us married.'

Robert Harrison says that Bobbie's sister Martha could also never forgive what happened to him. 'My father was born there, brought up there, worked there, served the community there, worked in that hospital for twenty-four years. Martha just couldn't believe why anyone would want to do that to him.'

Robert asks what sort of reaction I get from other people when I ask whether they are bitter. He is genuinely curious.

'Maybe I'm wrong. My father brought me up to be honest and go to church. I can't understand people who say, "I bear no malice." They are probably better than I am. It'll be forty-six years in February and I honestly couldn't forgive the people who did that. Nobody has any right to do that. I've got on with my life as you can see, I've a good family, but they ruin people's lives.'

He makes no distinction between loyalist and republican paramilitaries. 'As far as I'm concerned, a terrorist is a terrorist.'

***

Jim McAllister, a republican politician and poet from Crossmaglen in south Armagh, wrote a poem imagining his fate if the IRA were to shoot down a British Army helicopter in which he was being flown out as a prisoner. He would be at home and at peace, unlike the outsiders:

> And should my bones fall on McCooey's Creggan,
> Or the yellow hills of Lurgancullenboy
> Or my ancestral rocks at Carrigans,
> Slievenacapal, Carricknageera or the fortress of Lislea
> Should my bones smash on Sturgan Brae
> Or bleach in Camloch waters,
> I'd be at home in my land;
> The rest at map reference
> F13, Sheet 3, South Armagh.

The poem, which he recites in Ken Loach's film *Hidden Agenda*, comes to mind when writing about Bobbie Harrison. While McAllister was able to 'other' the British soldiers killed in south Armagh by highlighting that the locality where they died was just a grid reference to them, he wouldn't have been able to do the same with victims such as Bobbie Harrison in the RUC or UDR, who were as at home and familiar with the streets and fields as their killers, if not more so. Bobbie was murdered by the IRA in the village where he was born and reared, where his family had lived for generations, on a street where he could have named every shop and every shopkeeper.

Seventeen

A Cold House for Catholics

We were visiting family in Dublin when Bobbie Harrison was murdered. Mammy was particularly upset because she had known Bobbie since she was a child but our parents kept the news from us, shielding us from the Troubles as best they could. My nose was never out of a book but I was not street-smart. As people used to say after someone got a smack in the mouth, I was often talking when I should have been listening. Having grown up in a Catholic cocoon, I was oblivious to sectarianism. I was about to get a crash course.

As if the North needed another divide, the eleven-plus exam created a new one – streaming us into comprehensive or grammar schools. The unfairness of having your educational fate sealed at 11 years of age is stark. Ostensibly meritocratic, the test is won or lost on a playing field that is never level, where middle-class children will always have home advantage. In my case, this was literally so. For whatever reason, perhaps a lack of numbers sitting the test from my school, we were bussed to another school to do the exam. The eleven-plus was a snake for many children but turned out to be a ladder for me.

Just as looms had replaced loam as a fertile means for Catholics to prosper, Stormont's 1947 Education Act, introduced in the face of fierce Orange opposition, offered an equal opportunity to escape the factory floor.

Most from Laurencetown who passed the exam went to Catholic grammar schools in Newry. Like my siblings and most of my cousins, I went to Banbridge Academy, a State grammar and thus effectively a Protestant one. Catholics made up roughly 10 per cent – it was not so much mixed as slightly diluted Orange. Newry was twelve miles further away and suffered much more from bomb and gun attacks than Banbridge. But I think our parents' primary motivation was a perhaps naive ecumenism.

In the village, passing the eleven-plus marked you out as a minority; going to the Academy doubly so. However, in much the same way as the only grief I ever got when going out with a Protestant was from members of her community, I heard more anti-Catholic abuse said to my face at school than I ever heard anti-Protestant abuse expressed in exclusively Catholic company. It was easier for me to marry an English Jew than it would have been to marry a Northern Protestant.

Make friends, my mother told me ahead of my first day. Ask someone to sit beside you. Unfortunately, I chose someone from Hilltown, a Protestant from a predominantly Catholic village. Now that the boot was on the other foot – and he was in the majority – he was going to kick with it. He spat in my face once during some chasing game that term, which crossed a line, and his fellow Protestants told him so.

Days later, I was sitting on the high beam outside the gym with the rest of the boys in my class, before our first PE class, when a pupil asked us what religion we were. My heart sank but I took some vague comfort that although I was the only Catholic, the questioner was the only Baptist. Of course, that distinction meant nothing: it was a Catholic versus Protestant thing, full stop. Two Protestant boys had a Catholic parent, yet one was still sectarian.

Every day someone called me a Fenian, a rebel or a Taig – that, for the name-callers, was the underclass. The bigots were a minority, perhaps a dozen in each year, but allies, other than friends, who called them out were even fewer. Most pupils chose to be non-aligned. Sectarianism was not an undercurrent, it was a rip tide so vicious I still find it hard to believe that something the North was notorious for went unnoticed among teachers, yet it was never addressed.

It spiked when a local RUC or UDR man was murdered, but parents and pulpits fuelled it too. It peaked with the hunger strikes in 1981, when their enemy's self-sacrifice intolerably won international support. I was 13. 'Could you eat a chicken supper, Bobby Sands?' classmates chanted. 'Could you eat a chicken supper, you dirty Fenian fucker?'

One of the most brazenly bigoted pupils in my year was a Free Presbyterian. I sometimes wondered was it my imagination or as the week progressed was he becoming almost civil, while on a Monday, fresh from his pew, he was almost puce with prejudice?

I naively wondered whether pupils who were Church of Ireland would be less anti-Catholic than the Presbyterians. After all, their roots were in England, which had largely abandoned its hatred and suspicion of Rome, rather than Scotland, which was still evolving from sectarianism to secularism. Also, the Anglican brand of Christianity was closer in form to Catholicism. Years later, when I moved to London, I sat through half of Mass in the first church I came to on Willesden High Road before it dawned on me that – despite the smells and bells – this was High Anglican, not Catholic. Some unfortunates say that you can tell whether someone is Catholic or Protestant by how they look. That is, of course, nonsense. But I think I could identify a Protestant who disliked Catholics by the way they looked at me.

I had plenty of friends who happened to be Protestant. One of my fondest memories is of walking a mate round the car park of the Coach nightclub to sober him up, the half-cut leading the cut, before his dad arrived to give us a lift home. The next stage of the plan was for me to sit in the front passenger seat and make polite conversation while he slept it off in the back. I thought I had executed my part pretty well but his review on Monday morning was not great. 'He said you swore a lot and talked about Celtic the whole time.'

My friend Peter was a Catholic but had an English accent – he had only just moved from London to his mother's native Banbridge after the death of his father. So when one of his new classmates informed him during his first week at school that he was a dirty Taig, he had to ask what that meant. Other Catholics opted to keep their heads down for seven years in the hope that their religious identity would not be noticed or commented upon.

One lunchtime, the deputy headmaster entertained pupils with a rendition of 'The Sash', an Orange ballad. I recall the headmaster stopping his car in the pouring rain to send a pupil from my village home for wearing a proletarian duffel coat, not the regulation posh gabardine. He wasn't the only pupil in non-regulation clothing, but he was the only Catholic. Catholics were admitted but not accommodated.

The Union flag flew from a flagpole by the entrance. Every so often a minor royal would descend in a helicopter, landing on a rugby pitch. Around Remembrance Day, the entire school body would troop down to the Anglican church to honour the war dead.

The address at the first annual prize day I attended was made by Enoch Powell, the local unionist MP, who had been expelled from the Shadow Cabinet in 1968 by British Conservative Party leader Edward Heath over his racist, anti-immigrant 'rivers of blood' speech. His wife presented me with the very on-brand book I had chosen as my prize, *The Book of Insults, Ancient and Modern*. I felt uncomfortable standing for the British national anthem. It made me feel I didn't belong. And I knew that the tradition I was expected to respect did not reciprocate.

I can't remember Powell's speech, but one of his pet projects was to remove the right to vote in UK elections, including in Northern Ireland, from people such as my father and many other neighbours who were born in the Republic. Under the front-page headline 'Ought to be treated like aliens', the *Banbridge Chronicle* in 1971 editorialised approvingly: 'We find overwhelming support for the views of Mr Enoch Powell, who on Wednesday attacked the "unhappy fictions" of the British Nationality

Act, 1948, which allows Eire citizens in the United Kingdom to be treated for all purposes, except military service, as if they belonged to it.' Ironically, the editorial above it expressed the fear that 'all too many of our people will retreat back into the old, bitter entrenched attitudes that we all thought had died away in recent years'.

In geography class I pored over my atlas, taking comfort in the fact that Catholicism was not always in the minority. I learned about oxbow lakes: meanders of a river that over time become silted up and cut off from the mainstream, which reminded me of the North, increasingly isolated from the South and Britain, left to stagnate. In maths, it was the Venn diagram that spoke to me. The North was the shaded area where the British and Irish circles intersected and overlapped. In RE, my teacher informed me that the Catholic Bible was the Douay-Rheims version. I was pretty sure my parents' copy was the Good News one. Someone got told off for spelling God with a small g. The same teacher taught us English and chastised a pupil who spelled grammar with an e. 'A grammar-school boy who can't spell grammar!'

We studied the poets of the First World War, Wilfred Owen and Siegfried Sassoon, but not Tom Kettle, an Irish nationalist who sacrificed his life in British uniform. Seamus Heaney's 'Docker' poem was in our anthology but was not studied in class:

> That fist would drop a hammer on a Catholic –
> Oh yes, that kind of thing could start again;
> The only Roman collar he tolerates
> Smiles all round his sleek pint of porter.

I wonder now whether the Troubles-related poetry of Heaney, Michael Longley, James Simmons and others should have been on the curriculum to provide teachable moments about our own conflict.

***

Football was the poor relation at school, behind rugby and even hockey. We played on a rugby pitch with rugby goals, modified with a second, lower crossbar to make a soccer net, like a double-exposure photograph.

I once played against St Patrick's, the local Catholic secondary. I felt a bit like the footballer returning to play against his former club who declines to celebrate when he scores to convey his conflicted emotions. Of course, when I did score – a rare enough event – I managed the double whammy of hitting a teacher's car with the ball because there was no net in the goal, so there were cheers all round.

Years later, I would also score on my debut for Canmore Saints, the Catholic chaplaincy team at the University of St Andrews. It was a rather scuffed effort but it earned us a draw in the first match of the season. The nuns had turned out to support us. A friend, the future Father Eugene O'Neill, recounted with glee the look on the head nun's face when I exclaimed after a controversial refereeing decision: 'Fuck me pink.' The nuns did not come back.

The team was a broad church. I recruited a fellow Banbridge Academy old boy, Tyrone Howe, who became an Ireland rugby international and an Ulster Unionist councillor before becoming principal of an English public school.

One winter we had a parish mission, which meant a week of attending Mass at 6.30 a.m. With an extra hour to kill before school, Colm 'Flea' Campbell and I played football on the road because a heavy frost had left a layer of icing on the lawn, my very own bleach green.

My village's crowning glory was an impressive GAA pitch. Woe the day you were caught playing soccer on it or, worse, cricket. Paul Ross, who was usually the ringleader of the latter game, joined the RUC and was bullied out of it for being Catholic. The middle ground was no man's land. I called once for a friend to play soccer and he said that it was a foreign game. We had played it all our lives. He had a Manchester United replica jersey. That's how wrong he was.

***

There was a lot of sectarian abuse at school but it was almost always verbal, not physical. Only once, after the last assembly of the school year, some boys from upper sixth, the year above me, roughed me up. The intention was not so much to hurt as to humiliate, I think. There was not a teacher in sight as they always retreated to the barracks of the staffroom at break time. But if there was a bigger divide than the sectarian one, it was the one that divided the pupil that ran to a teacher to tell tales from everyone else at the school.

I started out deferential but grew insubordinate as I became alienated. One teacher had got two of my cousins into trouble. They had been on the back seat of the bus to school one morning when they spotted him driving behind them. They mentioned it to two other brothers from the village, who went to St Patrick's. They gave him the finger for the rest of the journey. My cousins were disciplined and forced to name the other boys, who then got into trouble at their school, resulting in a big fight between all four boys.

This teacher had drawn every important diagram on the curriculum on a rolling chalkboard in his room and I fantasised about taking a duster to it. Dust to dust. I was fooling about in his physics class one day when he said, 'Doyle, you're all right most of the time but sometimes you can be a bit of a dick.' 'That's the difference between you and me, sir,' I replied, loudly enough for him to hear but quietly enough for him to pretend that he hadn't. 'I'm only a dick some of the time.'

Reading aloud a role in a play we were studying in English, I drew the line at saying the word papist: the abuse I experienced in the corridors would not be normalised in the classroom. Another day, I was messing about and my science teacher asked me what was so funny. Was it the colours of chalk he was using? I looked up. Green, white and orange, among others. Not my comedy jam, as it happened, but an insight into how his brain was wired. Another teacher always wore a Glasgow Rangers tie, highlighting his support for a football club that proudly hadn't fielded any Catholic since the First World War.

A new headmaster, Winston Breen, changed things when he arrived in 1984. He went out of his way to successfully prepare my brother Shane for Cambridge and, when his brother Harry became the most senior RUC officer to be murdered, he addressed the school on the evils of sectarianism.

In his contribution to the school history, Shane, now a professor of history at Leeds University, wrote, 'The petty sectarianism of life outside the classroom sharpened my academic ambition. Repeated reminders that Catholics were stupid provoked the desire to excel, and to leave.'

My father's American boss's daughter, honey blonde and tanned, a golden girl, was in my Spanish class. I didn't feel competitive. Even back then I realised nothing, not even a lack of ability, would hold her back. Form is temporary, class is permanent. And privilege rankled less than prejudice.

My German teacher had encouraged me to apply for Oxbridge, but I chippily said I didn't want to go to a foreign university. My narrowed mind had narrowed my options.

The *Derry Girls* blackboard differentiating between Catholics and Protestants was funny. But few would have laughed if Catholics had been called dirty, lazy, untrustworthy, priest-ridden, Virgin Mary-worshipping, IRA-supporting rebels.

A fellow shopkeeper once said to my mother, 'My son has got engaged to one of your sort if you don't mind, but I'll say nothing for I might be glad of her in my old age.' She didn't even realise how offensive she was being, my mother says. Another woman once listed all the tragedies that had befallen her children, including the death of a son after a fall. 'And to crown it all,' she said, 'one of them married a Catholic.'

'You could go from Dromore to Markethill and you could really say that the Protestants there hate Catholics,' a local unionist politician once told Éamon Phoenix. 'That was his take on his constituents,' the historian told me. 'We weren't even talking about the Glenanne gang. It chilled me a bit.' Northern Catholics were treated not how Protestants were treated south of the border but how Travellers were treated.

***

I do not know whether the school now has a specific anti-sectarian strategy. When it comes to bullying, there is an ingrained resistance among pupils to inform on their peers, an act that in itself can lead to bullying and ostracising. I think it is unreasonable to put the onus on children to lead by example, when the authorities – the adults in the room – are conspicuously silent. No teacher ever raised the subject, warned perpetrators of the consequences or encouraged victims to come forward. If you cannot be what you cannot see, perhaps likewise, you cannot tell what is not asked.

By the time I started secondary school, hundreds of people had been murdered, many of them locally, exacerbating the sectarianism that was already endemic. The Alliance Party has had an admirable record of fighting sectarianism. Banbridge Academy, in my time, did not. My mother once stood as an Alliance candidate. She also had to ring Winston Breen to give out to him after my brother Garry came home distressed in his first year after another day of sectarian abuse. My instinct is that very few teachers in my time were sectarian but was that enough? Was it too much to expect them to be actively anti-sectarian?

I don't think my English teacher was sectarian when she expected me to say the word 'papist'. But I don't think she was anti-sectarian, or her antennae might have twitched. It is insufficient not to be racist in a racist society. You must be anti-racist. You would not expect a pupil of colour to say the N-word. Would it be plausible for a teacher in England in the 1970s to argue that they had no idea that pupils of colour might have been subject to racism?

It turns out that when the deputy headmaster played 'The Sash', teachers did protest and it did not happen again. But there was no public acknowledgement of how inappropriate his behaviour was. A civic lesson went untaught.

My cousin Julie left the Academy after three years because she couldn't stick the abuse. Perhaps if the school had conducted exit interviews to find out why pupils were leaving, the staff might have learned a thing or two. 'I was the only Catholic girl in my class,' Julie says. 'The first week I was there, age 11, my RE teacher made me stand up on my chair so the rest of the class could see what a Catholic looked like. I think the intention was to single me out: she's a Catholic, don't be friends with her.

'I felt totally ostracised for three years. Because I've done well I always have this fantasy of going back and saying, up yours. I was called a Fenian on a daily basis, mainly by the Dromore and Rathfriland ones, older ones because I had older siblings. I feel like I've carried through my life: keep your head down, never let on, people will pick on you. I feel ashamed, I wish I had stood up more for myself. I just remember it as the most unhappy time of my life, that school, just a horrible, isolating experience. It made me very determined that my children would not be subjected to that.'

Other Catholics probably got off far more lightly than Julie and me, by keeping their heads down and their mouths shut; by conforming; by being apolitical; shielded by wealth or privilege. Sectarianism was not the sole issue. A former pupil of Chinese origin told me about the racist abuse she suffered.

On publication of my essay 'Dirty Linen' in *The Irish Times*, one of my former teachers, David Griffin, wrote to me to complain that he and many of his caring, compassionate and committed colleagues would under no circumstances have turned a blind eye to the abuse I described. I – an advocate of reconciliation and tolerance – had caused hurt to some fine teachers who had served their pupils well in those difficult years.

David had lived in the area for over fifty years and no one had ever raised the issue of sectarian bullying with him. He did, however, concede that many important and necessary reforms, particularly in the field of pastoral care, had been introduced. Of course there had been failings, but huge efforts had been made to promote and encourage tolerance and understanding. The Academy was one of the first State schools to make Irish history a core feature.

He cited an impressive list of cross-community initiatives in which the school had been involved, but all after my time. David was one of the good guys and so it felt churlish to have bitten the hand that wasn't a fist.

I got in touch with him and he invited me to his home. I had forgotten how strong his Southern brogue is. A native of Tipperary, he was raised by his uncle, a Church of Ireland minister, in Inishannon, County Cork. After studying history at Trinity College Dublin, in the late 1960s David taught history at an integrated comprehensive school in Fivemiletown, County Tyrone.

'I wasn't there a week until I walked up the street with [a senior colleague] and went to buy my meat in Vincent McMahon's butcher's shop, who advertised in the school magazine. This gentleman said, "You're shopping on the wrong side of the street [i.e., buying from a Catholic]." So [the integrated school] was doomed from the outset.'

He became head of history at Banbridge Academy. 'There was much more obvious suspicion of Catholics at the Academy. If there was prejudice in Fivemiletown, it was hidden, but in Banbridge Academy, I think the older generation was perhaps defensive. Maybe I'm trying to apologise for their attitude. They perhaps felt that the Catholic Church had chosen to maintain their own section and instead of seeing it as a State school, they saw it as a Protestant school.'

'How do we treat people from the nationalist community? Those questions were not raised at staff meetings. Where pupils were concerned, particularly among the older generation [of teachers], there was definitely a feeling, we need to keep these people a little bit in check, when it came for example to the appointment of prefects.' This was not policy, just individual prejudice. 'I remember one teacher leaning over [a colleague's] shoulder and telling him he was picking too many of those Catholics. [The colleague] told him he couldn't pick his own nose.'

That teacher may have been bitter, David says, but he treated Catholic pupils well. However, when John Dunlop, an ecumenical former Presbyterian Moderator and peacemaker, was guest speaker at a prize day, this teacher refused to meet him.

The teachers did not leave their politics at the gate, not in David's early years anyway. 'In the seventies we had a very hot staffroom. When Bloody Sunday and other incidents happened there was tension, very strong voices on both sides.'

Was sectarianism properly addressed in my time there? 'It wasn't. I would accuse myself of perhaps not being aware.'

After Winston Breen became headmaster, a Catholic pupil who became head boy complained about a pupil calling him names. Mr Breen and Mr Griffin made the bully apologise before his class.

David was a founder member of the cross-community, anti-sectarian Alliance Party in 1970. Knowing that the North was deeply divided and sectarianism was rife, surely he must have been aware that bigotry would be a problem among pupils? If he was hearing prejudice in the staffroom, why would he not think it was in the classroom too? Did no one ever think, How is our small minority of Catholic pupils being treated?

'I suppose it's something you both imagine doesn't exist and you don't want to see it and you kid yourself it isn't there. Certainly there was a complacency: Banbridge Academy is a *nice* school. Will drawing attention exacerbate the problem? Sometimes people fear that by raising an issue you bring it to life? I wasn't observant, critical enough.

'I think what defines Banbridge Academy is it is very middle class. There was no graffiti in the toilets or on schoolbooks. The teachers and the typical pupil were middle class. We did discuss the failure of pupils from working-class backgrounds to do as well. If you looked closely enough, and only Winston Breen did, it took two generations to jump up. There was a culture change with Breen. He had a sharpness of vision.

'The perception was if there were tensions, they were more likely to come from Rathfriland or Dromore.' The suggestion is that Banbridge was above all that sort of thing.

Years after I left, two pupils erected loyalist paramilitary flags on the rugby posts. They also carved graffiti on trees, threatening that anyone who took the flags down would be shot. The caretakers removed the flags and the culprits foolishly incriminated themselves by asking for them back. The school magazine obliquely referred to a prefect who had broken the record for the time taken to lose his badge.

David remembers one more traumatic incident. Sean Quinn, a Catholic policeman, was killed in an IRA bombing in 1982. His children attended the Academy, so David went to the funeral in Newry. Bishop Walsh gave a very brave sermon, he says, but 'while the coffin was being lowered, there were fellas shouting horrible abuse from the road. It was one of the ugliest incidents and I've never forgotten it.'

***

Paula Jordan has been principal of Sperrinview Special School in Dungannon, County Tyrone, for sixteen years, and in 2022, in recognition of her thirty-five years' service in special education, she was appointed MBE and attended Queen Elizabeth's funeral.

Paula, a Catholic from Laurencetown, also attended Banbridge Academy, two years ahead of me. Her experience was different. She did not encounter sectarianism from her fellow pupils but she did from a teacher, and from the headmaster.

She was 12 years old when her RE teacher 'said the reason Catholics went to Confession was that was where priests told them who they should kill next, that's who they get their orders from.

'I lost it. I knew there was thirty-one sets of eyes boring into me.

I just stood up, I so clearly remember myself saying that she was indoctrinating young children to hate and thinking I have no idea what that word means.

'I just said I wouldn't listen to this and I lifted the bag and the coat and went out through the door. I remember just leaning against the wall thinking, what have I done? I'm going to get expelled. Mummy and Daddy had put such a lot into education. Daddy left school at 13, Mummy left at 14. I thought, I'm going to disappoint them so much. There was just this silence in that corridor. The next thing there was a round of applause and the whole thirty-one of them trooped out behind me.'

The headmaster's solution was to remove all Catholics from RE classes.

Generally, Paula's time at the Academy was very positive. She got involved with drama, cross-country running, the school choir, achieved a bronze Duke of Edinburgh award, took part in a 24-hour forward roll to raise funds for a trampoline. She never experienced sectarianism because she was in a good class and pupils generally didn't know her religion.

The estate where Paula lived was predominantly Protestant, but the Jordans lived near two Catholic families, the Fegans and the Feeneys. Both had been left fatherless at the hands of paramilitaries – Joe Fegan was killed at Newry Customs Clearance Centre in August 1972, and John Michael Feeney at Bleary Darts Club in April 1975.

Paula's best friend was Mary Fegan, while her younger sister palled around with Mary's youngest sister, Denise, who has Down syndrome. The four half-lived in each other's houses and are all friends still. When Paula was 12, the Gateway Club was set up in Banbridge to help people with learning disabilities participate in leisure, social and creative activities. Denise's mother, Christine, asked Paula to accompany Denise to the club, which led to her volunteering for two periods a week at Donard Special School in her last two years at Banbridge Academy. Paula received a handwritten letter from her headmaster, Frank Dorman, thanking her for volunteering at Donard rather than playing a sport as most students did. 'He wrote that as the parent of a special child, he really appreciated this.' Paula was also voted the Scripture Union's pupil of the year.

However, Paula's career in special education was almost sabotaged before it even began. She had applied to teacher-training colleges at St Mary's, Jordanstown and Ulster University but received no offers, even though she knew students with lower grades had been offered places. A cousin who was a teacher asked a friend at St Mary's to look at her application, which included a report from her headmaster, Mr Dorman.

'The reports written about me and sent to universities along with my applications were blatantly dishonest and painted me in a very poor light. The report basically said I had been a troublemaker, had played truant on a regular basis. I wouldn't even have been late for class, never mind not go to one. I missed two days in fifteen years, one was P1 [primary one or junior infants] and one was P7, both for grandparents' deaths. But I don't think it was just me, I think it happened to lots of people.'

She was advised to repeat her A levels – even though her grades should have been good enough to secure a place – and get an honest report from a Catholic school.

Her sister Lynn had just started second year at the Academy. Naturally, her parents decided to remove her. 'Lynn was happy with this,' says Paula, 'as, unlike me, she had never been happy in the Academy, with only two members of her class speaking to her once they realised that she was a Catholic.'

Paula asked her parents if she could take Lynn out of school and they agreed.

'When we entered the headmaster's office he briefly looked up at us. I told him that I would be collecting Lynn from school at lunchtime as she was leaving the Academy and had to go to get her new uniform. He never once asked why she was leaving, where she was going or how I had got on with my applications. I waited a few moments and it was obvious that he was not going to engage with us, I told him which school Lynn would be going to and that, at least there, she would be treated appropriately. His only response was "Fine!" I think this says much more about him than I ever could.'

Paula went to Sacred Heart grammar school in Newry to repeat her exams – the curriculum was different but David Griffin helped her with history and an English teacher helped her on her tea-break – and a year later, she got offers from all three colleges.

'At the time it was horrific, but looking back it was the making of me. That year in the Sacred Heart I grew up very fast and I wouldn't have the group of friends from there otherwise. They do say God moves in mysterious ways. Certainly at the time I thought it was the worst thing that ever happened to me. It worked out for me, but it still shouldn't have happened.'

***

The Academy is a fine school, but in the period Julie, Paula, Lynn and I were there, it sorely failed its small and unconsidered minority of Catholic pupils, giving no thought to our vulnerability nor taking the appropriate steps to protect us.

I support integrated education, provided the cultural identities of all pupils are equally respected and recognised. It is depressing to learn that only 7 per cent of pupils in the North attend integrated schools.

Given the North's troubled recent history, I am uncomfortable that many State schools, including Banbridge Academy, host branches of the Army Cadets, a national youth organisation sponsored by the British Ministry of Defence and the British Army. In the case of Banbridge Academy, the town already has its own Army Cadets branch.

Andrea and I are graduates of the University of St Andrews, Shane of Cambridge University and Garry of Trinity College Dublin, which is at least partly down to our school having been an academic hothouse. But the fact that none of us returned to the North is at least partly down to the fact that it was a cold house for Catholics.

Eighteen

All Traders Are Targets

At about 2 p.m. on Monday, 15 March 1982, a man was about to cross the border near Forkhill in south Armagh to cash a cheque at his bank in Dundalk when armed men ambushed him and hijacked his car. Two sat either side of him in the front while a third in the back put a black bin bag over his head. He thought he was going to be shot.

Instead, the IRA let him go. Others that day would not be so fortunate. The car, now carrying a 500lb bomb, was driven north to Banbridge and parked outside Fred Elliott's butcher's shop on Victoria Street, just off Bridge Street. At 5.30 p.m. it exploded, one of five bombs set off by the IRA that day in the North in acts of human butchery. Pointlessly, a bomb warning was telephoned to Dundalk Garda Station minutes later. The explosion was heard seven miles north in Dromore, where some people thought it was thunder. In Poyntzpass, eight miles south, a farmer was almost trampled by his cattle, who panicked at the sound of the blast.

Alan McCrum – an 11-year-old farmer's son from Loughbrickland, middle child in a family of five, in his first year at Banbridge High School – had just finished a piano lesson and was waiting for a lift home from Mary McMullan, who worked in Rodney Watson's jeweller's.

'Alan was standing beside a chair at the counter, in line with the door,' Watson told the *Banbridge Chronicle*. 'I was over at the counter and Mary had just gone through to the back. I was chatting to Alan

WE ARE FITTING SPECIALISTS FOR CLARKS CHILDREN'S SHOES

Phone 23750

Banbridge Chronicle

Also circulating in DROMORE, RATHFRILAND, POYNTZPASS, SCARVA, TANDRAGEE

112th Year — THURSDAY, 18th MARCH, 1982 — Price 20p

BULK PURCHASE in HAND-BAGS

Approx. 1/2 price

HOUSTONS

Banbridge 22447

CHILD KILLED —STREET DEVASTATED

PICTURES AND FULL

about a watch he got from me a couple of months ago. Alan had just said, "It's going great," when bang, end of story.'

Everything seemed to happen in slow motion. The jeweller had ducked at the sound of the explosion. When he got back up, he saw Alan was in a sitting position on the floor. Blood was pouring out of him and then he fell over. 'I heard Mary say, "Oh my God, Alan," and I went immediately and dialled 999,' Watson said. 'That was the only call I got out – the line went dead after that.' Alan had been killed.

Dickson McCrum, the victim's uncle, said on the family's behalf, 'We want no retaliation. We are a sincere Christian family and accept Alan's death as something which the Lord himself has allowed.' Such faithful stoicism and peaceful restraint should not be taken lightly. That this Christian charity was commonplace after such atrocities does not make it any less remarkable or significant. It was the bedrock, the backstop that saved the North from sliding into all-out civil war.

At Alan's funeral in Banbridge Baptist Church, Pastor Carson likened him to Samuel in the Old Testament. But Samuel grew to be a prophet 'while Alan was like a bud, plucked as it was about to break forth'.

Francis Brooks, the Catholic Bishop of Dromore, said, 'Words cannot describe the revulsion felt by all who believe in God's law of love on hearing of yet more bomb and murder attacks in our province.

'In a week when all Irish people are preparing to honour St Patrick, who first brought us the good news of our brotherhood in Christ, those who plan and help carry out such deeds are working to cause dissension and fear in our country. Once again, their actions must be condemned as grievously sinful in themselves. No possible motive can justify them.'

On behalf of the Catholic community in Banbridge, he expressed deep sympathy to the injured and heartfelt compassion to the parents and family of Alan McCrum, 'whose young life, full of promise, was so violently taken from him'. 'May the God of compassion help those who have suffered,' he said, 'and touch the consciences of those responsible for these evil deeds.'

Jim Lyttle, owner of a home-furnishing shop, criticised the RUC's failure to enforce parking restrictions and, at a more profound level, said, 'What appals me is that people are ushered into Eternity without warning. The men who do these terrible things should give thought to the fact that they have a judge – God – to meet, sooner or later.'

Junior McCrum, who was 18 when his brother Alan was murdered, and went on to become a DUP councillor, spoke about the family's loss as they marked the twentieth anniversary of his death.

'You never forget the memories,' he said. 'It happened on Monday, 15 March 1982, at 5.30 p.m. and he wasn't buried until the Thursday and I could take you through all that in great detail. You never forget it until the day you die. Alan was always a very outgoing, bubbly fellow, he was full of fun. He had a comical sense of humour, he was always witty.

'It's going to be a difficult time for us. It's something that the family doesn't forget, even though it was twenty years ago. Life has to go on, but there is still that doubt in your mind. What would Alan be doing now? Would he have a job? You always see him as he was on the last day.'

I was in fourth year at Banbridge Academy in March 1982. Most days I got the bus home from the stop beside the heavily fortified RUC station but occasionally, if there was a match or some other after-school activity, I too would walk up the town to get a lift home, past Fred Elliott's, where a girl in my class had a Saturday job, to either Mammy's shop, Arcade Fashions, just off Newry Street, or my uncle Joe's insurance brokers on Scarva Street.

There is something obscene about bombing a town centre. The IRA's euphemism was to call it a commercial target. You might as well twist the hateful loyalist slogan 'All Taigs Are Targets' to say 'All Traders Are Targets'. If the conflict was a war, then this was a war crime.

Someone found the hands of jeweller George Armstrong's ornamental clock, which had told the time to passers-by since the 1890s. Those hands would be put back on and time would tick once more. But human body parts could not be so easily restored. And an 11-year-old's life was stopped dead that day.

Rodney Watson was not injured in the explosion, but the next day, while dusting a display case, a sliver of glass cut his finger.

***

When the dust settles after an explosion, how does an artist get under the skin of the public, callused perhaps by the relentless abrasiveness of violence, the deadening daily diet of grim news – not unfeeling, just emotionally spent?

Perhaps the two most powerful artistic responses to the Troubles are the *Women of Belfast* sculpture series, Banbridge-born artist F.E. McWilliam's reaction to the IRA's Abercorn restaurant bombing in Belfast in 1972, which killed two and maimed many more; and *Silent*

F.E. McWilliam, Woman in a Bomb Blast, *bronze in an edition of 5, 132 x 58 x 58 cm, 1974, Private Collection on loan to the F.E. McWilliam Gallery & Studio. © Estate of F.E. McWilliam*

Testimony, Colin Davidson's series of oil-on-linen portraits of Troubles victims and their relatives, including Margaret Yeaman, who was blinded by the same IRA bomb that killed Alan McCrum.

Jennifer McNern, a Catholic from north Belfast, lost both her legs in the Abercorn bombing. She and Margaret, a Protestant from rural County Down, met and became friends through WAVE, the charity that supports victims of the Troubles and campaigns on their behalf. Colin Davidson is its patron.

We meet in Jennifer's Belfast home, where the kitchen is full of art. By coincidence, it is 31 July, the anniversary of both the IRA's bombing of Claudy, which killed nine people in the County Derry village in 1972, and the UVF's Miami Showband massacre. Thirty years of violence accumulated so many atrocities that they do not even always have a date on the calendar to themselves.

Margaret worked as an estate agent for Raymond Armstrong, whose office was above Fred Elliott's shop in Victoria Street, Banbridge.

Somehow we start chatting about Suzy Lamplugh, an estate agent who disappeared in London in 1986 and who is believed to have been kidnapped and murdered by the man she was showing a house to. Margaret recalls taking basic precautions such as letting the client go upstairs first and waiting outside the door while he viewed a bedroom. Harm, however, would come her way not in an isolated property but in the office where she worked on a busy shopping street.

Before the bombing, the Troubles were noises off, an urban phenomenon. Margaret thinks country people are different. Catholics and Protestants get along better, mix together, help each other out. 'Everybody got on. If anybody needed a hand out or somebody had died – many a wake I went to, helped make the tea. My mother would have gone to [social evenings] in the chapel.'

When she went to work in Banbridge, she thought it was safe. 'It wasn't Belfast or Lisburn, it was a quiet market town.' Life at home, out in the countryside, was good but busy, chauffeuring the kids to youth club or roller disco as well as looking after two ponies and four dogs. 'There wasn't enough hours in the day. Many a time I never got my coat off me.'

On Monday, 15 March 1982, Margaret's day began with dropping her children off to school in Dromore: Karen and Ian to primary school, and Linda and Paul to secondary. She then arrived at the office at around nine. She officially worked until five but she often had to stay a bit late as, she says, you couldn't push customers out the door.

Next door to Margaret's office was one belonging to Bill Craig, a solicitor and a hard-line unionist politician.

Fifteen minutes before the explosion, Craig had come into Margaret's office because a car was blocking him in. Margaret went to the window and confirmed what he had said. Craig was in a side office with her boss and two customers when the bomb went off. It was twenty-six minutes past five, Margaret remembers. How could she forget?

'I never heard the bomb going off but I felt all the effects of it,' says

Margaret. 'It was like an electric shock and I thought it was something I had touched, electricity. But I found out later it was the rays. If they had got to your heart, they would have just stopped it.

'I remember just getting threw right across the office on my knees and my sight went there and then. I couldn't see. I said to myself, now, if I keep breathing, I'll maybe live. It's just strange the things that go through your head. I was unconscious and then I came back, you know, back and forth. Because I remember the ambulance men coming up and then getting onto the stretcher. And then there was somebody that brought me a blanket.

'But I could hear somebody screaming and it wasn't for a while till I realised that it was myself. All my teeth fell into the bottom of my mouth, they were all broken. And my finger, that finger, my boss came out and he tied his tie around it.'

The bomb blast blew the window to smithereens and the shards shredded Margaret's face. Some were so deeply embedded that they still surface decades later, rejected foreign bodies. (I think of how some extremists still see their Protestant neighbours as planters to be expelled. How Enoch Powell wanted Southerners like my father living in the North to be treated as aliens.) 'My lip and my face, I'd over a hundred stitches in my face. I could feel along my lip there, it was all cut right up to my nose. And my hands, I could feel them hurt too.'

William Craig, interviewed by the *Banbridge Chronicle* minutes after the blast, still covered in grey dust and bleeding from a cut to the forehead, said, 'There was a tremendous bang and then everything went dark.' Craig's hearing was affected, Margaret says. 'Weeks later, he was driving his car when he heard a ticking and thought it was a bomb in his car so he stopped. He realised his hearing had cleared and that it was only a clock.' Several shoppers in the butcher's were wounded by flying glass. One woman lost half her foot and an eye, Margaret says, which triggers my memory.

Margaret Doyle, a 25-year-old housewife and mother of four, lost a foot and a finger in the explosion and her left eye was badly damaged. My mother's name is Marie Doyle and a customer came into her shop after the bombing and said to her, 'Oh, thank God, I thought it was you.' Fred Elliott, the butcher, described the effect of the bomb as like being electrocuted. The back of his head required several stitches.

Margaret says she thought she was going to wake up and it be only a dream, but it wasn't. 'I thought it was my eyelids that had got damaged. I didn't realise that it was my eyes. So, one of them they had to take out completely. And the other one, they left it in but there's nothing they can do with it. It is just dead. But they didn't want to leave me with no eyes. It was more like a psychological thing because now it's starting to give me trouble. They said it would shrink – and it has shrunk quite a lot – and then it will give you a lot of pain and then they'll have to do something, maybe take it out. But I'm not looking forward to that day.'

Her artificial eye is blue, although her eyes were brown, because her damaged eye had turned a beigey-blue colour.

I wonder how Margaret processed the specialists' terrible prognosis that her sight was gone for good.

'Oh, my goodness,' she replies, with a gentle politeness that is deeply affecting. 'I didn't want to come out of the hospital; I wanted to stay. Because I thought they would be able to operate and even get me one eye, but no. And it's an awful thing to walk out of the eye hospital surgery having been told there's nothing they can do.

'When my husband came to take me home, I said, "No, I'm not going home." He says, "You have to." I says, "No, I can't go home till I get my eyes sorted." But I had to go home. And I didn't like it. I wanted to stay. Strange somebody wanting to stay in the hospital.'

Their mother's injuries had a devastating effect on the children. It was weeks before Linda, her eldest but still only 15, came to see her. 'And of course she just fainted. She just went right down, and my mum says, "Oh, Linda has tripped over something." But I knew she hadn't. It was just so hard on them.

'And I now have grandchildren and I can't … I always pictured grannies as taking them in the car, giving them a few pence – or more than a few pence now – and taking them out to buy them things and to go places with, but no. I feel as though I have let them down too.'

Like many mothers during the Troubles, Margaret worried that her sons would get involved with paramilitaries as a reaction to what had happened. 'I had said to the two boys, I don't want you to get into any organisation. I don't want yous to do anything. Because that would hurt me far more.' So they didn't. But her eldest son would still become upset and cry about her injuries, even when he was 20. And I says, "Look, I'm all right." "You're not," he says. "You're not all right."'

It is not enough that Margaret has lost her sight. Others take away her dignity. Once, as she was leaving her doctor's surgery, having injured herself, the GP pushed her in the back as a crude way of guiding her out the door. 'I says to him, "Doctor, just give me your arm." But he was pushing me out. He didn't know what way to deal with somebody who was blind.'

There is another thing she doesn't like. 'People come up to you and say, "Hello, Margaret, guess who this is." And I say, "I don't know. Who are you?" And then they'd say their name, but, you know, it's not a guessing game. Another of my gripes is to walk into a room and nobody speaks to me. Because then I don't know who's in the room. I suppose they wait for me to say hello. But I could be talking to myself.'

Margaret's husband, Richard, has been selfless in his support, but he has suffered terribly too. He said that when they met anybody, he saw the horror on their face when they saw Margaret. 'Now he's only told me that lately. He knew not to tell me at the time, because I wouldn't even have left the house to go to the hospital. And for a long, long time, I would never go into Hillsborough or Dromore or Moira. Because they were places that I would have gone to before. And when anybody asked, "What happened your wife?" No matter where it was, I couldn't answer, I would have just burst into tears. He had to tell it.'

Their grandson got married in Crete in 2021. Richard said, 'If only you had even one eye, you would be able to see the grandchildren, see them at their wedding.' She hasn't seen any of her grandchildren. She has to say to somebody, 'Who does he look like?' More than that. 'I can't really visualise my youngest son, Ian. He'll be coming up on 50. He was only nine.'

Adjusting to life outside hospital was hard in other ways. 'Even the kettle boiling frightened me. All the sounds frightened me. If there's a car alarm goes off, I would nearly jump out of my skin. I don't like balloons going off either. Or fireworks. It was very, very tough. I didn't like anybody to see me eating so I would have gone away into the kitchen. And now I'm not allowed to do anything. My husband, he says, "You'll burn yourself if you lift that kettle."'

Years later, it would emerge that Eamon Collins, an IRA man from Newry, was responsible for driving the bomb car to Banbridge. He became an informer and later wrote a book, *Killing Rage*, about his time in the IRA. He was brutally murdered by former comrades in 1999, who stabbed and slashed his face repeatedly, to take revenge and with the apparent aim of ensuring he couldn't have an open coffin.

Knowing the identity of one of the people who had blinded her 'really shook me up an awful lot', says Margaret. 'I was sorry that he had such a horrible death although, mind you, when I was so badly knocked down, and couldn't see, if I had have got him, I could have finished him off. But then after that I said to myself, no point in it. Because bitterness only ruins yourself. So I just put them out of my mind.

'A lot of people, and men of the cloth, have said to me, "I'm sure you're bitter." I said, "No." I don't be bitter because the bitterness would eat me up. And I don't want that because then they would have made their point.'

Margaret was sceptical about counselling. 'You get somebody opening Pandora's box, then your time's up and they just leave you like that. Which is very unfair.'

But two sessions with a counsellor called Martin from Barnardo's did help. His method was to go through the time from the day of the bombing until she left hospital. 'And then he said, "I want you to do it as if you're not in it, you're the person who's watching it." And do you know it helped me a lot. It helped me that there wasn't so many nightmares. I still get nightmares, but there wasn't just as many, or flashbacks.'

My understanding of this is that the counsellor, by making Margaret an eyewitness to her own trauma, helped her redirect her natural compassion for others inward towards herself, the person who needed it most.

After the bombing, Margaret's mother stayed with her every day for two years from nine in the morning until nine at night. But then her mother got breast cancer. Life takes. And it takes.

'I would have prayed and said look, I don't want my sight back, as long as my mum gets cured. And she didn't.'

'That's so cruel,' I say.

'Oh, it was so cruel. Really. And between the two things, it took such a long time even to get over her passing away. When she was ill, I didn't care about myself, as long as she would have got the treatment for the cancer. And was all right. I bargained. I know you're not supposed to but I bargained.'

Margaret went to see anyone who might cure her, faith healers, nuns. 'I went to them all. When mum had the cancer, we went round them again, the seventh son of the seventh son, and then there was other ones that laid hands on you, on my eyes.'

She was genuinely hoping for a miracle. 'Oh yes. Oh, my God.'

But Margaret's mother died just three months after her diagnosis, aged only 62. It was the morning of the Enniskillen bombing, 8 November 1987, when the IRA bombed a Remembrance Day service, killing twelve people.

Margaret had lost her mother, her carer and companion.

'When she came into Craigavon [Hospital] to see me I wouldn't let her go, you know, to go home. I just wanted her to stay. No matter what it is, you're always looking for your mum. Or no matter what age you are.'

Margaret had no hesitation supporting the Good Friday Agreement. 'I thought if it would stop the Troubles that my family could go out and go somewhere, that you weren't worried about them all the time.'

With the passing of time, I ask, does it get easier or does it feel that she is always in the same place?

'It doesn't get any easier. No, it doesn't. But I can laugh. People will say if I'm in the passenger seat, "Look out there to see if there's any cars coming." And I just say, "Remember, I can't see them!" But you do have to have a laugh. Jennifer and I do. Otherwise you couldn't get up and out of bed in the morning.'

Nineteen

Women as Victims of Man's Stupidity

Jennifer McNern is from north Belfast. Her parents, Hugh and Teresa (née Blaney), were from Donegal. Her father had been working in the shipyards in Scotland but they moved to Belfast where he worked at Harland & Wolff. He and a colleague were killed in 1965 when the safety bar on the scaffolding they were standing on to paint the outside of a ship gave way and they fell to their deaths. Jennifer regards her father's death as suspicious, given the circumstances – 'to me it was always fishy that both sides gave way' – and the history of attacks on Catholic shipyard workers.

Her widowed mother received about £1,000 in compensation and had to work three jobs to raise her five children. Rosaleen at 17 was the eldest, only fourteen months older than Jennifer, then their brothers Hugh and Pat, and Bernie, who was only six.

By 1972, Rosaleen was private secretary to the head of the Confederation of British Industry. Jennifer had studied catering management and now managed school meals in the Holy Rosary school, off the Ormeau Road, but even though she was 21, she still kept on her Saturday job in a local launderette. Both sisters still lived at home. Rosaleen was engaged to be married and so she persuaded Jennifer to skip her afternoon shift and accompany her to town to shop for clothes. After leaving Wallis's clothes shop, they walked round Cornmarket and then decided to join the queue for the Abercorn restaurant. There were just two girls in front of them, who, when a table did become free, were lifting their stuff to go to it when two other girls appeared from nowhere, skipped the queue and took their seats.

'Now, within about three minutes they left. They didn't order anything. So the two girls in front of us took their seats and that was Anne Owens and Janet Bereen. And then another table came free and it was on the left-hand side as well. I remember we had our coffee and apple tart and fresh cream and we were just about to leave and the next thing I remember was I woke up and I didn't know where I was and a nurse walked past, and I said, "Where am I?" And she said, "You're in the Royal Victoria Hospital in Ward 17. You've been in a bomb explosion." But seemingly I had asked that question every day and then forgot. It must have been the medication.'

Jennifer's arm was broken and in a cast, and she was in traction because she had fractures down the side of her body. One day, her mother, who had been visiting her along with the owners of the launderette and Bernie, her younger sister, was walking down the corridor when she heard an almighty scream and she said, 'That's Jennifer.' She came running back into the ward and everybody was round Jennifer's bed.

'I had been sitting up and then I went to go to sleep and I lifted up the blankets and I noticed my right leg was missing. Because I didn't know, like. I can still wriggle my toes and everything, even to this day. I had obviously been sedated and I didn't know that I had other injuries. Mummy said, "Everything's going to be okay." So, they must have knocked me out then at that point. And then the next day the doctor on the ward came down and he pulled the curtains round and he said, "Jennifer, you haven't just lost your right leg; you've lost your left leg as well." And I really don't remember my reaction.'

Then one day a nurse said to her, 'Your sister's photograph was in the paper.' 'I hadn't even been asking why Rosaleen wasn't coming in to visit me. Just shows you where your head is at.' She asked her mother to bring in the paper. 'I don't think she realised I was going to read what was underneath, but I read the little print and it said that she had lost both legs, an arm and the sight of one eye.' Jennifer's mother explained that Rosaleen was very ill and on a respirator in intensive care. 'I got into a very distressed state. Because I wanted to see her. I wanted to speak to her. All of a sudden all hell just broke loose.'

It was decided to bring Rosaleen up out of intensive care up to Ward 17. There was great excitement. Everybody was waiting to see what was going to happen when the two sisters met. 'So, Rosaleen appeared in through the doors. And she was ashen. She looked about half the size that she normally would have been. And they pushed her towards my bed, and there she was, no legs and just one arm, and I knew to look at her she was spaced out. So, I said hello and she just looked at me and said, "That's mine, that's mine and that's mine."'

In true, age-old sibling tradition, Rosaleen was inspecting what was on top of Jennifer's bedside locker. 'It was her soap bag that she had bought for her honeymoon. You know the way you go into the hospital and everything's new, well of course Mummy just grabbed stuff for me because I was the one that was probably getting washed every day. And it was all put onto her lap and off she went. Swear to God. But everybody just sort of looked at one another as if to say, well, that was short and sweet. I laugh at it now but at the time it was ...'

Not the reunion she was hoping for.

Jennifer now also knew that before her mother came to see her, she would have been down in intensive care with Rosaleen.

When the girls did not come home that day, and news of the Abercorn bombing broke, their mother went looking for them because she knew that was their favourite café. She and a neighbour went to the Royal Victoria Hospital. Nobody knew any names at that point. 'But she was shown a table with people's wares on it. And Rosaleen's engagement ring was on it. So, she knew Rosaleen was there. But there was nothing of mine and she said, maybe Jennifer went off somewhere else. But no. Imagine, like, your mummy being told that news.'

Her mother's ashen face made Jennifer realise the impact that her and Rosaleen's injuries were having. 'I remember watching her and thinking, this is not just all about me.' So she asked her mother to bring in her make-up bag, and Jennifer put on her make-up and lipstick every day in time for her mother's visit. She was literally putting a brave face on things.

Jennifer really believed that the Abercorn bombing would be a watershed, the atrocity that would end all atrocities. Bloody Sunday had happened only two months previously and the Troubles were still in their infancy.

'It was the first time that the IRA had attacked civilians in such a way. I remember thinking when I heard about all the other injuries of the people and the two girls [Anne Owens and Janet Bereen] that were killed, that that must be the end of it now, they [the IRA] must be totally shocked by what had happened. And it was just the beginning of it.' Looking back fifty years on, she feels as though she's 'nearly talking about what happened to other people. Did you really come through all that?'

Jennifer's illusions that what had been done to her and her sister and all those other women would influence the IRA were soon shattered. She was discharged from hospital on 21 July 1972, the day that would become known as Bloody Friday. Starting at 2.10 p.m. the IRA set off twenty-two bombs in Belfast city centre in eighty minutes, killing nine people and injuring 130.

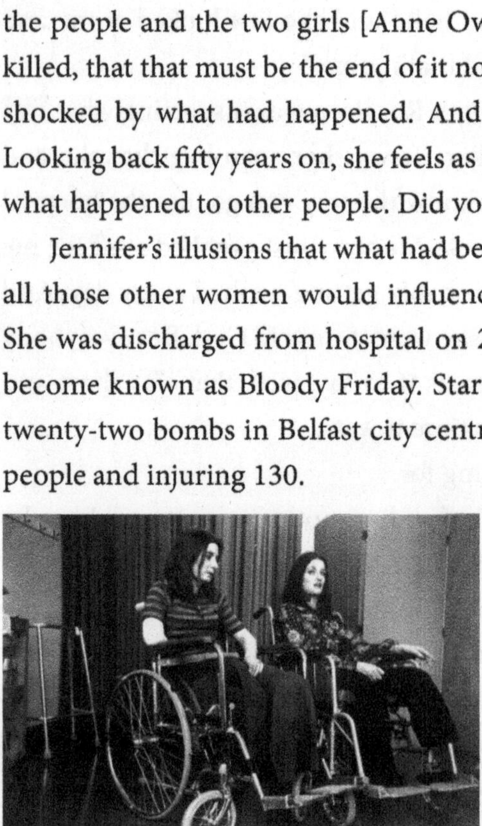

Rosaleen and Jennifer McNern after the Abercorn bombing in 1972.

'Bombs were everywhere. Coming home that day, the traffic was a nightmare. And I remember thinking to myself, God, I'd just love to go back to the hospital.'

Jennifer also had to deal with the media. 'I remember at the very beginning the press used to ask, "Do you forgive them?" And, of course, you had to say yes, because you thought, oh, God, if you didn't say yes, you were a bad person, whereas now I would say no, I don't forgive them. I don't wish anybody any harm but I certainly wouldn't use the word "forgiveness". You know, you're supposed to forgive everybody now. I don't think so.'

In a similar way, even in private, people learned to put up a front.

'The only thing my mother ever said about what happened was, "Thank God your father wasn't here to witness this. He could never have coped." It's very difficult for people to understand ... We didn't talk about what had happened in case somebody got upset. It wasn't wise at all. And that carried on for thirty years.'

Everybody was pretending, everyone was trying to protect the other's feelings. It was after the peace agreement in 1998 that Jennifer began to get angry. 'I thought it was great that there's peace but people like me and Rosaleen and others I met afterwards, we're left behind and not a mention. I loved being angry,' Jennifer says. 'I was getting high on it. But running alongside that was depression.'

One of the most uplifting things that happened after the atrocity was that Rosaleen did still get married to her fiancé, Brendan Murrin, a Donegal man, during the year she spent in hospital. They have one son, who lives in Connemara, and two grandchildren, 'lovely weans', Duilleog (Irish for leaf) and Carrick. Jennifer, too, had a child when she was 32. Emer studied marketing but gave it all up and now works in the nursing home that her grandmother Teresa was in, caring for the elderly. She wants to go and live in Donegal and raise llamas. 'I just said, "You know, Emer, do whatever you want. As long as you're happy, anything at all."' Emer would be quite angry, too, about what happened to her mother. 'I don't go there with her at all,' says Jennifer. 'She wouldn't miss and hit the walls if she met some of them, you know.'

***

Margaret and Jennifer became friends at a Christmas dinner organised by WAVE. 'I was sitting beside Jennifer and she says to me, "You're eating the decorations."' They had fallen onto her plate from the ceiling.

Jennifer and Margaret gained strength from coming together as part of a victims' forum, leaving anger behind to focus on their right to proper support. The British government set up a memorial fund for victims after the Good Friday Agreement. 'A memorial fund? I thought memorials are for people who are dead,' was Jennifer's response. 'I'm very much alive, thank you.' That December she got a £50 cheque inside a Christmas card 'and it was all signed, you know the way an office would sign Merry Christmas'. She got on the phone and a car was sent round to take it back.

Campaigning was not without its challenges, however. When they met Martin McGuinness, IRA leader turned Sinn Féin deputy First Minister, Margaret was initially a bit shaken.

'It was twice I met him and shook hands with him,' Margaret says. 'And I lost friends – after all he has done, and you sitting there blind and you're shaking hands with him. And when he was ill, I felt really sorry for him, and when he died, I thought, now, he shouldn't have died. It would have been far better if he had been alive.'

They joined forces to gather signatures for a petition as part of a campaign for a victims' pension. In Newry one day, Jennifer explained to a woman what had happened to them and what the campaign was about. '"Oh," she said. "A bomb went off in Newry and I was three streets away and I'll never forget it."' Jennifer was unimpressed. 'You got a shock, I felt like saying. Get over yourself.'

Margaret remembers another day asking people to sign the petition in the snow in Belfast. 'And people wouldn't even put their signatures down. "Yous have got enough [financial support]," that's what they would have said. And then Jennifer would say, "Aye, this woman has no eyes," and I would say, "And this woman has no legs."'

There was political resistance to the idea of a victims' pension. Michelle O'Neill, Sinn Féin's leader in the North, said, 'There'll be no hierarchy of victims,' objecting to the exclusion of paramilitaries who had been injured while committing an act of violence.

'We had to take them to court.' The top payment is £10,000 a year, about £200 a week.

***

Colin Davidson is one of Ireland's leading portrait painters. Everyone from Queen Elizabeth II to President Michael D. Higgins, from Seamus Heaney to Ed Sheeran, has sat for him. His most powerful, soulful portraits, however, are not of the great and the good but of the grieving and the wounded, a series of portraits of eighteen relatives of Troubles victims and survivors entitled *Silent Testimony*, which was first exhibited at the Ulster Museum in Belfast in 2015, then in Paris, Dublin Castle, Derry, UN headquarters in New York and Britain's National Memorial Arboretum.

The saying goes that by the age of 40 you have the face you deserve. *Silent Testimony* dwells on people whose faces reflect suffering that no one deserves.

'Something very unwelcome and toxic and traumatic has been thrust upon them and that has defined them,' Davidson says. These are portraits of the loved ones left behind, who were overlooked in the euphoria of the ceasefires, still traumatised, 'paying the price for your peace'. This carries an echo of the First World War idea that the fallen gave their todays for our tomorrows. 'Except we acknowledge those who gave their lives in the war,' Davidson says.

'*Silent Testimony* was purely about now,' says Davidson. 'It wasn't about the past. It was looking at the legacy of what we have left behind in this place. *Silent Testimony* is one big question. It's not a statement.'

Davidson knew Alan McBride, who had lost family in the Shankill bombing, and told him he was interested in making portraits of people who had suffered loss. He was worried it might be a patronising or unhelpful idea but McBride reassured him and WAVE, the victims' and survivors' pressure group, of which Alan is coordinator, offered to become a partner. They drew up a balanced matrix of people who had not yet told their stories.

Margaret was initially reluctant to have her portrait painted. 'I wanted to just blend in the background.' The artist asked her about the bombing as he sketched her, but there were jokes too. 'It wasn't all doom and gloom.'

Margaret would not dream of touching a person's face to visualise them from its contours as she would hate anyone doing the same to her, as inappropriately overfamiliar perhaps as touching a pregnant woman's bump. However, she did feel her own face, or rather, Davidson's portrait of her, as she alone of all his subjects could not see the result.

'He said to me, "I'll let you touch the painting. Nobody else is to put their hands on it." He put my hands right round it all and described it all.'

'I was aware that Margaret was the only person that I had painted who was never going to be able to see their painting,' Davidson said. 'And so, I brought her over to the painting and I lifted her hand and I just ran it over the surface and I said, "Right, here is where I've painted your mouth, here's where I've painted your hair," and I brought her in close to the painting to smell the linseed oil. And that was very poignant for us both actually.'

Davidson asked her if she would take off the dark glasses she normally wears for the portrait. 'I don't wear them about the house but if I'm going anywhere: the first thing, glasses are on,' Margaret said. 'I

Portrait of Margaret Yeaman by Colin Davidson, oil on linen, part of his Silent Testimony *series. © Colin Davidson*

wouldn't go anywhere without them. Because well, I suppose I hide behind them, I don't like people seeing the state of my eyes.'

The eyes are supposed to be the windows of the soul and Davidson starts his portraits with the eyes. So Margaret's shattered, shuttered eye was central to the artist's particular vision for this portrait.

'I paint what I see,' he says. 'Margaret has a glass eye and in some ways I was painting a glass eye, a lifeless eye, but that was the point and Margaret was aware of and understanding it was going to be part and parcel of the portrait that I made of her. And part and parcel of the reason why I was choosing to paint her as well. That actually, you know, do people question whenever they look at the painting that a large part of her life has gone? I think they probably do. Because that's the reality. But also, it's staring at us whenever we look at that image of a human being. Here is somebody who through no fault of their own had their future, sight, normal life that we are gifted with, stolen from them in such a horrific, traumatic way.'

Davidson is also known for his shop-window reflection portraits that capture the kaleidoscopic colour and bustle of urban, commercial life, a rich blur of colours. A shattered shop window cost Margaret her sight.

'People have an understandable habit,' says Davidson, 'of saying that people like Margaret and Jennifer were in the wrong place at the wrong time. The fact is, Jennifer and Margaret were in the right place at the right time. It was the people who came in to snuff life out who were in the wrong place at the wrong time.'

***

Sweltering my way through the petrified streets of Pompeii in the summer of 2022, I stopped short at the sight of a woman stretched out under a table, her slender fingers splayed as if seeking a shelter that is eternally beyond her grasp.

My feelings were complicated: empathy for her terrible fate; an uneasy sense of trespassing on someone else's tragedy; an appreciation for the effort that had gone in to preserving this warning from history; but also an unlikely epiphany or cultural connection.

This horizontal female form, caught in extremis for all time, immortalised victim of a remorseless, violent force oblivious and indifferent to every humane sentiment, reminded me forcefully of F.E. McWilliam's *Women of Belfast* series of figurative sculptures depicting women caught in a bomb blast.

This was his artistic response to the horror of the Troubles, specifically the Abercorn restaurant bombing in Belfast in 1972. 'These sculptures are concerned with violence,' he wrote, 'with one particular aspect, bomb-blast – the women as victims of man's stupidity.'

The political engagement was out of character but showed the pull of an exile's roots, claimed critic Judy Marle, the formal restraint in contrast to the joyful inventiveness of his earlier work, bodies 'defined not by folds of Classical drapery but by decorous chain store dresses blown apart by the blast'.

The first of the series was called *Coffee at the Abercorn*. 'The chummy cosiness of the title,' wrote Marle, 'as reassuring as the title of a Betjeman verse, was attached to the figure of a woman caught and hurled in the air by bomb blast ... the title underlines the peculiar horror of the event, that happened in a room Mac himself knew well.'

'The images that F.E. McWilliam forged out of the Northern Ireland conflict are expressive,' his friend and fellow artist T.P. Flanagan wrote. 'The shock-waves emanating from Belfast established links of compassion and involvement. For me the poignancy of that expression is that it is twofold: the women are victims of a storm of hatred; the artist was born in the country where the storm arose.

'Patterns in art and life often touch with alarming similarity. The ghastly photographs of charred bodies from the La Mon firebomb disaster in 1978 invite comparison with the statue-like fragments of victims of Vesuvius at Pompeii two thousand years before.'

Davidson too is a huge admirer of F.E. McWilliam's *Women of Belfast* series. 'It's one of the most powerful reactions to atrocity that in honesty has ever been created in art. The other one that comes to mind is Picasso's *Guernica*. It is without doubt the seminal body of work of his as far as I'm concerned. Not least because he had utterly mastered his craft of being able to breathe life into his human forms at that stage in his career. I think he was living in London in those days, so having a benefit of a bit of distance maybe was helpful.'

Jennifer went to look at F.E. McWilliam's *Women of Belfast* series in the Ulster Museum after WAVE's chief executive Sandra Peake told her about the connection to the Abercorn bombing.

Did it mean anything to her? 'No. I suppose, unlike Margaret, I don't have any memories. People say they have flashbacks about what happened. My vision of what happened starts in the hospital, basically.'

In his artist's note accompanying the exhibition in July 1973, McWilliam wrote, 'I left Ireland when I was eighteen, and although I seldom return, what happens there concerns me closely, not just because most of my relations and many friends are there, but because my early roots remain unbroken – especially the roots of memory. I can recall clearly what happened in my home town during the former "troubles", this left me with a lasting awareness and hatred of intolerance and religious bigotry.

'I did not choose the subject consciously. It happened I suppose, because the situation in Ulster is inescapable, even at this safe remove, something that is always nagging at the back of one's mind.

'Inevitably the figures clothed themselves. The drapery used obeys the nature of drapery but is used schematically in the sense that it is intended to further the emotion of the experience rather than to depict actual clothing. In a way, although it looks real, I have taken more liberties with the drapery than with the human form. I would like the drapery itself to be a sort of metaphor for the event.

'As they have a common subject matter these sculptures have no titles – women affected by violence – women of Belfast.'

McWilliam had been born in Newry Street, Banbridge in 1909. 'Banbridge was a linen town,' he told Marle. 'The mill dams gave us swimming pools and in summer blue fields when the flax was in flower, and white fields when the linen was spread out to bleach, magical intrusions in the normal patchwork of green.'

For McWilliam, the local landscape was innately sculptural, 'like a basket of eggs, with scarcely a flat field anywhere', Bryan Robertson wrote in his obituary in the *Independent*.

He was the son of a GP whose practice was on the high street, at the time as much a place of manufacture as of commerce. He grew up surrounded by coopers, carpenters and rope-makers, who produced in their backyards what they sold out front.

'It was a fascinating place for a small boy to grow up, and I think it had a bearing on my subsequent activities because of the constant sight of craftsmanship in action … the whole idea of people making things with their hands.'

The future sculptor also witnessed first-hand people destroying things with their hands – a Protestant mob attacking Catholic shops and businesses on his street and surrounding ones in revenge for the IRA's assassination of Colonel Smyth in Cork in 1920. He also saw his father tend to a boy who had been shot, perhaps William Sterritt, killed as a mob attacked the Monaghan family business in 1920. It had a lasting effect on him.

The anger that fuelled *Women of Belfast* worked itself out in his later *Banner* series – inspired in part by the Peace People protest marches against violence, some of which he participated in in London – in which people are obliterated by the slogans they support. In the series he portrays women as survivors and campaigners for peace. *Peace B* depicts two women using peace banners as weapons to attack each other. The first of the series was based on a famous Belfast graffito, 'Is there life before death?'

***

Margaret and Jennifer are both fans of true crime. 'The saucier the better for Margaret and the gorier the better,' says Jennifer. Margaret's librarian has her card marked.

'"You're down here for serial killers," she said. I says, "Aye. I was listening to Maeve Binchy and Danielle Steele but I think I'm tired of that now."'

Jennifer has little patience for serial killers' sob stories. 'I says, well, a lot of people have awful childhoods, they're not serial killers. And even if they are damaged people they still need to be taken out of society. You can't go round killing people.'

The same might be said for people who grew up in staunchly republican or loyalist families.

Jennifer is concerned that a new generation is growing up nostalgic for the excitement of the street violence that characterised the Troubles – that they are too young to remember. 'They've no idea and some of them are ready to roll. "God, yous were lucky to have lived through the Troubles, we missed it all." They thought it was fun with the army on the streets. Can you imagine? They haven't a clue, they see it as romantic.'

Margaret copes because, 'What is the alternative? You either go on or else you just go and throw yourself in a river. There's many a day

Jennifer McNern and Margaret Yeaman in Jennifer's home in Belfast, 2022. © Martin Doyle

that maybe I can't find something, I've set it down and I can't find it and then I go about cursing for a wee while and then I will go into the bathroom and sit and have a cry that nobody would hear me. I didn't want to annoy my children.'

'[Silence] becomes the norm nearly,' says Jennifer, 'but it's a shaky norm. If something happens to trigger, I can fall apart very quickly. It was the peace that was my trigger. But it wasn't actually peace. It was the fact that they didn't include everybody. They were in such a rush to sort of calm things with the paramilitaries. They were placated. I remember watching on television and they were coming out of prison joyful, yahooing. They shouldn't really have been allowed, especially when there was nothing to balance it on the other end.'

Margaret was once at a meeting in Warrenpoint. As she was leaving a man opened her car door and said to her, 'I'm an ex-IRA man, will you pray for me?' 'Well, I couldn't speak. And I cried the whole way home. That this man had the cheek to ask me to pray for him. But after I got over my anger, I did. I said, well, he asked me to pray for him and I will.'

Twenty

'Why couldn't it have been me?'

When Alan Gourley tries to explain what attracted him to pipe bands, the funny thing is that his first memory is not the sound of the bagpipes but the smell of wet wool, the evocative combination of kilts and northern rain.

'I didn't join the pipe band to get marching on the Twelfth of July, to go out and kick the Pope as they say. I joined the pipe band because I can remember the smell. The uniforms, you see, they would have got soaked and boys hung them up but when a pipe band walked past you got this smell ...'

Then of course there was the smell of dope. No, not cannabis, but the nickname for a product pipers applied to their bags to stop air escaping.

'The pipes in the olden days used to have sheepskin bags. They're synthetic now. You used to have to keep them moist by putting on this thing we called dope to seal the seam but there was an awful smell off it. Airtight you called it, came in a wee tin. You used to have to boil it on your stove, put it into hot water and that melted it down, and the house would have been stinking, and your mummy would have been going, "What is that auld smell?" And I have heard instances of boys putting honey into the bag to seal it and on the Twelfth of July the wasps would have been flying.'

We are getting into the weeds of bagpipe-playing now, discussing the price of reeds and how moisture plays a big part in the sound of your instrument. Alan would be classed as a wet blower, he tells me, which means moisture gathers round his reed, affecting the sound, whereas others in the band would be a wee bit drier. In the same way as Prince Andrew doesn't sweat? I joke, but this conversation is triggering for me. I am having a flashback to playing the recorder at primary school once a week. You were supposed to clean it with a rod that had knitting wool wrapped around it, and of course I never bothered. By the time next week's class came around, my recorder stank of stale saliva. I think I may have been a wet blower too. It's too late for my musical career but bagpipes now have a canister to collect all that excess saliva, and a meter to help you tune your drones and chanter.

Alan's father's is from Cookstown, County Tyrone, and his mother from just up the road in Moneymore, County Derry, yet they didn't meet until they came to Banbridge. Alan's dad was the manager of Houston's shoe shop and his mother worked in the same store. His father was a founder member of the Banbridge Pipe Band, and Alan and his two brothers followed the family tradition.

The Banbridge Pipe Band folded a decade ago and now Alan plays with the McDonald Memorial Band, run by his best friend Gary McDonald, who is a grandson of the Battle of the Somme veteran the band is named after, and business editor of the nationalist *Irish News* newspaper in Belfast.

While pipe bands are a predominantly Ulster-Scots tradition and therefore most of their members are from a Protestant background, Alan and Gary are keen to emphasise that the bands are cross-community and distinct from the loyalist band tradition. While the best band in Ireland is the Field Marshal Montgomery in Belfast, not far behind it is the St Laurence O'Toole Pipe Band, founded in Dublin in 1910 at a meeting attended by Pádraig Pearse, Thomas Clarke, Seán McDermott, Arthur Griffith and Douglas Hyde. Its first secretary was Seán O'Casey. The band played at the funerals of Thomas Ashe, O'Donovan Rossa, Arthur Griffith and Michael Collins. Now based in Maynooth, a significant percentage of the band are Protestants from the North. 'That shows you how pipe bands transcend politics,' says Alan.

'Pipe bands are non-sectarian,' says Gary. 'It's not one of these blood-and-thunder type things.' They would mostly march in their local district. 'We would play at church fêtes and on the Twelfth of July. But we also play St Patrick's Day.' In 2021 they played at both in Newry. Despite the name, a pipe band can have almost as many drummers as pipers.

There are two types of competition sets. The main one is a march, strathspey and a reel, called an MSR for short, the bread and butter for a pipe band. The other is a medley selection, a mixture of reels, jigs, hornpipes, slow marches.

Solicitor Kevin Winters' father, Jimmy, was one of three Catholics who played bagpipes in the McDonald Memorial Pipe Band, 'all down to the sheer love of music', he says. Kevin's father and two uncles were all traditional musicians and so they took up the bagpipes too. Ballela Pipe Band, based in the village five miles east of Banbridge, was entirely Catholic with many GAA members, Kevin says. 'For me as a child it was not unusual to go to a pipe bands competition on a Saturday and then go to Clones for a GAA match on a Sunday.' Orangemen marching on the Twelfth used to go to his great-uncle's to borrow drums; Kevin and his brother went regularly to world championships in Scotland. He has promised Gary McDonald that he will write an article for *The Irish News* about it. 'The working title is "And what takes you here?" Sometimes it is said as a bit of a joke. It still felt a wee bit uncomfortable, though, but then I am able to bore them with my knowledge.'

***

Alan joined the 4th Royal Irish Rangers regiment of the Territorial Army (TA) and Volunteer Reserve, which was based in Portadown, to play the pipes, not to play with guns. Having played in pipe band concerts over the years, he had heard the regimental band play.

'The TA wasn't set up to serve in Northern Ireland, not like the UDR. The TA was in the event of a third world war to go to Europe, and that's where it was to be deployed. I didn't particularly join it because I wanted to go to war in Europe. No, I joined it for the pipe band.'

When he attended the barracks, it was for band practice, playing MSRs, not firing SLRs (self-loading rifles). When he first joined, he had to go to Ballymena for a fortnight for training, 'to learn how to shoot, fire machine guns and all. And my target practice wasn't that good. I think with a lot of regiments now, a lot of musicians are maybe medics, things like that as well; maybe not fighting soldiers, but sort of stretcher-bearers or whatever, like. But that part of it was never for me.'

Back in 1984, Alan worked for British Telecom at the telephone exchange in Newry, along with two other TA colleagues who lived in Tullylish: Jim Bell, who had the rank of major, and Trevor May, who was a corporal. Trevor and Jim had served together in the TA for about eight years, at home and abroad, often on NATO exercises acting as umpires. They were both married with children, but Alan was still single back then. Jim was the senior colleague, so he drove the others to work in his yellow Volvo, picking Trevor up first, then collecting Alan in Banbridge, right outside the café where we are chatting, Blend & Batch, facing the war memorial.

On the morning of 9 May 1984, Jim collected Trevor first as usual, so he was in the front passenger seat and Alan got in the back when they picked him up in Banbridge. When they got to Newry, Jim parked near the exchange, outside a school, across the road from the police station, facing in towards the town centre. They thought it was a relatively safe place: an open position in plain view of passers-by, on a wide street with nothing to obstruct the view. However, at some point that day, a bomb was placed under the front wheel arch on the passenger's side.

Jim, Trevor and Alan nipped off a wee bit early that afternoon, about a quarter to three, as Jim had a lawnmower to collect on the way home.

'We went over and got into the car,' recalls Alan. 'Normal. Nothing.

Turned the ignition, everything hunky-dory. Now, because Jim was facing into Newry, obviously he had to turn the car, so there's a wee side road, Windsor Avenue, I think, runs up beside the school, so he was reversing the car into this street to head to Banbridge. I heard this almighty bang and my first reaction was: he's reversed into something. You know? He hasn't, though because I'm watching, I was looking. And I turned round and the inside of the car was filled with a sort of a white powdery smoke. But I could see Jim Bell, the driver, his seat, he was threw flat. And I could see his elbow. Actually, if you picture white, the whitest white, I could see the bone in his elbow.'

'Trevor's seat, it went forward. And it, from what I can recollect, nearly went flat like that. Trevor was a fair build of a fella, six foot, and I remember thinking to myself, how could that seat have gone like that?

'Obviously then a crowd gathered. Boys from the telephone exchange come running over. They tried to get me out of the door. My door wouldn't open. Then I don't know whether the back window had shattered or what, but they were asking, can you get out the back window? As soon as I put pressure on my right ankle, I knew. I said I can't. So they got crowbars, got the door open, they got me out of the car that way. The ankle had wee cuts and lacerations, singe marks and that, you know. They sat me on this wee low wall, and obviously then at that stage the police, ambulance had arrived. There's quite a crowd about.

'One of the policemen was from Banbridge and had been in our pipe band, so he talked away to me and asked if I wanted him to go and tell my parents. So I said, well, that's all right. The ambulance crew obviously gave me a bit of a check-up – they told me that because I was the least injured of the three, they would hold me here, get the other two into the ambulance first and get them away to hospital. I thought, that's fair enough. So, I don't know how long it was, like. And I sat and I waited, and we waited, and there was nothing.

'Next thing, they took me and Jim Bell in the ambulance. And

I suspected then, I says, there's something seriously wrong here with Trevor; they don't want us to see him. I didn't know he was dead, but I thought he's that badly injured that they don't actually want us to see him. So, they whipped me and Jim off to hospital. To Daisy Hill [in Newry] first of all. Then they took Jim to the Royal, and I went to the military wing of Musgrave Park Hospital.'

Trevor had been killed. He was 28 years old, originally from Portadown, and left behind a wife, Lyn (née Metcalfe, from Gilford), and a two-year-old son, Stephen.

Alan's right ankle had been shattered. 'It wasn't just a clean break. It still gives me pain to this day. They just put it in plaster. Sometimes I think because I was in the military hospital it was just patch them up and get them out. Sometimes I wonder – Jim was taken to the Royal and obviously I could understand why, but if I had been maybe taken on the NHS or somewhere like that, might have been a wee bit more specialised or something.'

Was Alan in shock after the incident? 'I probably was at the time. Sometimes I look back and say, how have I been so calm about all this, you know? And I just put it down to the fact that there was people killed in the Troubles. There's people far worse. I got off with my life and again in those days it just seemed to be, well, it's no worse than a car accident sort of thing. You know? I suppose if you come through something like that you're thankful for every day you have after that. I tell younger ones in the band now that didn't even live through the Troubles. I would maybe be limping a wee bit and some of them would say, "Did you hurt your ankle?" And I tell them what happened. They're shocked and they can't believe actually what our generation went through.'

Alan missed Trevor's funeral in All Saints' Parish Church, Tullylish but saw coverage of it on the television news from his hospital bed. 'I can still see that picture of the funeral, the church in Tullylish there and the crowds on that wee road.'

When I read the words that the Bishop of Down and Dromore, Dr

Robin Eames, spoke at the funeral, I realise Trevor May's widow and son were not there either.

'We are gathered here in a beautiful part of the province to pay our respects to a young man who, because of the time in which he lived and the way in which he sought to serve his community, has paid a severe penalty. I speak for the whole community when I reflect on the sense of shock, outrage and frustration which unites us all. My thoughts and prayers are not in this building but up the road with Lyn and her little son, who like so many before have been asked to carry a cross that is not of their choosing. They have something more than our sympathy – they have our support.'

Dr Eames referred to 'an ever-widening net of so-called justified murder by the terrorists. This is a widening net the terrorist seeks to justify so easily. We are accustomed to justification each time a life is taken.'

The minister who conducted Trevor's funeral said, 'I am speaking on behalf of his wife when I say that Trevor never imagined himself as a threat. The community is shocked and dismayed. The Territorial Army was a hobby. His wife is devastated.'

Can Alan remember what he felt watching it? 'I was sad. I was in the ward with five or six other squaddies but they were English or Scottish and I was telling them that was my mate that was killed. It was emotional to see it.'

He doesn't remember being angry. (Alan comes across as a very even-tempered man.)

'I don't know. I mind going with a girl years afterwards and we talked about the Troubles and it was still ongoing, I says till her like, "You know, I still maintain to this day the IRA did more to put off a united Ireland than to get a united Ireland." People like myself would say, I'll never vote for a united Ireland, but try and persuade me. Tell me you'll live a better life. I'd be open to persuasion. If it was a fair and reasonable argument, I'll listen till it. You know? I might say I still don't think, but at least try and persuade me. But this trying to coerce people into something, it's the wrong way to go.'

Did he feel that the motivation for the attack on him was primarily political or sectarian or a bit of both? 'I think it was political,' he says, 'I don't think it was sectarian. I think sectarian's more if a Protestant goes out and kills a Catholic for absolutely no reason or vice versa. But ours was probably more political because they assumed, not because we were Prods or this or the other, but because, they thought, members of the British security forces.'

He says his family were not embittered. 'Probably more thankful. My parents were more thankful that I survived.'

He mentions Fred Baxter, though, a DUP councillor in Banbridge. 'He was the cleaner in the telephone exchange in Banbridge and he had a locker there and if you opened the door of the locker, he had the front page of the *Chronicle* of that incident in Newry – basically a statement saying don't ever forget this. So, he would have been DUP so probably people like that, it would have hardened them. And the fact that he obviously knew the three of us.'

His colleagues in Newry were full of sympathy for what had happened to him. From both sides of the community. 'Well, I worked with Catholics. Some of my best mates. We used to hang out at the Coach and all. So there was no animosity. I think being brought up in this town went a long way.'

It had never crossed his mind that joining the TA might make him a target for republican paramilitaries. He suspects that the IRA thought they were in the UDR, the locally raised, regular British Army regiment.

'To go back to why we were targeted, Jim Bell's nickname was The Major. Now, when you look back, you think: how stupid. We were going in and out of Newry Telephone Exchange. Now nobody was ever caught for this, but they reckon that somebody overheard Jim being called The Major and assumed we were in the UDR. I've heard names mentioned, people that I worked with before and after the incident, that would be nice to your face but always in the back of your mind … But you said nothing because there was no proof, no evidence. And you just had to get on with it.'

The IRA's South Down Brigade threatened further attacks on Territorials. It said, 'The IRA sees no distinction between members of the RUC, British Army, UDR or Territorial Army. All are enemies of the Irish people.'

The IRA had, in fact, killed several members of the Territorial Army before. Given their elastic, ever-expanding definition of what constituted a 'legitimate target', it was not always clear which category their victims fell into. However, before Trevor May was murdered, the Provisionals had cited TA membership as justification for assassination. In other cases, it was clear TA membership was the only reason why a victim had been killed.

On 3 October 1973, Ivor Vennard, a 33-year-old Protestant postman, married with two children, was shot dead in a sub-post office by two IRA gunmen in Lurgan's nationalist Kilwilkie estate, eight months after he had left the UDR. The IRA issued a statement that he had been shot because he was a TA member. His widow responded, 'When murdered he was a member of none of the security forces, neither had he any political involvement. This was nothing more than another senseless killing. It is a downright lie to attempt to justify it by claiming that my husband had TA connections.' Hugh McGinn, a 40-year-old Catholic, married with six children, was shot dead by the INLA in Armagh city on 28 December 1980. He was a part-time sergeant major in the TA, having joined in 1960. In April 1983, Trevor Elliott, 38, married with five children, was shot dead by the IRA in Keady, County Armagh, near the shop where he worked. He was a drummer in the TA's pipe band. He was also press officer of the Armagh branch of the DUP. A senior TA officer in Armagh said, 'We would like to emphasise and stress that we have no connection and no involvement in the security situation here in Northern Ireland.'

I had a friend at school who joined the TA in Banbridge and I worried for his safety, even if he didn't. He used to call it the SAS – Saturdays and Sundays, playing soldiers at weekends. Happily, nothing ever happened to him and he ended up joining the police in England.

The brother-in-law of one of Alan's aunts was also shot by the IRA because he did building work on an army base, part of the ever-widening gyre of 'legitimate targets'.

Alan voted for the Good Friday Agreement. 'That incident in Newry didn't sway me. I was glad to see there was some kind of peace coming. I never thought, after what happened to me, people have got to pay, why should I vote for this? For the sake of the next generation, the young ones, let's see if we get to the end of this. I would be an Ulster Unionist through and through. David Trimble passed away recently there. I think it's only now people are recognising and realising just what he went through and what he did. And I tell you, of all those politicians, John Hume and Gerry Adams, David Trimble got the hardest time, I think. Because Paisley and the DUP … what riles me is that the Ulster Unionists and Trimble took the step and the DUP were outside: "No, no, no, no." As soon as they become the big party, they change. The two parties, the SDLP and the Ulster Unionists, that took that step are now the smallest parties and the two polar opposites are now the big ones.

'Any Catholics that I worked with had this aspiration for a united Ireland. You might not like it but you respect that people have their own opinions. I know things needed to change in Northern Ireland, gerrymandering and all this. I can understand why some people thought: we're not getting anywhere politically, we're going to have to do something more. When that all started to come about, power-sharing, I said what's wrong with that, like? I often thought: what if there was never partition? If in some way the Republic had stayed within the Commonwealth or something …'

***

Alan received £25,000 in compensation and had six months' sick leave to recuperate. Towards the end, he was asked to attend a medical board, but he couldn't as he was going to a band competition in Scotland. The boss initially told him he couldn't leave the country while on sick leave. If I were a unionist, I would have taken umbrage at this but Alan didn't press the point. In any case, the boss came back and said, 'Alan, I've got that cleared. I've told them I think this would be good for your mental health, for your recovery to get away.'

***

'People often ask me what happened,' says Alan, 'how has it affected you and do you lose sleep over it? And I say well no, I don't, because I think in the back of my mind I accept that it's one of those things. It was a way of life, you know? I was lucky that I got away with my life.

'I suppose in a way I would probably feel some guilt because I wasn't married at the time but Trevor had been recently married and in actual fact had a wee child. And Jim Bell was married and had a family and all and at the end of it you think to yourself why couldn't it have been me really, like, if it was any of us? Because yes, obviously I have a family, I would have been missed and that, but you wouldn't be leaving a child without a father.

'And in actual fact, I remember when we were leaving the exchange I was going to say, it crossed my mind, it shows you how in a split second a decision you can make can change your life, I was going to suggest that I would sit in the front on the way home. Uh-huh, but then I didn't bother, because I thought, it's stupid, I'm getting out first anyway. It would mean chopping and changing. But if I had put the question and Trevor says, "Aye, if you want to, you sit in the front …"'

'So, it really could have been you?'

'It could have been, you know.'

***

Jim Bell credits an Official IRA man with saving his life after the Provisional IRA attempted to murder him. His colleague, the exchange's first aid officer, rushed to the scene of the explosion and applied a tourniquet to Jim's mutilated left arm to prevent a fatal haemorrhage.

'My recollection is of being blown backwards,' he says of the explosion. 'I thought I'd been hit by a car. I'm told my language left a lot to be desired.' He credits the make of car, one renowned for its safety features, for his survival. 'Only it was a Volvo 240, we were all dead.' That said, he still suffered terrible injuries, which affect him to this day.

Apart from a broken leg, which healed, although the muscle still bulges through the soft tissue, most of his injuries were to his upper body – a mangled arm, perforated eardrums and a damaged eye. He can joke about it without making light of it: 'I had that many holes in my ass because of the shrapnel, I often said they could have carried me out of there like a six-pack. They were going to cut the arm off, but the surgeon said a second-class arm is better than a first-class prosthetic.'

As his left arm had lost almost all its tissue, the surgeon attached it to his chest wall beneath a flap of skin for several weeks to generate new tissue, then grafted skin from his backside to cover it. Jim, modifying the saying that some people don't know their arse from their elbow, jokes: 'My ass *is* my elbow.'

He was told that his arm would never go up past 90 degrees, but by carrying a paint tin with gradually more water each day he got that down to 45 degrees. However, he can't pick anything up from the floor on his left side. 'I sleep on a waterbed because if it's cold my hand claws, it locks up and I can't use it.'

The vertebrae in his lower back were also damaged. 'Two and a half pounds of Semtex up your arse doesn't do you a lot of good. There are days I can hardly kneel or use my arm. I have hearing aids and suffer badly from tinnitus. My wife can hear the TV at volume 7, I can only hear it at 21.'

As well as his physical injuries, there were mental scars. 'For years

I wore a long-sleeved shirt to cover my injuries. It was only after I got my head straight I said, "Up yours, mate, I've nothing to hide, I've done nothing wrong."' On this wet summer's day, he is in short sleeves and, in the middle of describing the hole in his chest, he decides to show, not tell, pulling up his shirt to reveal the blanched hollow in his torso.

'Terrorism is done by very few,' he says. 'It mesmerises many and terrorises many more.'

Neither Jim nor his family received any counselling. His children, Jason and Joanne, were in their early teens. He was sent to see a psychiatrist to tick a box. 'I refused to sit with my back to the door, I smoked most of his cigarettes and I was armed, which scared the shit out of him. My marriage fell apart, as everything had to be my way and I was self-medicating on alcohol. I wanted revenge on the bastard who did this. It took me a long time to realise that it was pointless, that the only person I was screwing up was me.'

But the toughest thing for Jim to deal with was the trauma of coming home. 'Survivor's guilt is a big thing,' he says. He had been badly injured, but he was still alive. Trevor, his friend, colleague and neighbour, was dead. He felt a duty of care towards Trevor's widow, installing a security alarm on her house, and was on call if ever she felt scared, but, eventually, 'She said, "Jim, I don't want you coming round any more" and that really hurt. She's blaming me, I can understand that: "You got him to join the TA; you brought him to Newry; you got him killed in your car" – is that what she's thinking? That's what goes on in your head. It was hurting too much to see me walking around when her husband wasn't.

'It's coming up to forty years now. These thoughts will reappear over the next few weeks and I'll have to put them to bed again. The outcome could have been a lot worse. Fifteen minutes earlier, the kids would have been coming out of school. How many of them would we have killed in the blast?'

I gently correct him: 'They, not we.' He might bear the scars, but should not have to bear the blame, even subconsciously.

On the twenty-fifth anniversary of the bombing, Jim returned to Newry and put a wreath against the wall near where his Volvo was parked. 'It didn't last a day. I suppose people just want to forget.'

He is originally from Lurgan. 'My father had a draper's shop in William Street. My mother was a terrorist.' He pauses for effect. 'She used to beat the crap out of me with a leather strap.' He would hide it in the bin and the binman would return it to his mother. 'I still hate binmen.' He is grateful, though, that he was brought up free of prejudice. 'I have been to the chapel in Lurgan many times for the funerals of my mother's friends, to show respect. That's the way I was brought up.' He shows me round his workshop and I spot a crate addressed to Sister Bernadette Duffy, a nun from the parish who spent her adult life as a missionary in Africa. He is shipping her a bicycle.

Jim was always interested in the military. His uncle Eddie was one of the last to make it out of Dunkirk during the Second World War. 'I felt so proud to be walking round Lurgan with him.' Jim's grandfather and five great-uncles fought in the First World War. His grandfather lost a leg and a brother. Jim graduated from the scouts to the TA just before the Troubles began. He convinced Trevor to join the TA and they did a lot of war games together in Germany with the British Army of the Rhine. Jim's specialty was identifying Russian vehicles and weapons. Trevor was his radio operator.

Back home, they helped each other out with domestic jobs, slagged each other off. 'I always remember him getting conifer trees to plant round his garden and when they arrived they were about an inch long. Poor old Trevor was one of the nicest people you could ever meet, very quiet, refined, very seldom lost his temper, a family man, just an effing good guy.'

Jim has both Irish and British passports and is very proud of his service to the Queen. 'I'm a royalist. I wouldn't say I'm a loyalist by any stretch of the imagination.' He insisted that his team make it to work every day during the Ulster Workers' Council Strike, leading by example. He was stopped by a barricade in Gilford. 'I said, "You're blocking the road. How is the ambulance going to get through?" What ambulance? "The ambulance that is going to have to come for you if you don't get out of the effing way."'

He has no time for politics, he says, but that doesn't mean he was blind to injustice. 'To say we didn't have discrimination before the Troubles is a lie.'

He sees himself as a European and thinks leaving the EU is 'the worst thing we ever did. Everything was levelling up nicely. We are now in a great position for trade, but no, we want to be tied by the umbilical cord to Britain, who would shite on you as soon as look at you. I don't see anything wrong with a united Ireland as long as it's done democratically. But I know I couldn't afford to live in the South.'

Jim lives in a converted linen mill built in 1702 by the River Bann, part of the old Uprichard estate. Daddy was passing one day and persuaded him to join the local cross-community group, the Laurencetown, Lenaderg & Tullylish Community Association.

'I believed in it. I saw it as another chance to stabilise society. Laurencetown was seen at the time as a republican or nationalist area because it had the tricolour flying. We applied for the Queen's Award for Voluntary Service and the Lord Lieutenant came down in full dress uniform to present it, which meant we could put the crown on our letterhead. The next morning about seventeen republican flags went up but by 10 a.m. all the flags were gone. I thought, "Fuck, we've won."'

He served as chairman for five years and is still on the committee along with my father, my cousin Mel Byrne, a former SDLP councillor, and Kevin Savage, a Sinn Féin councillor: 'He's dead straight, a nicer guy you'd never meet.'

Somehow it doesn't surprise me when Jim quotes Clint Eastwood: 'Don't let the old man in.' 'You could sit in your chair and say, "Woe is me, look what they've done to me", but I say to myself, "Get off your ass." There are two types of people – survivors and non-survivors. I've every intention of going to my grave saying, "What a ride."'

Twenty-one

Delinquent Juvenilia

I was a slow learner when it came to realising that the best thing for me to do was to leave the North. I had started studying French and German at Queen's University Belfast in October 1985. On 15 November that year Margaret Thatcher and Garret FitzGerald had signed the Anglo-Irish Agreement, resulting in a wave of unionist protests and increased tension. Belfast was not buzzing back then. It was ticking.

I attended a talk by an SDLP politician held, inappropriately, in the Catholic student chaplaincy. As I entered, after walking from my home off the Lisburn Road, I looked over my shoulder, worried about more than my street cred. Only four other students had turned up. Surveying this, the politician, instead of turning the lecture into a seminar by offering to buy us all a drink, turned tail.

Political activism at Queen's was a dangerous business. Edgar Graham – a 29-year-old law lecturer and a rising star in the Ulster Unionist Party – was murdered by the IRA, shot dead outside the university library on 7 December 1983, two years before I matriculated.

Sheena Campbell – a 29-year-old law student and a rising star in Sinn Féin – was murdered by the UVF, shot dead in the York Hotel on Botanic Avenue near Queen's on 16 October 1992, two years after I graduated. Her mother was from Tullylish.

Having tried the year before to persuade one of my best friends,

Andy, to stay and study in Belfast, I now was thinking of following in his footsteps and transferring to Edinburgh University, where he was a student, or to the University of St Andrews, where my sister Andrea was studying.

I saw myself as a moderate. I had a relative in the police and we played squash together in the bowels of the fortress that was Lurgan RUC station. In my time at Queen's, I played snooker in the Felons Club on the Falls with a student whose father had been a republican prisoner, a requirement for membership. I was an equal-opportunity sportsman. I lived near the loyalist Village area and faced a moral dilemma when neighbours knocked, collecting for a loyalist band. Inspiration struck. 'Thon student doesn't even understand decimal currency,' they must have said when they emptied their tin. In truth, though, I did not feel safe living in Belfast.

It is here that I must admit that I used to write poems or songs, or a misconceived combination of – or hesitation between – the two, which I shall christen pongs. I wish I had kept a diary instead but there you go. Most are truly terrible, delinquent juvenilia. One or two, though, at least capture something of how I felt at the time. A summer or two later a friend recorded himself singing this, accompanying himself on the guitar, with the accidental sound effect of someone ringing the doorbell in the middle of it … and it wasn't bad, honestly:

Staring through a slit in the curtains
Wondering if it's curtains for me
Hearing a crash or loud voices outside
But there's no place to hide
Behind the settee
Walking down rundown streets
Wanting to run down rundown streets
Almost embarrassed to be always alert
Wary of a slowing car.

The hate of the day clouds my mind gets in my way
Stops me from sleeping then poisons my dreams
A drought of tears is all that keeps me from weeping
A draught of fear sends me creeping into my jeans
And I guess I am just an unpicked victim
Waiting in the wings
An unselected statistic, hoping that
Peace is what tomorrow brings.

When I did transfer to study in St Andrews, I attended a creative writing class with the poet Douglas Dunn, who commented on the musicality of my work and compared it (not necessarily favourably) to 'Bagpipe Music' by Louis MacNeice. When Thomas McCarthy mentioned in his book, *Poetry, Memory and the Party: Journals 1974–2014*, that he'd met Dunn and found him rather depressed, I must admit checking whether the date coincided with my time in his writing class.

***

At St Andrews, where in 2001 the heir to the British throne would follow in my footsteps, I began to notice posh people. It is wrong to make fun of people because of their accents – but they were commonly called Yahs. They tied their sweaters round their shoulders, not their waists. They were loud. Even their trousers were loud. They wore Barbour jackets and Icelandic fishermen's jerseys.

I spoke fast and kept having to repeat myself: I learned to speak more slowly so that English people could understand me. The misunderstanding was mutual. When my then girlfriend, Natalie, came to visit and introduced herself to Granny, her clipped, public-school vowels caused confusion. 'Nettle-y? Daughter dear, what sort of parents call their child after a weed?'

Natalie insisted on giving me a cutlery lesson before we visited her parents. I was now in a world where what mattered was not which foot you dug with but how you held your knife and fork. Great.

A lecturer corrected me when I defined limbo as a Catholic concept of a post-death state or place that no longer existed. 'It never existed,' he said, in a tone that did not hide his disdain, though his came from a sense of secular, not sectarian, superiority, which was novel.

I greenly took offence when a fellow student innocently asked if I would be crossing the snot-green sea for the holidays. He hastily explained the Joycean reference. I needed to up my reading game and sand down my chips.

I was living in a different world now, but I still tried to keep abreast of what was happening back home, combing the British dailies in my hall of residence's common room for their scant coverage of the North, where the violence was still comfortably outpacing political activity.

***

The first thing I did when I went to London after my first year at St Andrews was sign on; the same when I left school. Drawing the dole; signing on; doing the double; collecting the bru; claiming social security – the numerous euphemisms for unemployment benefit I acquired aren't quite up there with Inuit words for snow, but they speak to the centrality of the experience. There was a precariat before the word.

Before I left school, my first regular job was at was at my uncle's filling station. Bizarrely, in retrospect, clothes from army surplus stores were the height of fashion, in my circles anyway, so some of my wages were spent on a US Army jacket and combat trousers, although my being unable to open the knot I tied at the ankle and having to cut the lace to get the trousers off suggested that I might not in fact be combat material.

When my uncle opened his business he received a death threat from loyalist paramilitaries. But he survived and prospered, even if his nephew occasionally confused orders for petrol and diesel. Catholics did not have to join the IRA or Sinn Féin to pose a threat. Seeking to advance socially or economically was subversive enough. Croppies refusing to lie down.

I'd also once mitched off school with my friend Flea to earn a few bob gathering potatoes for a local farmer. We were the only boys from our village doing the work that day. All the others were Protestants recruited from elsewhere. We kept to ourselves, picking from our own furrow. Gathering potatoes is too much like hard work and I would not recommend it. Still, the money would always come in handy. Towards the end of the day, however, the other teenagers started to call us Fenians and pelt us with stones and potatoes and we had to run. We were local, but we weren't loyal. Imported Protestants clodding spuds at local Catholics felt like some sort of bad joke: a stereotype, a cliché and a metaphor walk into a bar …

When I was 13, we'd moved to a bungalow on the other side of the Bann. It would have been the other side of the tracks too, but the railway line was long gone. We had a ludicrously large front garden, in truth a field so full of weeds that the only cure – allegedly – was to plant it with potatoes, the picking of which was delegated downwards. If this back-breaking bending was social climbing, it felt counter-intuitive. My lower-middle-class life had got off to a very unpromising start.

Poor Shane had it worse. If there is one thing worse than lifting spuds, it is picking flax. A local entrepreneur needed labour and Mummy knew just the boy. Forget grinds. Nothing focuses a student's mind like the grind of agricultural labour.

Something was lost in the transition, though. My grandfather Bill 'Slater' Doyle was a roofer like his father before him and built himself a fine house. The thought of me or Daddy up on the roof, even of our bungalow, conjures up for me the fate of Rod Hull, who fell to his death adjusting an aerial in a storm, leaving Emu an orphan. The closest I have ever come to the roof is releasing the catch on the folding ladder to boldly go into the attic.

My upbringing – my class background – has not completely defined me, but it certainly colours how I perceive the world and understand society. Our sky was lower, our horizons closer. Our first and only family holiday abroad was to Brittany by boat, just before my sixteenth birthday. That said, we were lucky in that Daddy's parents lived near Courtown, the County Wexford seaside resort, and – bonus points – my aunt Kathleen owned the chip shop, meaning free chips. To replicate that buzz as an adult you'd need to be a gambler in Vegas.

At the time, alienation was the buzzword to describe how Catholics felt in a gerrymandered State designed to deny them their rights and identity. I felt the buzz of recognition when I read how Stephen Rea admired the 'appropriate disrespect' his fellow Queen's student Eamonn McCann had shown to the authorities in the late 1960s. But I never succumbed to the nihilistic extreme of nationalism that was happy for our gutters to run red while only our rivers ran free.

***

While studying at Erlangen, which was then in West Germany, I met the daughter of a leading Northern Ireland industrialist who could not have been nicer. She introduced me to her father, who took an interest in my modern languages degree, and encouraged me to come back to the North and start a career in marketing. The daughter and her boyfriend took me sailing on Lough Erne in Fermanagh in their boat. The Berlin Wall came down that year. There seemed little prospect then that our walls would come tumbling down or that our politicians might produce such seismic change, however.

I realised when I was at St Andrews that I could become a different, middle-class, person if I wanted. I didn't really. I spent the first decade of my career working for Irish community newspapers in London – a vocation, not just a job, recognising in the Irish diaspora an even more marginalised out-group of the nation. I had contemplated a career in the law but was also captivated by investigative reporting into miscarriages of justice.

During my final year at university, one trip to London for an interview with a City law firm in October 1989 coincided with the dramatic release of the Guildford Four. I returned to St Andrews with a 'Free the Birmingham Six' poster I'd picked up at the GAA club in Ruislip. In 1991, I reported from the Old Bailey on the release of the Birmingham Six. A colleague spotted me in a photograph in the *Daily Express* the next day in the middle of a crowd of well-wishers, celebrating with one of the Six. I later interviewed Paddy Hill about his charitable work helping other victims of miscarriages of justice. But I also published a front-page photograph by our Midlands correspondent Brendan Farrell on the twenty-fifth anniversary of the Birmingham bombings that showed Bridget Reilly laying a wreath in memory of her sons Eugene and Desmond, who were among the victims murdered that night by the IRA. Bridget looked so like my granny, Bridget Doyle, and her grief reminded me of Granny's helpless sorrow when my Granda Bill died.

As arts editor of *The Irish Post*, I interviewed many authors who review for me now as books editor of *The Irish Times*. My finest hour was appearing as an extra in the final episode of *Father Ted*. I was at a party in the green room of London Studios on the South Bank after the recording of an earlier episode in February 1996 when a newsflash announced that a huge bomb had gone off in the Docklands, a few miles upriver. The IRA had broken its ceasefire. Tragedy had trumped farce once more. When I was made deputy editor, my successor as arts editor was Joe Crilly, from Derrymacash, part of an area known as the Montiaghs (pronounced Munchies) or boglands, which lies between Tullylish and Lough Neagh. Joe was an acclaimed playwright, whose plays are all set in our common hinterland and often explore its sectarian tensions. After his death by suicide in 2017, in a generous act of memorialisation, my *Irish Times* colleague Ronan McGreevy, who had worked with us both at *The Irish Post*, crowdfunded the publication of the Crilly Trilogy (*Second-Hand Thunder*; *On McQuillan's Hill*; and *Kitty & Damnation*). Queen's University Belfast academic Mark Phelan wrote in its foreword, 'Crilly's dialogue pithily captures the mulchy vernacular of Mid-Ulster speech,' an earthy mix of Elizabethan English, Ulster Scots and Irish.

Joe could be provocative in conversation too, once calling a freelance colleague of Northern Protestant stock who had embraced an Irish identity 'a tame Prod'. Perhaps for him they were a novelty, not having grown up or been schooled alongside them, whereas for me having benefited from such solidarity throughout my teens and been glad of it, to casually disparage those who crossed the aisle or lived comfortably on common ground felt off.

The Montiaghs also inspired this risqué limerick by Seamus Heaney, sent on a postcard from Emory to Michael Longley and signed in jest, R[obert] Lowell.

'There was a young man from the Munchies, Whose language would surely affront yez, It was fuck yez Hell roast yez, Yez fuckin whores' ghosts yez, Yez bollocks, yez bastards, yez cunts yez.'

***

The peace process, when it started, felt miraculous. The Troubles were all I had known; only the Christmas ceasefires gave an annual inkling of a life free of fear and horror. The Good Friday Agreement felt like a monumental compromise, endorsed by former extremists on both sides, leaving the reactionary naysayers of the DUP isolated. In time, even they would come on board, but in embracing Brexit they helped dismantle the European Union framework that provided a common European home for rival national identities. There must be no border between the North and Britain, they insist, except, hypocritically, on social issues such as abortion.

The prospect of a return to violence appals me. Equally, the rise of the middle ground and a more pluralist society and the rejection of the old binaries of religious and national identity give me hope. Regardless of whether a referendum on reunification is held and won, I would like to see ever closer links between North and South, and East and West for that matter. In such a scenario, everybody wins.

In the 1970s, ugly oil drums filled with concrete and linked by scaffolding poles used to divide Banbridge's high street from through traffic. Later, pretty flower beds in coffin-like troughs fulfilled that function. But every summer another hardy perennial is allowed to colonise what should be a shared civic space in a mixed town: the red, white and blue bunting and Union flags of one tradition are strung up along the street, and a triumphalist Orange arch spans it, while side streets sport loyalist paramilitary flags. A party that excludes 40 per cent of the population. What is that but Protestant privilege?

If discrimination and domination are bad, does it really have to be said that indiscriminate murder is so much worse? A fortnight before the Omagh bombing on 15 August 1998, in which twenty-nine people were murdered, the Real IRA planted a similar 500lb car bomb in Banbridge. Luckily no one was killed. For me, the deepest divide was and always will be between those on all sides (including the State) who supported the taking of life for political ends and those who opposed it.

As John Montague wrote in 'A Response to Omagh':

All I can do is curse, complain.
Who can endorse such violent men
As history creaks on its bloody hinge
and the unspeakable is done again.

With no peace after the deluge
no ease after the storm
we learn to live inside ruin
like a second home.

Every August, a human effigy is trundled up the Cut on a tumbril by the local branch of the Apprentice Boys of Derry, and set on fire on the Downshire Bridge, a human sacrifice, more *Wicker Man* than Burning Man, more folk horror than folk festival, like a Gothic fever dream from an Andrew Michael Hurley novel. The effigy is of Lundy, who wanted to surrender during the Siege of Derry. The contemporary message to Unionist leaders is: compromise at your peril.

A war memorial stands at the top of the town and a smaller one beside it honours members of the security services killed in the Troubles. But there is nothing to commemorate civilians such as Pat Campbell, no Stolpersteine to make a new generation stumble and turn away from bad old ways. You will find a memorial to the Miami Showband in Dublin, another just off the dual carriageway where the killings took place, and there is a plaque on lead singer Fran O'Toole's old home in Bray. But nothing in the town they played for the night they were murdered.

In the words of Kim Wagner, historian of the British Empire, 'We are not responsible for the past, but we are responsible for what we choose to remember and what we choose to forget.'

Twenty-two

'You'd not get a softer target than Pat'

Even before the name of the victim was released, when news broke on the night of Monday, 20 February 1989, that a security guard had been shot dead at the Ewart Liddell linen mill in Donaghcloney, it ricocheted around Laurencetown. Everyone knew that it was Pat Feeney who had been murdered.

His cousin Declan Feeney, whose father John Michael had been murdered in Bleary Darts Club in 1975, was at his friend Paddy Barry's house in Millar Park, just a few doors down from Pat's family home, when the TV programme they were watching was interrupted by a newsflash.

'And I immediately said, "What day is today?" And they said, "Monday." I said, "Pat Feeney does the security in the factory on a Monday."' Declan ran over to the house – his uncle Patsy had seen the news and was beside himself, trying to get through to the police. Declan took over and managed to get through to Banbridge police station. 'I said, "I want to know is it my cousin Pat? I'm with his father now." And he said to me, "Yes, I'm afraid to tell you it is." And then just at that, when I come out of the house to go over and tell my mother, a police car pulled up outside.'

Billy Duffy was a friend and neighbour of Pat's. He died in 2023, shortly after I interviewed him.

'I was in bed when the news came on,' he said. 'I sort of knew when they said security guard in Donaghcloney. I was actually after the same job that wee Pat got, even though Donaghcloney would have been considered a risky place [for a Catholic]. You'd not get a softer target than Pat. Pat just liked a bit of craic, liked his football, liked a pint. He was quiet enough, no badness in him. There wasn't a bad bone in his body.'

Donaghcloney is part of the Catholic parish of Tullylish but a separate Church of Ireland parish for the same reason the seat of the Catholic diocese of Dromore moved from the nearby mainly Protestant town to the predominantly Catholic city of Newry near the border. Catholics tended not to socialise there, although we celebrated our parents' twenty-fifth wedding anniversary in McCartans' pub in the village in 1990. It wasn't perhaps the most obvious place to hold the party, but we wanted to support a local family who'd had a hard time keeping their business afloat in a village where to be a Catholic was no advantage.

James McCartan was one of the finest Gaelic footballers of his generation, part of the 1960 Down team, which was the first from north of the border to win an All-Ireland football final. They won again the following year. He and his brother Dan, another future All-Ireland winner, had both attended the Protestant primary school in Donaghcloney. In his memoir, *The King of Down Football*, co-written with Seamus McRory, James remembers with affection his decent, fair-minded teachers.

He writes too of being ostracised by pupils who called them 'papishes' and often refused to let them join in a game of football. The main sport of the village, though, was cricket. 'Here discrimination raised its ugly head again. The other children would not allow us to bowl or bat. We were allowed, however, to act as fielders as this involved a lot of running and hard work.' Ironically, the fielding skills they developed would serve them well as Gaelic footballers.

As an adult, James combined a career as an elite amateur sportsman with managing the family quarry, farm and pub. He was a moderate nationalist: 'I believe in the concept of a united Ireland. However, that thinking would be based on a consensus only arrived at by democratic and constitutional means. The idea of either IRA or loyalist paramilitaries forcing their separate agendas of national unity or a sectarian statelet would be totally repugnant to me.

'It is easy to express republican ideals from the relative safety of south Armagh. When the IRA campaign of killings and bombing escalated it was the innocent Catholics living in unionist strongholds such as Donaghcloney who suffered most.'

In his memoir, he lists the campaign of harassment that he and his family endured. In 1973, on the day of Princess Anne's marriage to Mark Phillips, loyalist paramilitaries planted a large bomb outside the pub. Sectarian graffiti was repeatedly scrawled on the walls of the bar and their home, but no one was ever charged. Despite this, the village's older Protestants kept coming, as customers and friends. Regularly, however, they would leave to find black roses attached to the windscreens of their cars. Loyalists tried to extort £12,000 by threatening the McCartans' children, in particular their son, who shared his father's name: 'James' end will not be quick. It will be slow and painful.' In 1991, a huge IRA bomb blew out every window and door in their home and those of their neighbours, to whom the McCartans gave shelter overnight in the bar.

McCartan's was the only licensed premises in Donaghcloney but when the Twelfth of July demonstration was held in the village, locals stood outside advising visitors not to give business to 'the Fenian McCartans'. On another 12 July, 200 posters with the slogan 'It's unhealthy to drink in McCartans' were fixed to every pole in the village.

For thirty years they had a night-time security routine in the event of a gun or bomb attack. Sometimes they even slept in tracksuits in case they might have to evacuate in a hurry. When James's wife, Marie, walked through the village, young locals would spit as she passed.

James and Marie's five children attended the local Protestant school but were taunted by their classmates and excluded from games. 'Despite our protestations most of the teachers washed their hands of this,' he wrote. In 1981, they could stick it no longer and the children all transferred to the primary school in Laurencetown that I had attended.

The Good Friday peace agreement brought no respite so, having raised their family, the McCartans decided to sell up in 2001. The highest bidder was a local man, 'an exceptionally decent Protestant'. Local extremists tried to pressurise him into offering less but he stood firm and paid the market value.

While Laurencetown's Catholics could choose where they socialised, they had to take work where they could find it.

Patricia Donaghy lived next door to the Feeneys in Millar Park. Pat was about six years older than her, but they had got to know each other well as they walked to the bus stop at the crossroads every morning to wait for their factory buses. She worked in Spence Bryson's shirt factory in Portadown.

'People ask where you were when JFK was shot,' says Patricia. 'Well, I know exactly where I was when I heard about Pat. I was doing the dishes in the kitchen of Number 32, when the news came on the radio. My blood ran cold. The next thing I just heard the wails next door. It was February so the curtains would have been drawn, you wouldn't have seen the police car driving up. My mum and dad were very fond of Pat; he was like another son.'

Billy Duffy had a framed photograph of Pat Feeney on a coffee table in his living room. Pat was about ten years older than me, so he has the hairstyle of someone who came of age in the mid-1970s, and the trademark moustache I remember, which always gave him a rather mournful look. He is wearing a Celtic scarf that celebrated the club's centenary in 1988, the year before his murder. Billy let me remove the photo from its frame so I could make a copy without the glare from the glass. As I did so, I noticed the date on the back, January 7th, 1989, the month before Pat's murder. In the photo, someone's fortieth birthday card is on the mantelpiece behind him, marking a milestone he would never reach.

Pat wasn't really a Celtic fan, though, says Fergie Larkin, his cousin. 'Pat was a Chelsea fan. He was buried with a Chelsea scarf around his neck. Wait till I tell you about Pat and Celtic. Pat bought a Celtic jersey to play five-a-side with the Donaghcloney workers. They were all Rangers fans. I said, "Pat, do not, do not, do not, don't do it; you'll wind those boys up the wrong road." I says, "Wear your Chelsea jersey." But Pat went out and bought a Celtic jersey.'

That wasn't the only time Pat failed to heed a warning from Fergie.

'That Monday night [a week before Pat was shot], I was out at that factory to have the craic with him and I said to him, "Fuck me, Pat, I wouldn't stay here." There was nobody about. He was sitting in thon wee fucking hut with one wee bulb hanging down, down the lane by the factory gates. There wasn't a light [outside]. It was really eerie.'

When I was growing up in Millar Park, there were some older boys who threw their weight about. Others might have had a smart mouth. I can picture them hanging around the local shop – long hair and centre partings, all double denim and Doc Martens, drinking Lucozade to cure a Sunday morning hangover. Pat wasn't like that. Even though he was from a famous boxing clan, he wasn't a fighter, or a big mouth.

'Pat was the quietest cratur in the village,' says Fergie. 'We would have went for a pint, he would have had four pints before he would have spoke.'

Fergie has a framed photo of his cousin on display in his living room too. The haircut is the same – long, the ears half-covered – but this one is black and white, the expression solemn, the Adam's apple prominent.

What did Pat do outside work? 'He played a few darts in the pub, had a few pints, that was him. He'd come with me on a Tuesday night to watch me play pool for a bit of craic. He used to come to Leeds matches with us, he enjoyed himself, like. It's just a pity he went to work where he worked, or he'd probably still be here.'

Gilford Mill, which closed down in 1986.

Pat's first job was in Gilford Mill. Fergie remembers Pat telling him about witnessing a fellow worker lose his arm in a machine. Donaghcloney Mill would prove deadlier.

'He was saving to buy a car. I think he had a couple of thousand pounds in the credit union in Banbridge. I said, "Pat, that'll get you a car." He says, "No, no, Fergie, I'm trying to get to 4,000. I'm going to get a real good car and drive down the park and doot the horn at Kevin McGarry." Kevin had a wee Volkswagen. And God help him, he never seen it.'

Fergie was 30 when Pat was shot. Michael, Pat's brother, was 22. 'Michael took it bad,' says Fergie. He had been in the local shop when he heard the news. 'I remember him running up the back alley roaring and crying, the screams of him. It was hard on them all, such an innocent kid to go. It was terrible.'

Fergie accompanied his uncle Patsy to the trial of two of the five loyalists convicted of Pat's murder. One of them worked in the factory alongside Pat and set him up to be murdered, falsely claiming to the UVF that Pat was in the IRA.

'He [Pat's colleague] was at a UVF meeting in Lisburn and this boy says to him, "What are you doing here? Are you spying on us? You haven't spoken all night, you haven't mentioned one target for us. Do you know any IRA men?" And he says, "I do – Pat Feeney." The detective said to him, "Do you realise you were telling lies?" He said, "I did, but I had to say somebody." And he said, "And you knew that night that you had signed that lad's death certificate?" He said, "I did, but I didn't know to the Monday night before when it was happening." The detective told me and Patsy in court that morning, "In my opinion he's worse than the man who pulled the trigger. The gunman thought he was killing an IRA man, whereas *he* knew he was killing a totally innocent man."

'He walked past Pat that night and says to Pat, "I'll see you tomorrow," and Pat says, "All right, I'll see you tomorrow." He told the detective that.

'That night, God love Pat, he seen them and he run. He had a leather jacket on – I know cos I burned his clothes. They fired five shots, one, two, three, four, and one in the middle like the five in a deck of cards. The one in the middle took the legs from him and they trailed him up over the gravel, which was all stuck to him, and then they put one in his head.'

Keith Ogle, a 20-year-old Queen's University student who lived nearby, heard the shots and rushed from his house, stopping only to tell his mother, Maud, to call the police. He saw a car speeding off but could not see the killers' faces, he told the *Banbridge Chronicle*. 'When I looked down the path and saw the door of the security hut flapping in the wind, I knew something was wrong. It was a cold night and I knew that Pat wouldn't have left the door open.'

He walked round the back of the hut and saw Pat lying on the ground. 'He was still living when I saw him. His eyes were just staring but I could hear him breathing. I told him to hold on and I ran down to the factory to get help, but when I got back he was dead. Every time I walk past there I know I'm going to think about it.'

Although it must have been traumatic for Keith, who was a year or two behind me at Banbridge Academy, I'm glad the last voice Pat heard was a kind one, not his killer's.

Norman Hutton, Ewart Liddell's production director, said Pat only did security duty on Mondays from 6.30 p.m. to 11.30 p.m. 'His death has come as a great shock to us and at the minute the work force is dazed. There is a mood of sheer repulsion around the factory.'

The morning after the murder, says Fergie, someone wrote on the wall of the men's toilets in the factory: 'UVF 2 Feeneys 0', a reference to the murder of Pat's uncle John Michael fourteen years before.

Fergie went with Patsy to Keenan's undertakers in Banbridge with the clothes for Pat to be dressed in for the coffin. They were given a bag containing the clothes Pat had been wearing the night of the murder. Patsy didn't want them so Fergie threw them in the boot of his car. They lay there for a month till the load became unbearable. 'I said, "Patsy, what will I do with them?" He says, "Burn them." So I burned them in the Gaelic field. There was a wee Chelsea badge on his coat. I took it off and gave it to Michael.'

The chief mourners at Pat's funeral were his father, Patsy; stepmother, June; brother, Michael; his five sisters, Maureen, Magdalene, Anne, Christine and Catherine; his half-brothers, Martin and Gary; and half-sister, Joanne.

Dr Francis Gerard Brooks, the Bishop of Dromore, urged mourners to join the family in forgiving the killers and implored both communities to set aside thoughts of revenge or retaliation and unite to defeat terrorism and violence. 'Let us put aside our narrow prejudices, our thinking always of "our side" and "their side" and begin to think and work as fellow Christians for the good of all.' Terrorism and violence should no longer be looked on as evil coming from one community to be stamped out by the other. 'It is a common evil, threatening both our communities. In this parish, due no doubt to the efforts of many good people of both communities, the last number of years have been mainly without sectarian violence and tensions. We had all hoped the violence and murders of the early 1970s were over.'

The police got their first clue to the case when a dog dragged a gun out of the kennel where it had been hidden in the garden of a house in Dromore by a neighbour. The woman who found it thought it was part of a plot to murder her husband and reported it to the police, but it turned out to belong to her son, who was convicted of the murder.

One of the other men convicted of Pat's killing also received a life sentence for his involvement in the 1989 UFF murder of Loughlin Maginn in Rathfriland, which led to the first Stevens Inquiry into the leaking of security-force documents to loyalist paramilitaries. Two UDR soldiers were convicted of handing over intelligence information, which led to the murder of Mr Maginn.

Another of the men convicted of Pat's murder used to get a lift from outside Fergie's shop in Laurencetown, with one of Pat's friends, to the factory in Portadown where they both worked. He stuck his tongue out at Patsy and Fergie in the courtroom. After the trial, Patsy said to the security guard outside his holding cell to just give him fifteen minutes inside with his son's killer. The guard said nothing would give him greater pleasure, but if he opened that door he would lose his job and he needed his job. When the killer was released from prison, people queued up outside his house to get a photo with their arm around him.

I have known Fergie all my life, but it is only when I ask him about his general experience of growing up in the Troubles that I learn he was actually born in England. His mother, Mary, is a Feeney from Laurencetown but his dad, Jimmy, is from Greenore in County Louth, just over the border. All their children were born in England. 'I stood on Cheltenham High Street when I was in P1 waving a Union Jack at the Queen Mother going up the street in the car,' says Fergie. His mother had health problems, so they moved back to the North, where flag-waving has never been as innocent.

'My first encounter with this carry-on was in 1967. We were living up at Drummiller Lough, and I was walking up from Wee Minnie's pub, and these kids from Gilford called us Fenian bastards, stoned us. I was crying when Daddy came home from work. "I don't like it here," I says. "What is a Fenian?" He says, "It's just 'cause you're a Catholic." I says, "We'll go back to England, they're all Catholics there." He says, "Do you not realise all your friends in the street went to a different school? You were the only Catholic. The difference is it was never mentioned in England."'

One day, when Fergie was walking in Banbridge in his school uniform, which identified him as a Catholic, an older youth punched him in the head as he walked past. That weekend, Fergie's cousin Jimmy Feeney beat the older youth up in a pub in town. A few days later Fergie was driving with Pat Feeney when they were stopped by UDR soldiers, one of whom was the youth's father. After being held for ages, Fergie said to them, 'Why don't you go and catch some terrorists?' They were taken into custody and held overnight for questioning.

Fergie's mother-in-law lived in the same housing estate in Donaghcloney as Robin Jackson, 'the Jackal'. Her funeral was on a New Year's Day. That New Year's Eve, local loyalists painted the kerb outside her house red, white and blue. Fergie's wife, Maria, and her siblings used to be stoned as they walked to school to Laurencetown after they got off the bus in Lenaderg.

Having run the local shop in Laurencetown for years, Fergie decided to lease it out. Just a fortnight later, a man fitting the description of a leading loyalist paramilitary called in, claiming he had been to Banbridge Tech with Fergie, and asking where he might find him. 'Only I'd that shop let out, and that person [working in the shop] had the good sense not to say where I lived, you'd have been writing about me today,' says Fergie.

Fergie is worried about the stability of the peace process as agitators stir up hatred online and on the streets. 'I just hope it never comes back. I wouldn't want that. If they come down and try to wreck all round them, people will have to stand up again. I would not encourage anyone to stay here.'

But our conversation ends on a lighter note. Fergie tells a story about his dad, Jimmy, a bus driver, and Artie McDowell, his conductor, who were both inveterate gamblers. Their route included a lap of Killycomain estate in Portadown – Jimmy would drop Artie off to place a bet at the bookies and pick him up on the way back. One day, they had £20 on a horse but the race was delayed so Artie signalled to Jimmy to go round again, 'so my da took the people round Killycomain for a second spin.

'I remember my da wasn't well and Artie came in to see him in hospital. He said to the nurse, "Jaysus, look at Larkin, he's not well and it's not fair, for Larkin and me gave every shilling we had to sick animals, but we didn't know they were sick till the race was over."'

***

Billy Duffy was about three years older than Pat, but they grew up together first in Chapel Hill and then in Millar Park. Billy became a West Ham fan after Bobby Moore captained England to the World Cup, and remembers a great trip with Fergie, Pat and a few others to Elland Road to see Leeds versus the Hammers, playing cards coming home on the boat, just for a couple of pence. 'There wasn't much of Pat, he was slightly built but boy could he feed. He'd say, "Are you not finishing that? If you don't finish it, I'll finish it." He loved a pint and a bit of craic.

'He liked a bit of style, there was a programme back then, *Happy Days*, he got that nickname, The Fonz. Pat was always looking down at his feet, to see was he all right. He was going with a lovely wee girl, she wasn't local, she thought the world of him but something just happened.

'He was a quiet wee lad, he was a threat to nobody, such a soft target. But sure, that's the way it goes. It broke my heart when I heard about it. I couldn't even look at the young fella in the coffin, to tell you the truth. I went to the wake but I told Patsy I don't want to see Pat, I want to remember him the way he was.'

Iona, Billy's partner, recalled that Pat was planning to go on holiday with them to Blackpool. 'I had big regard for Pat. He was a real, good friend, gentle, there was no badness in Pat.'

Billy was called after his father's brother, who served with the Inniskilling Fusiliers in the Second World War. A photograph of him in uniform hangs on the wall. The ashes of two of Billy and Iona's pets rest on the coffee table beside Pat's photo. The past is ever present.

The Troubles began when Billy was 15, so they coloured his adult life. 'The Troubles hit everybody,' he said. 'I probably have as many Protestant friends as I have Catholics, if not more, but back then the things that were happening would have made you bitter, on both sides.

He worked in Down Shoes for six months in the warehouse, but the pay was poor unless you were on the production lines. His sisters worked there too. At the time of the Ulster Workers' Council strike, when they came back to their places after a tea break, 'their machines would be plastered with flags'.

Billy went to work in Moy Park in Moira. 'Moira would be right and staunch, you know what I mean. We had bomb scares in the factory regular, it just became the norm. Everybody was more or less told not to go to work, intimidated, you more or less run the gauntlet.'

He got to know boys from Lurgan's big Catholic estates, Kilwilkie and Shankill, so he and friends from Laurencetown started going over to Lurgan at the weekends for a couple of pints. 'God rest Mummy and Daddy, they would have been in nerves at the thought of me being in Lurgan, in case anything happened. One day, three or four of us from Laurencetown were drinking in this old bar in Church Place, right next to the old police station, having a great time. Next thing someone comes up the stairs saying, "Right, everybody out, there's a bomb been placed in a beer keg inside the pub." Apparently it was 50lb of explosives, we all had to shuffle out past it.'

They didn't run? 'I can hardly remember going out. Everybody tried to keep calm, there was a thirty-minute warning given. I never seen a bomb go off before or after. Exactly thirty minutes later, I never seen the like of it, the boom, all the debris going up in the air, it was really shocking like.'

There was rioting that night between Catholics and Protestants so there was no chance of getting a taxi and the lads had to walk home via Bleary. Another night, Billy was drinking in Joe P.'s pub in Hall's Mill when a bomb was thrown at the window, but it bounced off the metal grille and exploded harmlessly on the pavement. 'Everyone was really shaken but it got to the stage where everyone ... I won't say accepted it, but learned to live with it. There was bars in Banbridge you couldn't go into. They are all fine now and no one wants to know.'

He remembers he was drinking in Molly's Bar in Hall's Mill when news came through of the Central Bar bombing in Gilford. Sandy McCullough, whose wife Sylvia was among the victims, would have been a regular drinking companion over the years. 'Even after that happened to his wife, Sandy didn't seem to be bitter about it. Many a drink I had with Sandy.' Likewise, Sammy Walker, the local community policeman. 'Like myself, Sammy liked fishing, shooting, a pint. He drank in Laverty's. That's where the pigeon men drank.' The parish's other community policeman, Francie Craig, lived locally too and, although literally born and brought up in an Orange hall, was well regarded by Catholics as well as Protestants, and was a calming presence after a passing loyalist band stoned the shop in Laurencetown. His daughter married a Catholic.

Billy lived next door to Joe McCart, whose partner, Phyllis Beattie, had lost her husband in the Gilford pub bombing. He was a quiet, kind man who often knocked the door at night to offer Billy a couple of rainbow trout he had just caught in the Bann, already cleaned and ready for the pan. Another McCart, Stevie, was a barman in Harry's Bar in Banbridge. A bomb was planted in the bar one day and he carried it out across the car park. 'It takes some guts to do that.'

Back in 1974, during the loyalist workers' strike, Billy and his mate Vincie McCaffrey volunteered to guard the Catholic church in

Laurencetown overnight after an arson attack. 'Everyone was minding chapels in case they were hit. So one night me and Vincie, we were standing in the graveyard. It was pitch dark, there was no lights. Vincie had a big black Labrador, they called it Captain, and the dog had followed Vincie without him knowing. The next thing Captain jumped up on Vincie. We near died. Talk about being scared. It was funny, but it wasn't funny at the time.'

My father also spent one night on vigil in the aptly named mission hut, which once stood to the left of the chapel steps, so called because it sold publications (such as the magazine *St Martin de Porres*, the Peruvian saint after whom I was named) promoting the work of Irish missionaries spreading the Good News in the developing world. The bad news was that Catholics in the old world were having to protect their churches from arson attacks by fellow Christians. The Orange hall in Lenaderg was also set on fire. And yet for more than forty years from 1981, Lawrencetown House was home to Whitefield College of the Bible, a Free Presbyterian theological college for missionaries and ministers. It stood just a stone's throw from the site of the Mass Rock on Holymount Road, but no stone was ever thrown.

***

As well as living next door to the Donaghys, Pat Feeney was also a regular in the pub that they ran, Molly's Bar in Hall's Mill, and was on the darts team. Molly's always had a pot of soup on the go for regulars so they would have no need to go home. The Donaghys also bought sausages from Brian the butcher and fried them on the range. It was a home from home.

Patricia Donaghy worked for a predominantly Protestant firm. 'We were making uniforms for the MoD; we could have been a target. I could have been a target for being a Catholic working there.' Did she experience sectarianism? 'Everything was all right until a fortnight before July 12th then you would have got wee barbs from the older women, diehards, like, "Are you going to the field?" Or, "Mr Paisley was on the news last night; he's a great man isn't he?" I never rose to it. I just let it roll off my back.'

Patricia was 25 when Pat was murdered. The wake was terrible, she says. The oddest detail sticks in her mind. 'The main thing I noticed is the shroud had come apart a bit and Pat had no socks on. I thought to myself, he's going to be cold.'

She didn't know if her employer would give her the day off for the funeral but they did. A lot of colleagues did commiserate with her too.

Patricia, like all of Pat's friends and family interviewed here, had a strong connection to England. 'My mother was a Londoner, Joanie Boxall from King's Cross. I make a point of letting people know because I am proud of both heritages. Daddy was from Katesbridge, Corbet direction.'

The Troubles first came to their door in 1972 when Joe Fegan was blown up by the IRA at Newry customs post. Joe was a cousin of Patricia's father, Billy.

She remembers the loyalist strike in 1974, 'the electric going off, my father and a lot of fathers going down to the crossroads and barricading so no other factions could get in to Millar Park'.

Her brother Kevin was born in London but was far more republican than any of them, she says. He was radicalised by his brother Billy being abused by the British Army. 'Billy was stopped at gunpoint one night, asked his name, where he was born. He said, "Paddington Hospital." The soldier replied, "You're an effing liar, you Irish bastard."'

Patricia's son Jason is a soldier, but in the Irish Army. He went to Banbridge Academy, two decades after me, but got grief from some pupils and a teacher. 'Someone put a tricolour up in a classroom and he got the blame, was told it was inappropriate. He said, "You allowed someone to put up the Union Jack last week. How is that appropriate?"'

Patricia's family has suffered much more than its share of misfortune. When she goes to the cemetery, she has a lot of graves to visit.

'To be quite honest, I would cry more at Pat's grave than I would at my own three brothers because they all died naturally, even though it was hard to watch. Nicholas, he died of a brain tumour. Kevin and Billy died of asthmatic heart attacks, which is easier to bear than knowing someone who was so young when he was killed. I watched my own sister die of a brain tumour and her own daughter at only eight and a half. I could cry about them because they died horribly. With Pat, it's different, it happened so quick and so horribly.

'Funny enough, about April that year [the year that Pat was murdered] I met my husband. I just happened to say to him, one of my best friends had been shot. Over the years I've kept it inside, in a big storage box in my brain. Everyone has their own troubles.'

Less than a month after Pat's murder, RUC Chief Superintendent Harry Breen, 51, and a colleague were shot dead returning from Dundalk Garda Station. He was the highest-ranking RUC officer murdered in the Troubles. He was also the brother of my former headmaster, Winston Breen, and left behind a wife, June, and two children, Gillian, 24, and David, 20. David's best friend was the brother of one of my best friends from school, so we had socialised a bit together. SDLP councillor Jim Walsh condemned the 'senseless' atrocity. Referring to the recent murder of his relative Pat Feeney, he said, 'I have seen the suffering and sadness families are plunged into by murders and it is terrible.'

Twenty-three

King Larry

Larry McCartan was delivering for his electoral base many years before he won a seat on Banbridge Council in 1973. At a time when few working-class families could afford a car, his mobile shop provided a vital service in rural communities throughout the district.

'One fed into the other, that's why he was so well known,' says Larry's daughter Vivienne. 'People didn't have cars back then. The mobile shop was the main thing. There was the milkman, the breadman, the minerals man, the clothes man, the insurance man. People calling to your house was a very normal thing.'

These delivery men, with their patter and big personalities, were a defining feature of my childhood, providing entertainment as well as a service.

Brian the Butcher's face was the colour of a beef sausage. The memory of his unrefrigerated van with its trays of blood-red meat and pasty sausages, like something out of *The League of Gentlemen*, still gives me the shudders. A neighbour said you could eat for a week off his apron. The fishmonger called out, 'Hernahernahern', hawking herring as if campaigning for a future taoiseach. Two brothers sold vegetables, the earth still clinging to their potatoes, carrots and parsnips. The lemonade or minerals man had obviously never heard of Henry Ford, who once said you could have any colour of car so long as it was black. There was red, brown and white lemonade, orangeade, pineappleade, cream soda, cola, kali water. Petesy Duffy, who took over the O'Dowds' coal round, used to compare the quality of coal to the finest spuds. 'Missus, they're like balls of flour.' Ernie the breadman used to get his helper to throw sweets from the van as he passed the schoolyard to see us scramble for the craic, a bit like the Scottish wedding tradition in which the groom threw coins from the car as the couple left the church for the local urchins to chase. Ernie was a Protestant but went to see Pope John Paul II when he visited Ireland in 1979, the same as you would any other touring international celebrity.

Larry was a gregarious, sociable individual, who naturally built relationships with customers in his years running the mobile grocery shop, regardless of their religious background, so when he stood as an independent candidate, he attracted votes from both sides of the house. The SDLP tried to recruit him but Larry felt this would put off Protestant voters and – as he had what his youngest son, Gabriel, calls 'a stubborn, independent streak' – he would not have liked to have been told how to vote. And yet it was his priest, Father Gerard Conway, who had not only first persuaded Larry to stand for election in 1973 but even paid his deposit.

Gabriel says, 'My father worked for everyone in the community. He did his best for whoever came to his door.'

Larry had been brought up to respect everyone as part of a rural community that had always been interdependent. His father, Willie John, could not have managed without the support of his Protestant neighbours in Kernan when his wife, Sarah Ann, died in childbirth in 1918, aged 41, leaving one-year-old Larry, his three brothers and three sisters motherless. A neighbour, Mrs McGaffin, minded the children for him but advised Willie John to buy a handloom so he could work from home as the little children were very distressed.

Larry had a lifelong passion for sport. He followed Glenavon, the Lurgan football club, but his first love was the GAA. When St

Larry McCartan with his granddaughter Louise.

Patrick's Gaelic Football Club was established in Laurencetown on 17 July 1944, he was a founder member and first treasurer. Three years later he captained the team that beat Kilclief to win the County Junior Championship. Billy Phoenix, uncle of the late historian Éamon Phoenix, composed a song, 'The Laurencetown Paddies', to mark the occasion: 'Larry's captain of the clan / And he'll keep the boys in hand.' A teammate and goalscorer that day was Patsy Feeney, whose son Pat would be murdered in 1989. 'There's Patsy Feeney on the left / Like a rocket he can weft / There is no goalie has a chance / When from his toe, the ball will glance.'

St Patrick's merged with Geraldines of Gilford in 1961 to form Tullylish GFC. In 1973, the same year Larry was elected, the club grounds moved from the grandly named but rudimentary Shamrock Park on Chapel Hill – where tree trunks, bark and all, served as goalposts – to what I still remember as the barley field behind Millar Park. It has expanded over the years and now has three pitches and superb facilities. Larry, a keen Down supporter, witnessed his county become the first team from north of the border to win the All-Ireland in 1960, repeating their success in 1961, 1968, 1991 and 1994. But watching Down lift the Sam Maguire at Croke Park was for high days and holidays. Friends took him to Gaelic matches all over south Down. They would stop at Graham's in Rathfriland for an ice cream on the way there and a pint at the Angler's Rest in Corbet on the way back.

On 5 July 1974, the *Banbridge Chronicle* reported that an application by Tullylish GFC for a donation towards a children's sports day was rejected by Banbridge District Council. Unionist councillor Joseph

Gibson claimed it was 'a sectarian organisation'. 'The council might as well give something towards his church's Sunday school outing,' he said. He added that he was also opposed because, as a believer in Sabbath Day observance, he could not support any organisation that ran sports on a Sunday.

In January 1975, the council voted by nine to five to reject Larry's proposal that the town's new swimming pool be opened on Sunday afternoons. Hugh Anderson said it would be a disgrace and hypocrisy to shut the pool when the golf course was open and children were playing in the street. After the vote, Mr Gibson said, 'To prove my sincerity on this, I can state that I was offered a spot recently on *The Golden Shot* but turned it down because this programme is shown on a Sunday – I'm no hypocrite.' The swings in the park in Linenhall Street were also tied up on a Sunday.

***

'Daddy was a family man,' says Vivienne. 'We had a very happy upbringing. He was always there for us. He had a strong faith, but he treated everybody equally and wanted others to treat us equally too. He was very hard-working. We all helped Daddy, delivering groceries round the countryside. We never stopped to think what anyone's religion was and I don't think Daddy did either. He built up a relationship with all those families, he helped them and they helped him.'

'He worked seven days a week,' says Gabriel. 'On Sundays after 8.30 Mass, he'd have a cup of tea and a ginger biscuit, then he worked to dinner time.' To relax, he loved TV comedies: *Fawlty Towers, Some Mothers Do 'Ave 'Em, Steptoe and Son* and – 'you probably can't say that now', says Vivienne – Benny Hill.

Larry married Mary Rose Maguire in 1948 and they had five children, Dominick, Laurence, Malachy, Vivienne and Gabriel. They set up home first in an old farmhouse by the River Bann, moving to Millar

Park when it opened in 1967. Larry ran a shop in a wooden hut in the garden before a permanent shop was built at the entrance to the estate.

As a councillor, Larry delivered a tap in a field for a cattle trough, grit for an icy road, a bus pass for a nurse. He stood out in fields in all weathers to get planning permission for a site. He organised an ecumenical carol service each year to accompany the illumination of the Christmas tree lights at the crossroads and was instrumental in the opening of Laurencetown Community Centre in the old Bann Primary School building. He had also successfully campaigned for the Housing Executive to renovate Millar Park. One of his proudest moments was his election in 1991 as vice chairman of Banbridge Council, fruit of its power-sharing policy. He had friends on both sides of the chamber, including Seamus Doyle of the SDLP, fellow independent Jim Walsh, and unionists Jim McElroy and Willie Martin.

When he retired from the shop, he became the lollipop man, helping schoolchildren cross the road safely. 'He was always in social environments where he could be talking to people,' says Gabriel.

Larry and his wife, Mary, carried on the tradition of having Protestant neighbours as family friends without giving it a thought. Maudie and Jimmy Graham were lifelong friends who moved to Millar Park at the same time. Laurence's son Malachy would play piano at their house. The two couples would go to bingo together in Newry. Larry would drive Bertie and Martha Anderson, friends who didn't have a car, to the Twelfth every year and to Scarva for the Sham Fight, another Orange celebration, on 13 July.

However, eight miles away from Laurencetown in Drumcree, Portadown, another Orange march had become a flashpoint as Catholic residents objected to it passing through their area. In July 1996, the RUC chief constable, in response to unionist protests and loyalist threats, had reversed his decision to reroute the parade, prompting nationalist protests and republican riots. Controversial Orange parades posed an unwanted threat to a fragile peace process as efforts continued to secure a renewed IRA ceasefire. An Independent Review of Parades and Marches was set up, which, on 30 January 1997, recommended an independent commission to review contentious parades. Nationalists and the Alliance Party welcomed the review but unionists attacked it.

Three days later, on Sunday 2 February, Vivienne was making plans for Larry's big eightieth birthday party, which was to be held in the local Bannville Hotel on 13 March, less than six weeks away. The family had debated keeping it a secret but decided it would be better if he was involved. 'Oh my God, was he delighted or what?' says Vivienne.

'He was a showman,' says Gabriel. 'He loved socialising.'

'He wanted to have a seat in the Bannville so that he would greet the guests as they came in,' says Vivienne.

'King Larry,' says Gabriel. He had made a list of people and that night Vivienne had started ringing round to invite the guests.

At about midnight that Sunday, a caller claiming to represent the Mid-Ulster Loyalists, a previously unheard-of paramilitary group, claimed that they had planted a bomb in Laurencetown. Earlier, loyalists had contacted the Samaritans to say they had also left devices in Hilltown and a Catholic part of Portadown. So, although the devices turned out to be elaborate hoaxes, this was not just a prank. No one was ever arrested but the Loyalist Volunteer Force, a Portadown-based UVF splinter group led by Billy Wright, which had broken the loyalist ceasefire over the Drumcree dispute, was blamed.

The 'device' in Laurencetown had been left under my uncle Joe's car on School Terrace. The RUC reassured him that he wasn't the target, but he still wonders how the officers could have been so certain. The police decided to evacuate more than 200 local residents, including Larry and Mary. Some were able to seek shelter with relatives – Joe went to stay with my parents – while others were directed to the Catholic church, which the priest had opened after being alerted by the police. Among those forced to flee their homes were the grieving relatives of

Bridget Hoey, who had died earlier that day. Some elderly residents were initially too scared to open their doors and so neighbours were asked to assist the police. 'I won't be opening my door until I hear it from one of my neighbours,' one woman had said.

It was a bitter night with freezing fog. Larry had gone out to start the car, gone back in to fetch hot water to clear the windscreen, then again to help Mary, who suffered from arthritis, to get out to the car.

As they passed Eamon Campbell's home and shop at the Point, Eamon invited them in to warm themselves at the fire while they waited for the all-clear. Eamon had just offered Larry the choice of tea or something stronger when the 79-year-old suffered a heart attack and collapsed to the floor in the living room. Larry's family believes it was triggered by the stress of the situation, and the strain of coming in and out of the cold. He had had a heart attack previously but had made a full recovery.

Vivienne was asleep in Banbridge when she got a phone call telling her to come quickly as there had been an accident. When she got to Eamon Campbell's, a policeman met her at the door and explained that there had been a bomb scare and that her father had been taken unwell. He prepared her for what she was about to see: her father was lying on the living-room floor and the paramedics were working on him. 'The policeman was awful good to prepare me,' says Vivienne. Nonetheless, when she caught sight of the grey Fair Isle sweater that he always wore, she became upset. The memory distresses her again now and Gabriel comforts her.

The RUC officer advised her to contact the family. 'He said, "They are still working on your daddy – they are trying their best, I am only preparing you for the worst. Don't worry, if you give me the numbers, I will speak to them." It's a bit of a blur but through it all those police officers who were on the scene that night were very supportive. I don't think we could have coped without that.' Similarly, Uncle Joe was on first-name terms with the local RUC reservist who alerted him.

Sadly, Larry could not be resuscitated and died in the early hours of Monday 3 February.

Banbridge Council adjourned its monthly meeting that night and the flag hung at half mast. Larry's twenty-four years in local government made him the longest-serving councillor. His fellow councillors paid tribute. Cassie McDermott said she would miss him as both a friend and a colleague. 'In a way I'm glad he died in office,' she said. 'I know it's how he would have liked it.' Jim Walsh, who had been invited to Larry's birthday party, said of the hoaxers: 'I hope it haunts them all their lives. Larry worked for everybody.' Seamus Doyle said, 'It's terrible when a man like Larry gets to his time of life that such an incident should contribute to his death.' Chairman William McCracken said, 'Larry lived for the council. Even last year when his health wasn't as good, the minute he was out of hospital he was back attending meetings. He loved being a councillor and loved to help people.' Wilfred McFadden of the DUP said he was devastated. 'He was purely independent and hated politics being mentioned in the chamber. I can say with my hand on my heart he did his best for everyone.' John Dobson of the UUP called Larry 'a total gentleman and a thoroughly likeable man. I've never heard anyone say anything bad about Larry McCartan politically or personally.'

Bernadette O'Hagan, a founder member of the Civil Rights Association and Sinn Féin candidate for Upper Bann, said 'the circumstances surrounding Councillor McCartan's death raise wider questions about the integrity of the British and unionists. The recent show of strength of up to one hundred [loyalists] in Seapatrick shows the need for nationalist vigilance in an area which has borne the brunt of loyalist actions in recent years.'

The wake and the funeral were huge. All denominations came, including David Trimble, the leader of the Ulster Unionist Party and the local MP. Larry's son Malachy was co-opted on to the council and served for another eight years.

How did the traumatic death affect the family? 'We could have let that eat away at us and it could have ruined our lives, but we just supported Mammy and each other,' says Vivienne. 'Be the better people.'

Do they consider him to be a victim of the Troubles? His death is listed in *Lost Lives*, which is considered the definitive guide.

'I do,' says Gabriel.

'I do too,' says Vivienne. 'If that hadn't happened, we'd have had him for longer. I stood at many a thing with my children, maybe Mark playing hockey, and thought if your granda had have been here, he'd have loved this. We lost that. Our children were cheated of those years. They still remember him even though they were tiny – the big white head of hair.

'Daddy always had this lump on his finger. Amy went to Laurencetown playgroup and Daddy was Santa. She sat on his knee and recognised the lump on his finger and the Fair Isle jumper. She was only three.'

***

Violence continued to swirl around the Drumcree dispute. Deaths associated with it include that of Robert Hamill, a Catholic, who was fatally assaulted in May 1997 by loyalists in Portadown in a sectarian attack. RUC officers were accused of witnessing the assault and failing to intervene. A month later, Gregory Taylor, an off-duty RUC constable, died following a beating he received from a loyalist mob in Ballymoney. That year's Drumcree parade was permitted, resulting in more republican riots. The following year's parade was rerouted, however, and none has been held since.

On 2 July 1998, the LVF was blamed for setting fire to the Catholic church in Laurencetown. Over a ten-hour period, nine other Catholic churches were burnt: in Banbridge, Dromore, Tandragee, Lisburn, Crumlin and Dungannon. The attacks were believed to be a response to the rerouting of the Orange Order's Drumcree march. Ten days later, on 12 July 1998, three young brothers, Jason (7), Mark (9) and Richard (11) Quinn, were murdered in a UVF firebomb attack on their home in Ballymoney, County Antrim. The attack came after a week of protests by Orangemen demanding access to the mainly nationalist Garvaghy Road as part of their annual march at Drumcree church. The Orange Order's County Armagh chaplain, Reverend William Bingham, called for the protest to end, saying, 'No road is worth a life, let alone three lives of three little boys.'

The conflict, even in its own death throes, was still capable of destroying lives, both young and old. More than two decades later, in 2023, a granddaughter of John Michael Feeney and a grandson of Rosie McConville died by suicide within weeks of each other. The trauma of thirty years of violence is still surfacing.

Conclusion

When I return to Kernan Lough now, it feels more like a pilgrimage site than a picnic spot. A few anglers are spread out like sentinels, watchers on the shore. There is a path with a kissing gate around the perimeter that you could circumnavigate in half an hour but it hasn't been too prettified or tamed. As well as reeds and rushes, there are brambles and a cloud of midges.

'The midgets'll ate ya,' a man in Mayo told us once on holiday and I'm reminded of it every time I encounter the little pests. Something breaks the surface in a splash and flurry but I miss it and spot only ripples and bubbles. A fisherman in a camouflage jacket casts his line and his float lands like a thrown stone far out in the lake. A fair-sized fish lies on the wet grass beside him.

There is a golden sheen off the water at one end where the surface reflects the shorn yellow fields sloping down to its edge. A copse of trees rustles in the wind. The path here is submerged and my brogues won't do. I resolve to come back with wellingtons, or 'water boots' as a cousin calls them.

On the way back I stop to say hello to the angler, who has since caught another fish, and I realise that his yellow float is a plastic Jif lemon. The last time I saw one of those was Pancake Tuesday circa 1979. He tells me he makes his own lures from pheasant feathers, like Jimmy Feeney, and offers me a fish, reminding me of Billy Duffy's neighbour's generosity. I ask him if he ever heard of the massacre at the lough, but he hasn't. Perhaps that's for the best. He did hear tell of a plane crashing into the lough in the war, though, its linen skin back under water once more.

***

In 2014, I devised for *The Irish Times* an alternative Irish writers' poster, its twelve women a riposte to the familiar all-male version, a copy of which I had Blu-tacked to my bedroom wall at college, blind then to its bias. The iconography of the Troubles is also very masculine – so many of the heroes are male. My focus here has been on those who have been sidelined, women as well as men devoid of machismo, survivors either directly or indirectly of terrible acts of violence.

When you immerse yourself in a subject, you start to find connections everywhere. Roisín Higgins, a historian at Teesside University, wrote an article for *The Irish Times* on her project *Sensing the Troubles*, about people's sensory impressions of the conflict. 'Working on this project I have often had an image of myself walking through the wreckage of conflict, collecting debris,' she wrote. 'I have also come to realise however, that by starting with the senses, what I am salvaging are the pieces that make us human.'

Roisín recalled one of her contributors, whose story reminds me of Jennifer McNern: 'My heart aches at the thought of 17-year-old Marian, beginning her life as a student nurse fifty years ago in that awful year. She tells me about the hospital running out of clean gowns and sheets the weekend of the Abercorn bomb in March 1972. A little girl was lying in bed, on white paper sheets and in a white paper hospital gown. She caught hold of Marian's hand and said, "Have I died? Am I in heaven? I was in an explosion." Marian said, "No, pet, you're not in heaven. You're in the hospital."'

The Paris-based, Belfast-born author Robert McLiam Wilson wrote an outstanding essay for *The Guardian* on the murder trial relating to the 2016 Bastille Day truck attack in Nice, in which I recognised a reflection of the neighbours whose testimonies I was collecting:

'They were profoundly ordinary people, all luminously eloquent in their pain and loss. They were an unforgettable lesson in what it is to be human. I hadn't expected to report on a murder trial and learn almost everything there is to learn about love.'

Every time I picked up a HET report, I thought of Gail McConnell, whose award-winning poetry collection *The Sun Is Open* addresses the IRA's murder of her father, an assistant governor of the Maze prison. In an essay published in *The Irish Times* the day *The Sun Is Open* came out, Gail reflected on lives in the aftermath of horror: 'One morning as my mother and I stood in our east Belfast driveway to wave him off to work, he was shot and killed in front of our house. It was March 1984. The IRA claimed responsibility. I was three-and-a-half.

'It has been a lifetime's work, living in this aftermath and trying to find language not only for this event, but for all the textures of the childhood in which it took place. Bananaman, skateboards, holiday Bible clubs, Wendy Houses, helicopters, Tetris, bomb scares, north coast beaches, memory verses, breaking news, Alphabites …

'I first wrote about my father's murder in a long poem called "Type Face". Like thousands of others, I had received a Historical Enquiries Team report about my father's death, produced in Comic Sans. Trying to absorb phrases like "laceration of the brain" in a font that was giving me jazz hands was an overwhelmingly jarring experience.'

'There is something eternal in what we say and feel for them,' the author Ed O'Loughlin has written of the dead. 'Everyone who was here, will always have been here. Everyone who was loved will have been loved forever. There is permanence in that, a ghost in the grammar.'

In May 2022, I republished an Arrowsmith Press essay by Victoria Amelina about the Holocaust and the Holodomor and her native city of Lviv. This brave and brilliant Ukrainian writer, who was documenting Russian war crimes, died from injuries sustained in a Russian missile strike on a restaurant in Kramatorsk in June 2023. Her fate reminded me of Lyra McKee's. Lviv was once home to Raphael Lemkin and Hersch

Lauterpacht, the lawyers who played a key role at the Nuremberg trials, and in the process defined our modern concepts of human rights, celebrated by Philippe Sands in *East West Street: On the Origins of Genocide and Crimes against Humanity*: 'We still need to talk about the past. A lot. We can help each other mourn our dead, as Raphael Lemkin and Hersch Lauterpacht helped me and millions of others around the world, regardless of nationality ... As a writer what I can do is to listen to the silences rising from the city's ground, and do my best to translate them into a tongue the living understand.

'No city is doomed to be haunted forever. We break the spell not when we banish the ghosts, but when we invite them to breakfast. A true home is a place where you have neighbours you know by name. This includes those who were killed and those who helped kill them, those who survived and those who risked their families' lives to rescue the hunted. Today I have neighbours, both living and dead, from whom I learn, about whom I write, and to whom I address my writing.'

***

The Rosary is divided into five decades, and they seemed to last five decades when I was a child and time warped like Dalí's clocks as Granda led the prayers. More than five sorrowful decades have passed since violent death descended on Tullylish. As surely as time stopped dead for its victims, it was arrested and distorted, too, for their loved ones. Some, understandably, do not want to dwell on the moment of their loss publicly, perhaps even privately. Others, equally understandably, live their whole lives in the shadow of a dark hour and want others to remember too.

Bereavement comes with a whole-life tariff, grief without any promise of reprieve or release. I find I have become an inveterate collector of words of wisdom about grief and loss. 'How can the dead be truly dead when they still live in the souls of those who are left behind?' asks Carson McCullers rhetorically in *The Heart Is a Lonely Hunter*. 'Unable are the Loved to die / For Love is Immortality,' writes Emily Dickinson. 'This is what memory is: an abiding awareness that some things have vanished,' Mick Herron explains. 'And this is what consciousness is: the knowledge that more absences will come.' Wallace Stevens wrote of the 'nothing that is not there and the nothing that is'.

I must admit I sometimes find it painful to read hopeful stories of improved survival rates for breast cancer. A bit late now, I can't help thinking. But then I remember how much skin I still have in the game, not to mention the whole of humanity. So, too, perhaps for many of the bereaved of the Troubles: they ask only that it not be inflicted on a new generation. They have done such heavy lifting for us all.

When I pass Hall's Mill, sometimes in my mind's eye I see that old dog's-leg terrace of houses with its two pubs, now long gone. The present is a palimpsest overwriting the past, but our human software is glitchy and sometimes the earlier edition reasserts itself. If the pull of the past makes me conjure up old buildings, think how pervasive the presence of lost loved ones must be in the consciousness of the violently bereaved. Trauma has no expiry date.

I have tried to be mindful of the poet Damian Gorman's sage advice: 'The first rule in helping someone tell their story – especially a story involving trauma – is not to be a tube, as we used to say when we were young; not to be a tube in thinking that the story is essentially about you. That way lies further hurt as well as untruth, for you end up treating the other person as material. And what do you do with material? You cut it, tear it, stitch it and otherwise do violence as you make something out of it, and call it "yours". It isn't. It is the life story of someone else. And your job is to bring what you can to the telling of it and lay that at the other person's feet.'

Writing this book has brought me closer to my roots, helped me face up, in a way, to my almost forgotten fears. The low-level anxiety I lived with through the Troubles may have been all in my head but it wasn't my imagination. I have sat down with the people it actually happened to. Some of them were angry, some stoic, all of them heroic. *They* are my tribe. I am grateful to them for sharing their stories but above all I am in awe of their courage. It also makes me even more intolerant of the apologists on all sides for the violent actions of their comrades – their moral casuistry, their ideological blinkers, their capacity for accommodating atrocity.

'The practice of violence changes the world,' wrote Hannah Arendt, 'but the most probable change is to a more violent world.' Decades later, it is now obvious that violence was not inevitable, that peace was always possible. It is also apparent that the prejudice and the discrimination that necessitated the civil rights movement of the 1960s still stymie democratic and policing norms in the North. Those who most vehemently proclaim their loyalty to the UK blithely undermine it. Those who most loudly champion reunification regularly alienate those they must persuade.

Gilford, a mill town without a mill any more, to me feels similarly bereft. The images on hoardings that cover derelict buildings on its high street are not promoting some future development but hark back to its heyday. The street sign on the corner is covered with weeds. I pull them back like a curtain to reveal the words: Mill Street.

The panoramic view from Norman Kerr's farm in Drumnascamph is magnificent. The Mournes – he points out Donard and Spelga – are silhouetted against the skyline, then your gaze shifts across to Keady and the Cooleys. As you turn you get a glimpse of Lough Neagh, and on a clear day the steam rising from a factory in Cookstown, and finally Cave Hill above Belfast. 'That's four counties,' he says with pride, before showing me the flax he's planted, a rarity these days, for a charity fundraiser. A barn in his farmyard has been converted into a homespun museum, Bann Valley Heritage, celebrating the linen industry. Conversation circles back to those who are gone. 'Hugh Fegan was my best friend,' he says. 'I still miss him.'

Norman is typical of a country farmer who knows that if he is in trouble it is his neighbours, the Magees and McAvoys, who will give him a hand, regardless of their religion. His wife, Esther, reminisces about a time a few years ago when Father Loughran, the local priest, and the Presbyterian and Church of Ireland ministers used to meet for coffee and prayer mornings. On Easter Sunday, they celebrated a dawn light service at Lisleyard fort together, followed by tea and toast in the community centre. Father Loughran would ring the Kerrs up and say, 'I've been making these RC [rice crispy] buns. You'll have to have one.'

***

One thing that struck me while conducting these interviews was the recurring mention of children stillborn, dying young, being born with life-limiting conditions or having life-changing accidents. These domestic tragedies gave my neighbours enough crosses to bear without acts of terror adding to them. The weight of such trauma makes me wonder that we are not all in callipers.

While working on this book, I was taken by the hand, to quote Declan Feeney, by so many people, not least local historians Plunkett Campbell and Catherine McEvoy, as well as the late Éamon Phoenix, who died in November 2022 just three months after I interviewed him. He was not only the pre-eminent historian of Northern nationalism, but also, serendipitously, a local historian by dint of his family connections to Tullylish. I had the good fortune to hear him give a lecture at Belfast's Linen Hall Library one evening on the fateful years of 1922 and 1972, and then to have lunch at his home the next day where he showed me his Presbyterian grandfather's First World War death penny and his great-grandfather's Irish-language Bible, while he talked me through his family history in Tullylish and Belfast, using the history of this small place and its people to illuminate wider, deeper issues.

Eamon once recalled two pieces of advice. The first, from his mother, was: 'Education is easily carried'; the second came from historian F.S.L. Lyons: 'To understand the past is to cease to live in it.'

Whether the North remains part of the UK or is reunited with the rest of Ireland as a reimagined island, it will always be a place of many shades, not just orange and/or green, no more than the sky above it is merely blue (or grey). As the teacher in Anna Burns' *Milkman* demonstrates to the class, at sunset it is pink, lemon, mauve and orange-red.

Amid the bigotry and the bloodlust, there have been moments of hope in our history, when we have proved ourselves to be greater than the sum of our hurts, and confounded old boundaries and binaries of religious and national identity: the United Irishmen of 1798; the outdoor relief protests in 1932; the civil rights movement; the Sunningdale Agreement; the Peace People; and all those relatives of Troubles victims who in the depths of their own bereavement appealed for no retaliation and gave their blessing to the compromises of the Good Friday Agreement. In the words of Michael Longley's 'Ceasefire': 'I get down on my knees and do what must be done / And kiss Achilles' hand, the killer of my son.'

I have come to think of the material gathered for this book – from interviews, local and national newspaper archives, HET reports and history books – as the contents of a flax hole or retting dam, where flax bundles are steeped to break down the outer shell and expose the inner core to be smoothed out, spun and woven.

My grandfather was a storyteller, a local playwright and an insurance man, a moderate nationalist who believed in an independent Ireland but also in maintaining good relations with all his neighbours, even when some had hurt him greatly by putting him and his sister out of work. My mother inherited his gift for storytelling and I hope I have too, albeit late in life. But I hope this book might serve too as an insurance policy, a way of providing for a better future by reminding us of the perils of the past and the risks of the present.

Martin the smart 'un, Father Lynch used to call me when I was an altar server. (A friend queries whether that was meant as a compliment and now I'm smarting.) I probably thought back then that brains were what mattered most. But when I see the harm that ideology has done, give me a good heart any day.

'The North feels dead and rotting, like their flax when steeping in holes and ditches,' wrote William Drennan to his sister Martha McTier in 1807, after the hope of radical reform had been crushed with the defeat of the United Irishmen in 1798.

It is a pungent image and, in the context, an understandable counsel of despair. It reminds me, however, of an anecdote from my grandfather Arthur Pat, which was recorded just before he died in 1988.

At the outbreak of the Second World War there was great demand for linen for aeroplanes, and so farmers were encouraged to plant more flax. Every farm in our parish had once had a flax hole or dam. Someone remembered that there had been one at the Dog's Elbow, a bend in the road near the Bannville Hotel in Lenaderg, that hadn't been used in fifty years.

'They opened it up,' said Arthur Pat, 'and when they got to the bottom they got a beet or bundle of flax tied with a wristband. Someone said it will be a quare mess now. Someone else said it will be no quare mess. Just stook it there and we'll dry it and we'll scutch it. They scutched it out and it was as good after fifty years as if it had been last year's crop.'

It feels like a more optimistic metaphor somehow, of promise and goodness that have been submerged and forgotten but not drowned or destroyed. The husk may be rotten but the threads inside are well preserved and can still be woven into something strong and new and beautiful.

Select Bibliography

Beattie, Geoffrey, *We Are the People: Journeys Through the Heart of Protestant Ulster* (London, 1992)

Beiner, Guy, *Forgetful Remembrance: Social Forgetting and Vernacular Historiography of a Rebellion in Ulster* (Oxford, 2018)

Burke, David, *Kitson's Irish War: Mastermind of the Dirty War in Ireland* (Cork, 2021)

Cadwallader, Anne, *Lethal Allies: British Collusion in Ireland* (Cork, 2013)

Campbell, Plunkett, *A History of Tullylish* (Banbridge, 1984)

Canny, Nicholas, *Making Ireland British 1580–1650* (Oxford, 2001)

Carson, Ciaran, *Belfast Confetti* (Oldcastle, 1989)

Cobain, Ian, *Anatomy of a Killing: Life and Death on a Divided Island* (London, 2020)

Cohen, Marilyn, *Linen, Family and Community in Tullylish, County Down 1690–1914* (Dublin, 1997)

Craig, Patricia, *The Rattle of the North: An Anthology of Ulster Prose* (Belfast, 1992)

Crilly, Joseph, *The Crilly Trilogy* (Dublin, 2020)

Curtis, Liz, *Ireland: The Propaganda War* (London, 1984)

Davidson, Colin, *Selected Paintings 1986–2022* (Banbridge, 2022)

Diamond-Feeney, Doreen, *Dreams and Things* (Banbridge, 1996)

Donoghue, Denis, *Warrenpoint* (London, 1991)

English, Richard, *Armed Struggle: A History of the IRA* (London, 2003)

Farrell, Michael, *Arming the Protestants: The Formation of the Ulster Special Constabulary and the Royal Ulster Constabulary, 1920–27* (London, 1983)

Ferran, Denise, *F.E. McWilliam at Banbridge* (Banbridge, 2008)

Ferran, Denise, and Valerie Holman, *The Sculpture of F.E. McWilliam* (Farnham, 2012)

Foster, R.F., *Modern Ireland 1600–1972* (London, 1988)

Gébler, Carlo, *The Glass Curtain: Inside an Ulster Community* (London, 1991)

Gibney, John, *The Shadow of a Year: The 1641 Rebellion in Irish History & Memory* (Madison, 2013)

Gooding, Mel, *F.E. McWilliam: Sculpture 1932–1989* (London, 1989)

Harnden, Toby, *'Bandit Country': The IRA & South Armagh* (London, 1999)

Heenan, Kieran, and Poilin Ni Cleirigh, *The History of the GAA Clubs in County Down, Old & New* (Banbridge, 2017)

Holroyd, Fred, and Nick Burbridge, *War Without Honour: Military Intelligence in Northern Ireland, a True Story* (Hull, 1989)

Keefe, Patrick Radden, *Say Nothing: A True Story of Murder and Memory in Northern Ireland* (London, 2018)

Lawlor, Pearse, *The Burnings 1920* (Cork, 2009)

Leary, Peter, *Unapproved Roads: Histories of the Irish Border 1922–1972* (Oxford, 2016)

Logan, R.A., *A Window on the Past: A History of Gilford, County Down* (Banbridge, 2001)

Marle, Judy, and T.P. Flanagan, *F.E. McWilliam* (Belfast, 1981)

McBride, Doreen, *Banbridge: The Star of County Down* (Cheltenham, 2020)

McCann, Eamonn, *War & Peace in Northern Ireland* (Dublin, 1998)

McCartan, James, and Seamus McRory, *The King of Down Football* (Dublin, 2010)

McKay, Susan, *Bear in Mind These Dead* (London, 2008)

McKittrick, David, Seamus Kelters, Brian Feeney, and Chris Thornton, *Lost Lives: The Stories of the Men, Women and Children Who Died as a Result of the Northern Ireland Troubles* (Edinburgh, 1999)

McKittrick, David, and David McVea, *Making Sense of the Troubles* (Belfast, 2000)

Messenger, Betty, *Picking Up the Linen Threads: Life in Ulster's Mills* (Belfast, 1980)

Ní Aoláin, Fionnuala, *The Politics of Force: Conflict Management and State Violence in Northern Ireland* (Belfast, 2000)

O Connor, Fionnuala, *In Search of a State: Catholics in Northern Ireland* (Belfast, 1993)

Phoenix, Éamon, *Northern Nationalism: Nationalist Politics, Partition and the Catholic Minority in Northern Ireland 1890–1940* (Belfast, 1994)

Phoenix, Éamon, *A Century of Northern Life: The Irish News and 100 Years of Ulster History 1890s–1990s* (Belfast, 1995)

Rankin, Kathleen, *The Linen Houses of the Bann Valley: The Story of Their Families* (Belfast, 2007)

Smith, Micheál, *UDR Declassified* (Dublin, 2022)

Travers, Stephen, and Neil Fetherstonhaugh, *The Miami Showband Massacre: A Survivor's Search for the Truth* (Dublin, 2007)

Urwin, Margaret, *A State in Denial: British Collaboration with Loyalist Paramilitaries* (Cork, 2016)

Watson, Frederick Gilbert, *History into Poetry: The Works of James McKowen (1814–1889), The Bard of Lambeg* (Belfast, 2021)

Wharton, Ken, *To a Dark Place: Experiences from Survivors of the Troubles* (Cheltenham, 2022)

Young, Alex F., and Des Quail, *Old Gilford, Scarva, Loughbrickland and Lawrencetown* (Catrine, 2002)

Acknowledgements

It takes a village to create a book.

I owe everything to my parents, Marie and John, for their love and support throughout my life and for laying the foundations for this book with their own essays in *Once Alien Here* (John Hewitt Society, 2020).

My mother told the story of her father Arthur Pat's expulsion from the linen industry in 1920. My father documented the murders in our parish during the most recent Troubles. When I first conceived of stitching those two threads together, the respect in which my parents were held opened doors for me that might otherwise have been closed. And my mother's memories, including of her father's stories, were an invaluable resource of local and family history.

My children, Isobel, Ruairi and Martha, were selfless in their support and understanding as this project took me away from home and took away from time we might have spent together. I am touched by their commitment that they might even read the book.

Huge thanks to my sister, Andrea, and my brothers Shane and Garry for their support and for sharing their recollections of our childhood. As a professional historian, Shane was also a great source of advice and feedback. A historian from Tullylish confirming that I might just have written too much on the early history of Tullylish was advice I could not in conscience ignore.

For the generous sharing of their local knowledge, I am indebted to local historians Plunkett Campbell and Catherine McEvoy and the late Éamon Phoenix, whose loss I am far from alone in regretting deeply.

He was a historian of national standing but his Tullylish roots made him the ideal sounding board for my project. My thanks to Noel Doran, Editor of *The Irish News*, for introducing us and giving me access to his newspaper's archive.

This book would never have been written, however, if Paul McVeigh, editor of *The 32: An Anthology of Irish Working-Class Voices* (Unbound, 2021), had not asked me to contribute an essay to it back in 2020. His witty Belfast coming-of-age novel *The Good Son* was an inspiration too.

That essay helped bring me to the attention of Marianne Gunn O'Connor, who became my agent after 'A Ghost Estate and an Empty Grave' was published in *The Irish Times*. Marianne has proved a rock of sense, a voice of wisdom and a source of calm at times of stress.

My publisher, Conor Graham, is a Northerner like myself and our shared background as well as his success as a publisher with titles such as *Burned* by Sam McBride and *Old Ireland in Colour* by John Breslin and Sarah-Anne Buckley convinced me that Merrion Press was the right home for *Dirty Linen*. His passion for the project, thoughtful feedback, unstinting attention to detail and pursuit of excellence have proved me right.

Conor also recruited the people who made this book happen: constantly creative cover designer Fiachra McCarthy, mapmaker Kevin O'Sullivan, production manager Wendy Logue, commissioning editor Patrick O'Donoghue, copy editor Heidi Houlihan, proofreader Djinn von Noorden, publicist Peter O'Connell, marketing manager Maeve Convery and marketing executive Conor Holbrook. Leah Foley did sterling work transcribing interviews.

Prose is like hair; it shines with combing, wrote Gustave Flaubert. It is a long time since I had hair worth combing and despite decades as a journalist, I have never had the luxury of such close and careful attention to my written words. Helen Wright, my exemplary editor, devoted enormous effort, endless patience and incredible sensitivity to the task. By the end of the process, even though a surfeit of 40,000 words lay like beautiful tresses on the floor, I never once felt like one of the demon barber Geordie Berry's victims.

Trusted readers are such a gift to writers and I felt blessed to be supported by readers who are also writers, as well as friends or colleagues. Fintan O'Toole, Ronan McGreevy, Brendan O'Leary and Daniel Geary made invaluable suggestions as the draft neared completion but from the start I was able to rely on the helpful but honest feedback of three good friends from different but complementary fields: the poet and author Martina Evans, the historian Breandán Mac Suibhne and the journalist Steven McCaffery. Sometimes, when my prose got a little flowery, the back of the hairbrush also came in handy.

Thank you to Anne Cadwallader, Susan McKay, Dieter Reinisch, Eoin McNamee, John Gibney, Nicholas Canny, Christopher Reid, Paddy Mulroe, David Dickson, Alan Hayes of Arlen House, Niall Ó Dochartaigh, Nicholas Allen, Ruth Hegarty, Michael Cronin, Jason Diamond and Brian Campbell variously for their own writing, for recommending further reading, lending books and suggesting lines of enquiry and apt quotations.

Thanks to the staff of Libraries Ireland for their brilliant service, delivering often obscure titles promptly to my local library from all over the State, and, ahem, for abolishing fines for overdue books. Thanks also to Belfast Central Library's Newspaper Library. Second only to eyewitness testimony, nothing brings the past alive more vividly than leafing through bound volumes of old newspapers. Switching from the *Banbridge Chronicle* to the *Lurgan Mail* was a salutary reminder that it is not only accents that change every few miles in the North. Neighbouring towns experienced wildly different levels of violence.

Thanks also to Cécile Chemin, Senior Archivist at the Military Archives of Ireland and Director of the Military Service (1916–1923) Pensions Collection Project, for unearthing files on Seamus Monaghan and his comrades.

I am very grateful to Catherine Heaney of the Seamus Heaney estate and his publishers Faber & Faber for permission to use the excerpt from 'Lint Water'; to Michael Longley for his generosity in allowing me to reproduce his poem 'The Linen Industry'; to Maureen Boyle and Arlen House for the excerpt from her poem 'Strabane'; and to Elizabeth Wassell Montague and Gallery Press for permission to reproduce John Montague's poem 'A Response to Omagh'.

Steven McCaffery introduced me to Padraic Quirk, deputy director of the Social Change Initiative, who invited me to take part in its Peacebuilding Leadership Programme, which provided me with invaluable support in the early days of this project and introduced me to his inspirational colleagues Avila Kilmurray and Eleanor Gill. They and the peers who I met and got to know on the programme give me confidence that the North is in good hands.

I would like to thank my colleagues at *The Irish Times* for their support and interest in this project, especially my editors, Paul O'Neill and Ruadhán MacCormaic, Deputy Editor Conor Goodman, Brian Kilmartin, Freya McClements, Seanín Graham, Hugh Linehan, Mary Minihan and Patrick Freyne.

Most of this book was written at home but when I needed to work intensively, I was lucky enough to retreat for a few days to the idyllic River Mill in County Down and Tyrone Guthrie Centre in County Monaghan. My thanks to Paul Maddern and Éimear O'Connor respectively.

Thank you to Sandra Peake and Colin Davidson, chief executive and patron respectively of the victims' charity WAVE, and William McKeown of Stramore Community Association for their assistance. Above all, however, I owe everything to the victims and victims' friends and relatives, who are of course victims too, who shared their stories and memories, sometimes joyful but often painful. I am in awe of their resilient spirit and hope I have done them justice. I owe a particular debt to Noel O'Dowd, who entrusted me with his personal archive and was equally generous with his time. He, more than anyone, opened my eyes to the extent of the trauma in my home place.